WITHDRAWN

UNLUCKY TO THE END

UNLUCKY
TO THE END

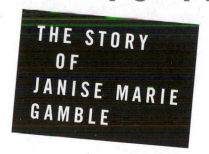

THE STORY
OF
JANISE MARIE
GAMBLE

RICHARD W. POUND

34

McGILL-QUEEN'S UNIVERSITY PRESS   MONTREAL & KINGSTON • LONDON • ITHACA

ISBN 978-0-7735-3300-4

Legal deposit fourth quarter 2007
Bibliothèque nationale du Québec

Printed in Canada on acid-free paper that is 100% ancient forest free
(100% post-consumer recycled), processed chlorine free.

McGill-Queen's University Press acknowledges the support of the Canada
Council for the Arts for our publishing program. We also acknowledge the
financial support of the Government of Canada through the Book Publishing
Industry Development Program (BPIDP) for our publishing activities.

Library and Archives Canada Cataloguing in Publication

Pound, Richard W
Unlucky to the end : the story of Janise Gamble / Richard W. Pound.

Includes index.
ISBN 978-0-7735-3300-4

1. Gamble, Janise. 2. Gamble, Janise—Trials, litigation, etc. 3. Police mur-
ders—Alberta—Calgary—History—20th century. 4. Bank robberies—
Alberta—Calgary—History—20th century. 5. Judicial error—Canada. 6.
Female offenders—Canada—Biography. I. Title.

HV6535.C33C34 2007   364.3092   C2007-902894-2

This book was designed and typeset by studio oneonone in Adobe Garamond
11.5/13

CONTENTS

Acknowledgments | vii

Introduction | ix

1 Prologue | 3

2 Vancouver | 8

3 Robbery and Shootout | 25

4 Initial Contacts and Opening Negotiations | 40

5 Hostage Siege | 58

6 End Game | 74

7 On Trial for Murder | 93

8 Legal Submissions, Charge to the Jury, and Verdict | 132

9 Appeal and Rejection | 155

10 Second Thoughts | 170

11 Plan B | 184

12 Supreme Court of Canada | 198

13 Unlucky to the End | 216

14 Conclusion | 222

Index | 235

ACKNOWLEDGMENTS

There are many people who have helped to make it possible for this work to be as comprehensive as possible. My principal worry is that by including a page or two of this nature, I risk omitting someone who deserves mention. If that happens, I hope anyone so ignored will forgive me and that we can hope for a second printing, in which the omission can be rectified – on the first bounce.

As a general consideration, when the subject of a work centres on legal matters and court cases and involves lawyers, things inevitably get complicated. For the lawyers, there are obvious limits to what they can do and say because of solicitor-client privilege, which, as a lawyer, I fully understand, even though I would have liked to have been more of a fly on the wall than they would (quite properly) allow. I confess to having been gently reminded by some of them, even if only by "one of those looks," that I was not going to get an answer to my occasional attempt to go further than was appropriate. The same is true of public authorities, such as the police forces, who have a duty to protect information subject to privacy legislation. I also understand those limitations and have tried to work within them.

All these impediments aside, however, I have greatly appreciated the generosity of those who have assisted me. Everyone, to the extent of the knowledge that they were able to share, was very helpful in enabling me to get the best possible triangulation on what happened and why. The Janise Gamble story, on whatever side they had happened to be, was compelling enough that they were interested in having it told.

I had come into the story at the end and worked back, so the first thanks go to Colin Irving and Allan Manson, who made their files available and were willing to discuss the strategies they had employed. Allan Manson had, fortunately, kept the transcripts of the murder trial and the bulk of the telephone intercepts recorded during the hostage siege, as well as records of his own efforts to obtain relief for Janise, and kindly allowed me to review them.

In Calgary, I was assisted by Cara-Lynn Stelmack and Marija Bicanic of the Calgary Police Department, who sorted through the material that could be disclosed and found some of the photographs that had been part of the public record of the trial, providing me with copies. The photos, in particular, have added much to the story and I am grateful for that assistance.

I received a great deal of assistance from the Crown prosecutor, Paul (now Mr Justice) Chrumka and tremendous insight and background from then Staff Inspector (later Chief of Police) Ernie Reimer, who headed up the hostage negotiations and arranged for me to meet or speak with some of his police colleagues who were involved at the time of the events. Webster Macdonald, who defended Janise Gamble, provided some helpful background and parts of the official records that had not been in the material obtained from either Colin Irving or Allan Manson. He was limited (and possibly a bit frustrated) by the solicitor-client privilege and had no one to whom he could turn to determine whether the waiver given by Janise and filed years before with the federal Department of Justice would permit him to speak freely. My thanks go to Danny Russell, who participated at the preliminary inquiry, and to Ralph Klein, who was engaged as part of the media during the hostage siege, well before he went on to become mayor of Calgary and premier of Alberta.

Jim Hogan, in Vancouver, helped with my understanding of the characters of John Gamble and William Nichols and their backgrounds, as well as some of the decisions taken during the crisis. Linda McLaren of Corrections Canada delivered my (unsuccessful) effort to engage William Nichols in the process of writing the book. Holly Dale was cautiously helpful in painting the picture of Janise Gamble during her confinement in Kingston's Prison for Women.

Ivan Whitehall and Ronald Fainstein of the federal Department of Justice shared what they were authorized to share and explained the federal interest in the case and the reasons why no administrative or political actions were taken to release Janise Gamble, as well as the concerns they had regarding possible retrospective application of the Charter of Rights and Freedoms.

The Right Honourable Antonio Lamer, later chief justice of Canada, who sat on the appeal of Janise Gamble, was helpful in describing the general atmosphere of the hearing and how it had proceeded but quite understandably declined to enter into the process by which the decisions, majority and minority, had been reached.

Blessed with all this help, I can only exonerate those mentioned from any errors in the work. Those are mine alone, as are the conclusions I have reached.

INTRODUCTION

On 12 March 1976 police officer Allan Keith Harrison was shot and killed following a robbery at the Ingleside Credit Union in Calgary. By the end of that year Janise Marie Gamble, a twenty-one-year-old girl from the Peterborough area of Ontario, had been jointly convicted of the murder, along with the man who fired the fatal shot. Janise was sentenced to life in prison with no possibility of parole for twenty-five years. It was clear that she had neither shot at nor killed the police officer. It was less clear whether she had participated in the robbery and subsequent confrontation that led to Keith Harrison's death. This book is an examination of the circumstances of the robbery, the flight of the suspects, the killing of the police officer, a hostage scene that lasted for forty-eight hours, the death of one of the bank robbers, the Calgary trial and conviction of Janise Gamble, and the efforts that later led to her parole after fourteen years in the desolate Kingston Prison for Women.

The case attracted the attention not only of Calgary, where the victim of the shooting had been a popular member of the community, but the entire country. The murder and hostage drama occupied the media for several days, not only because of the horror of the events but also because many of the surrounding facts were known by the public: news reporters were in regular contact with the criminals by telephone

during the standoff. The Calgary police, for their part, handled the
hostage situation with considerable restraint, negotiating patiently with
the captors and taking no precipitous actions that might have increased the danger to the hostages.

The main characters in the robbery, shooting, and hostage-taking
were John Frederick Gamble and William John Nichols, both of them
out of jail on bail while awaiting trial on charges, respectively, of murder and attempted murder. They had jumped bail and were heading
east, armed with weapons they had stolen in Vancouver. They were
resolved not to go back to jail. They knew they had shot a police officer, and when they were later told that he had died as a result of the
gunshot wound, this added to the urgency for the police of arranging
a solution that would not put other lives at risk. Once the two men
knew there would be no escape, they decided to kill themselves rather
than be taken into custody. Gamble succeeded, while Nichols was saved
from cardiac arrest at the last moment by action of the Calgary police
and medical authorities.

Nichols and Janise Gamble, now the widow of John Gamble, were
tried and convicted of the murder. The result for Nichols was not sur-
prising. It was he who had fired the shot that killed Harrison. John
Gamble had also fired shots in the exchange but apparently without
effect. In fact, he had been grazed by a bullet or a ricochet from a bullet fired by the police officer. There was no evidence that Janise had
fired a gun and some doubt as to whether she ever had one. Her fingerprints were found on none of the weapons involved in the crime.
There was conflicting evidence as to whether she had been involved in
the robbery as a lookout, although she was certainly involved in the
subsequent activities and the hostage-taking. She was, however, convicted of Harrison's murder by the Calgary jury that heard the case and
sentenced to life imprisonment with no eligibility for parole for twenty-
five years. This result was not overturned when the case went before
the Alberta Court of Appeal, and the Supreme Court of Canada refused leave to appeal.

The legal landscape was made more difficult in the circumstances
by amendments to the Canadian Criminal Code that became effective
after the murder but prior to the joint trial of the two accused. At the
time the events occurred, a person who killed a police officer acting in
the course of his duties was liable to capital punishment, even though,
as a practical matter, Canada had for some time ceased carrying out
death sentences, even when imposed by the courts as required by law.

The charges were eventually laid under the new law, which saved Nichols from a death sentence but exposed Janise to even harsher penalties than under the former law. It was this aspect that proved crucial to her earlier release on parole, without affecting the validity of her original conviction.

If not for a program that appeared on the CBC's *the fifth estate* some six years after her conviction, Janise would almost certainly have served the full twenty-five years before being granted a parole that would have by then been all but automatic, since she could not conceivably have been regarded as a threat to society. A Montreal lawyer, Colin Irving, saw the program and became convinced that there was an ongoing miscarriage of justice in her continued detention under those conditions. He offered to help, and thus began a fascinating and hard-fought legal saga that led to her release on parole in 1990.

The legal issues were complicated. They hung on whether or not the Canadian Charter of Human Rights and Freedoms, which had come into effect several years after Janise's trial and conviction, could be invoked to help her. There was determined opposition to her early release, even on parole, from the authorities in Alberta where the crime had been committed, and from those in Ontario where she was in custody. There was also opposition from the federal authorities, who were concerned because a considerable body of law had already rejected retroactive application of the Charter. The case was argued and lost in the Supreme Court of Ontario. It was lost again before the Ontario Court of Appeal. Leave to appeal was obtained from the Supreme Court of Canada, and by the narrowest of margins that court eventually decided that Janise should be declared eligible for parole. Her case still stands for some of the important principles that must be considered whenever the Charter is invoked.

I have been fortunate to be able to examine the records of the events, including the transcripts of the telephone conversations between the criminals and the police and others, which were not part of the evidence admitted during the trial. I had access to the trial transcripts and appeal briefs and many other documents bearing on the disposition of the case. I have used, where appropriate, the words of the people involved, especially during the hostage siege, to try to impart the flavour of what was happening during an intense and volatile situation, with professionals on one side and desperate fugitives on the other. Others involved in portions of the events, including the police, the prosecutors, Janise's defence, and those eventually connected with her release, have been generous in sharing their knowledge and helping me to understand as much as possible about what happened, especially those aspects that may never be known for certain. I express my thanks to them, since without their help, it would not have been possible to piece together as much as I have been able to record. The conclusions are, of course, my own.

The idea to write this book came from my following the efforts of Colin Irving to obtain Janise Gamble's early release. From time to time, in and around the games of squash we played together, Colin would mention how things were going. I confess to having had then only a mild interest, being an adept of neither criminal nor Charter law, but nevertheless I was intrigued that he was attempting to right what he obviously considered to be an injustice. I was pleased for him when the Supreme Court of Canada decided in his favour and, indirectly, pleased for Janise, having met her only vicariously through his recounting of her circumstances. It was learning some time later of her death only a few months after being released that set me to thinking there might be a story worth telling.

I asked Irving if he would let me see whatever materials he had available. Thus began my own serious interest in unravelling a complicated series of facts and trying to see how it was that what had first appeared to be a standard legal windmill-tilt managed in the end to be successful. Irving had come in at act 3, and to tell the story properly involved going back to the beginning, to see what had happened and, to some extent, how and why.

Janise Gamble, 3 March 1976, in the Calgary police station after her arrest

Allan Keith Harrison, the police officer killed in the shootout

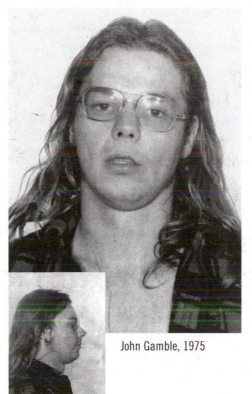

John Gamble, 1975

Bill Nichols, 1975

Inglewood Credit Union, March 1976

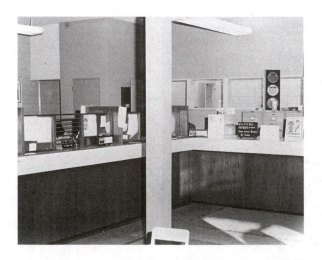

Sergeant Harrison's car on the roadside following the shootout

Pearl-handled .38 revolver found on the roadside near John Gamble's glasses following the shootout that killed Sergeant Keith Harrison

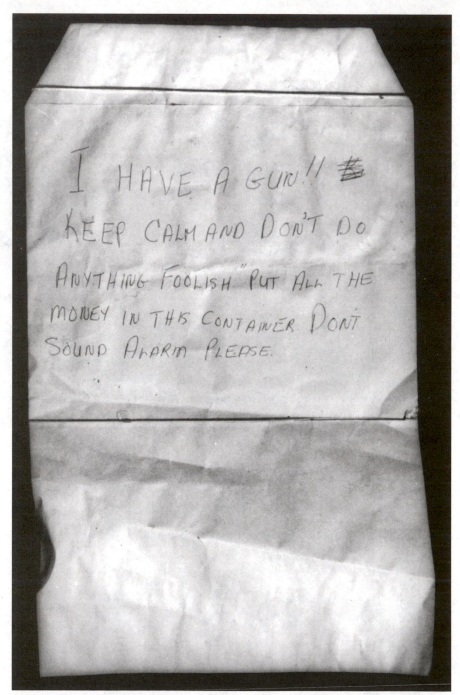

Envelope with note used in the holdup at the credit union, recovered by police after it was thrown from the getaway car. Police found Janise's fingerprint on it.

Two-tone 1974 Pontiac LeMans, the rental car used as getaway vehicle

Thunderbird Restaurant, 104 Meridian Ave. S.E., Calgary, where owners Rahim and
Laila Jivraj were taken hostage

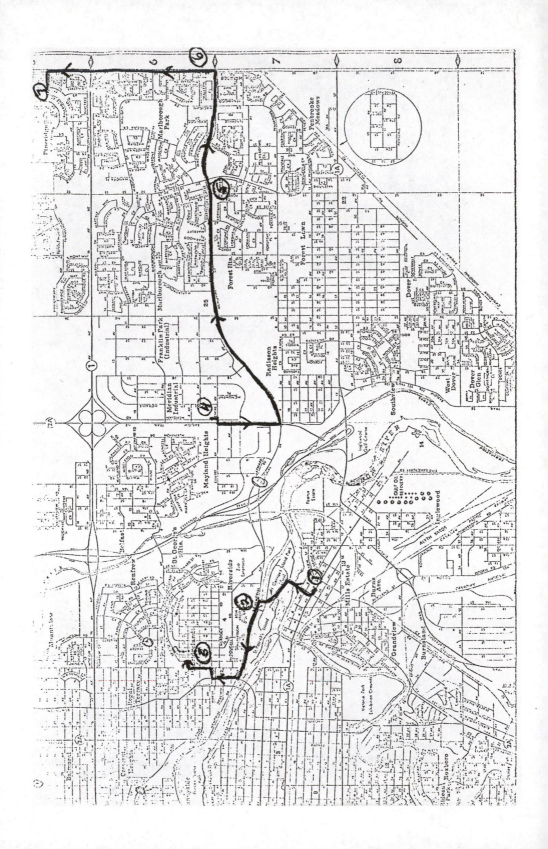

Route from the Inglewood Credit Union in Calgary to the siege site.

1 Armed robbery, Inglewood Credit Union, 1328 9 Ave. S.E., reported 12 March 1976, 3:17 P.M., two males and one female described.

2 S/Sgt. Keith Harrison, involved in shootout 1000 block Memorial Dr. N.E. reported at 3:17 P.M. At least three culprits, operating a 1975 Pontiac beige and white British Columbia licence RWE-973. S/Sgt. Harrison died in General Hospital 6:30 P.M.

3 Suspect vehicle followed for short distance by P.C. Austin. Brown envelope thrown from suspect vehicle in 400 block, 6 Steet N.E., recovered and found to be holdup note.

4 Thunderbird Restaurant, 104 Meridian Rd. S.E., entered by two male and two female culprits at 3:45. P.M. Rahim Jivraj and wife Laila Jivraj taken hostage. 1975 Pontiac abandoned at this location, and Bell taxi phoned. Culprits and two hostages, accompanied by taxi driver, leave this location a short time later.

5 Bell taxi stopped for gas at Texaco Service 52 Street and Memorial Dr. N.E. Taxi driver Douglas Moran entered service station followed by one male culprit. Driver refuses to drive any further. Taxi keys grabbed from driver, and culprits steal Bell cab at this point.

6 Approx. 4 Ave. 68 Street N.E.: private auto, a 1965 Pontiac KTG-638, forced off road. Driver of auto, Diane Lynn Perry, taken hostage at gunpoint. Bell taxi abandoned at this location and subjects continue in Perry auto.

7 6540 22 Ave. N.E. Culprits and three hostages forced front door of home at this location. Occupants of house, woman and two children, escaped through rear door prior to entry. Culprits holed up inside house. One hostage, Rahim Jivraj, released at 11:00 P.M., 12 March 1976. Standoff continues at this time. Six persons in house, two hostages.

Site of the hostage siege, the Ingram home at 6540 22nd Ave. N.E., Calgary, with hostage Diane Perry's 1965 Pontiac on the lawn

Interior shot of the Ingram home after the siege, taken by Calgary police

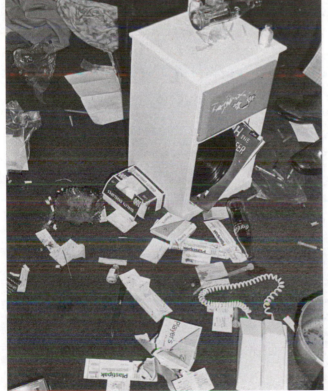

Left: Interior, showing the telephone used by the fugitives and negotiators, along with drug paraphernalia

John Gamble's body

The three significant guns: the "missing" pearl-handled revolver, the .38 used by Nichols to shoot Harrison, John Gamble's 9 mm Luger

Police lineup, showing Janise Gamble (number 10) and Tracie Perry (number 20)

Allan Manson   Colin Irving

UNLUCKY TO THE END

CHAPTER 1

PROLOGUE

Every prison inmate, even those in Kingston's notorious Prison for Women, has an innocent enough beginning. Certainly some start life with one or more strikes against them – poverty and abuse, for example, can mark an individual out for trouble in later life. But for others, the difference that leads to winning or losing is harder to pinpoint. A few small events or a couple of wrong choices – the sort of thing that could happen to anyone – may be enough to steer someone off the path of a normal, happy existence. In the same way, a butterfly stirring the air in Southeast Asia may affect whole storm systems a month later in North America.

For Janise Marie Gamble, the beginning was a happy home in small-town Ontario. She was born on 13 September 1954 in Trenton, Ontario, and lived there with her parents, Mary and Robert Yerek, until she was five years old. The family then moved, first to Toronto, then to Bowmanville, and finally to Peterborough. It was in Peterborough that her parents separated and later divorced. Her mother remarried, this time to Kenneth Sanderson, a correctional officer at the Peterborough Jail.

Janise was short, blonde, and cute. One of her teachers, Beryl Ofirskey, described her as a "physically very petite little girl – very happy

nature, very anxious to please everybody and be liked by everybody."
Janise herself recalled a relatively happy life – she never had any serious
problems, and she never went without. "I was happy. I was a happy kid.
I could just never have anything really throw me off." Her dreams were
typical small-town girl's dreams: "And all I ever wanted was a little white
picket fence, a house, and three or four kids, and someone who loved me
as much as I loved them – like a fantasy dream."

She left school in 1972, halfway through Grade 12 at the Peterborough Collegiate and Vocational Institute. She got her first job as a
salesclerk at Belts'n Bottoms in Peterborough in March. For the next
two years she seems to have had no trouble finding and keeping jobs.
She worked as a billing clerk and receptionist, sales clerk, and accounting clerk at a variety of businesses in Ottawa and Toronto. In her off
hours, she shared the normal round of teenage parties and evenings in
local bars with lots of friends.

If one had to mark the first beat of the butterfly's wing for Janise,
it would be the appearance in this crowd of a stranger from Toronto
named John Gamble. Pat Gallagher, a mutual friend, introduced Janise
to Gamble in 1974. Gallagher told her that he and Gamble had done
time together in Millbrook, the maximum security prison some thirty
miles south of Peterborough. During the day Gamble was working for
a roofer in Peterborough. In his off hours, he became a feature on the
local bar circuit, especially at the Red Dog.

Gamble and Janise did not get along well at first. In fact, he would
not stay in the same room with her. And Janise was far from impressed
with the twenty-two-year-old Gamble. The first time she met him, she
observed, "He had jeans on, and a little brown leather jacket. He
looked great. I just didn't like him." But other women definitely
seemed to be attracted to him. He was good-looking, with long blond
hair and a passing resemblance to rock star Jim Morrison. His Toronto landlady commented, "Maybe they were all animal trainers, you
know. You see something beautiful and wild and a little bit crazy and
everything like that, and some women, I guess, grow up wanting to
have that kind of hero. They'll change him ..."

Change him? Perhaps, in the weeks and months that followed, that
was what nineteen-year-old Janise thought she could do. In any event,
by April 1975 she had overcome her initial dislike of the sophisticated
stranger. "When he wanted, he could just charm the boots right off
somebody," she explained later. "And I guess at that point in time he

really wanted to because he did a darn good job. You know, he could just be sweet and nice. You couldn't help but fall in love with him."

The charm certainly worked on Janise. Once she fell, she fell hard. After three weeks in which she kept coming back from Toronto every weekend, she and Gamble started dating. The following week she missed a day of work and lost her job at Speedy Muffler.

Another beat of the butterfly's wing.

Gamble moved back to his mother's home in Toronto to be near Janise. Every morning at nine o'clock the couple would meet at the subway and spend the day in the park together. They seldom drank because neither of them was working now and they had no money. They just passed the time together, returning to their homes about nine o'-clock in the evening.

DARK SIDE

There was, however, a dark side – a very dark side – to John Gamble that Janise had not yet encountered. "All I knew was the way he was with me. What he did when he wasn't with me I didn't know about. He was a very private person."

Gamble did confess that he had once spent some time in jail on a conviction for breaking and entering – for which love-struck Janise instantly forgave him. What he did not tell her was that he had been in prison many times, not only for burglary but for robbery with violence. He had also been a patient in the Ontario Institution for the Criminally Insane at Penetanguishene.

The summary of his clinical record at Penetanguishene is chilling. It starts with the fact that his name was not Gamble, but John Frederick Koster. He was born on 20 January 1953 and lived with his mother, stepfather, and three siblings. To the Penetanguishene staff he appeared to have experienced emotional deprivation, and he acknowledged that he grew up in an environment of conflict and physical abuse, with very little emotional support.

At the time of his admission to the facility in July 1971, he was about seven months into a two-year sentence. After an attempted escape (he had a history of these), he had served part of his time in the maximum-security Millbrook Reformatory. He was eighteen years old. He admitted to the use of marijuana and hallucinogenic street drugs as well as heroin and amphetamines from early adolescence. He had already accumulated an extensive antisocial history that had resulted in contact with the police since age fourteen.

Psychological testing revealed that he had average intelligence and did not suffer from disordered thinking or mental illness. He was, however, impulsive, aggressive, belligerent, and disdainful of authority. Perhaps the most alarming observation made in the psychiatric report on him concerns his seeming lack of emotional connectedness. He appeared to have only superficial feelings about most events in his life and towards most people. The one exception was his conflict with his mother, which often extended to women in general and affected his ability to enter into a loving relationship. The diagnosis: anti-social-personality disorder.

GATHERING CLOUDS

If Janise had known what was in that report, would she have thought twice when Gamble asked her to marry him in the second week in May, less than two months after they started going out? Possibly. But subsequent events showed she was willing to forgive him for just about anything.

As it was, she said yes and excitedly announced her engagement to her parents. They naturally insisted on meeting her fiancé immediately, so the couple arranged to visit Peterborough that weekend. Gamble told Janise that he wanted to play it straight with her parents and confess that he had spent a year in jail. During the meeting he also told them how badly he wanted to put the past behind him, move to Vancouver, and start a new life with Janise.

Not surprisingly, Janise's parents gave him a hard time, but eventually they relented. Mary and Ken offered the two young people a choice. They could have a large wedding if they wanted, and Janise's parents would pay for it, or they could go for a smaller celebration, and use the extra $500 to start their new lives together.

At first the wedding was set for August, but soon Gamble started pressing for an earlier date. He confessed to Janise that he had once been a speed addict and was afraid he would start using again if he did not get away from the city. And so it was agreed: they would have a small, quick wedding and use the extra $500 to pay their fares to Vancouver.

Another beat of the butterfly's wing.

For the week before the wedding, the couple stayed with Janise's parents. Her mother questioned Gamble continuously, but he stuck to his story – he was going straight and turning into a family man. The wedding took place on 6 June 1975. The following day the newlyweds flew across the continent to Vancouver, thousands of kilometres from Janise's family and everyone she knew.

The storm clouds were gathering. It was not a question of whether, but of when, those clouds would burst.

CHAPTER 2

VANCOUVER

When they first arrived in Vancouver, Janise and John Gamble stayed for a number of weeks at the Vogue Hotel on Granville Street, where housekeeping rooms could be had for three dollars per night. It was well short of the best, but it was clean. Janise got a job with Pemberton Securities in Vancouver, starting in July 1975, about a month after their arrival. From July until early October she was the Toronto Stock Exchange coordinator, converting negotiable securities into non-negotiable securities for clients. For the balance of October until the end of the year she was on Unemployment Insurance but attended secretarial school in Vancouver to try to upgrade her typing.

Within a short time, reality of life with Gamble had set in with a vengeance. He started to drink every night, even though for the first month neither of them had a job and they had little to spare to buy liquor. Janise had never really noticed any change in him when he drank, until one night they were drinking Canadian Club rye – which she later learned brought out the worst in him. He said that he had not told her the whole truth about himself because he was afraid he would lose her. He wanted to be honest with her now, and he wanted her to help him. He told her about his mother and how he hated her. She had made him what he was because he was illegitimate and she had been a whore. She had given him to his aunt for four years, and then when she got married, took him back. Whenever he was bad, both she and his stepfather told him he was no good and never would be. He used to run away all the time because his mother told him she never loved him. When he was eleven, he stole a car, and she sent him to reform school because she couldn't handle him. The policeman who came to take him away told him they were just going for a hamburger. From then on until he had met Janise, he had been in and out of jail.

He said he was telling her all this to explain the bitterness and hate he had inside him because of his mother and jail. Then he began talking about "old John" – the one who went to jail, who used to beat up all his girlfriends, who had been a speed freak since he was fifteen and at one time had a thirty-two cap a day habit on junk. Janise didn't remember how they got on to the subject of her dating past, but he started getting very hostile, calling her names and saying that she was just like his mother and that she never really loved him.

Before she knew what was happening, he leapt out of his chair onto the bed and began strangling her. She struggled, but he seemed to like that. She passed out. When she recovered consciousness and thought it was over, he came at her again. Before she passed out again, she shouted at him to stop. Why was he doing this? After she came to for the third time, she scrambled off the bed and onto the radiator beside the third-storey window. She was so afraid that she almost jumped out of the window to get away from him, but he caught her. He took his belt off and, putting one end through the buckle, he started to tighten it around her neck.

Suddenly he stared at her and let her go. He fell back on the bed, crying and saying, "My God, why do I do these things? I'm so sorry, Jannie, please help me."

Janise got down off the radiator and went to him. He begged her not to leave him because he would never get better without her. He also told her not to look in the mirror. When she looked, it seemed that every single blood vessel in her face and neck had burst. Gamble cried like a baby for hours before finally passing out. In the morning he did not remember what had happened, and she had to tell him.

He explained that it was the "old John" who had done that to her. He said that when he drank Canadian Club, "old John" could become really strong and he couldn't stop him. But he was learning to control him since he had met Janise, because she meant so much to him. If she left him, he would be nothing.

Janise told him she wouldn't leave him and would help all she could. Then Gamble said that that was good, because there were two little nerves on each side of your eyes and if they were cut, your whole faced puckered and they could never be fixed.

She asked if he was threatening her. He said she could take it whichever way she wanted but that her face would not look too nice all puckered. He also told her that he had a detective friend in Toronto who could trace anybody, if she had any idea of hiding from him.

For a brief interlude after the first episode, things appeared to improve. Janise stayed in the Vogue Hotel recovering from the attack. Gamble treated her very well and assured her a hundred times a day how much he loved her and needed her. He tried to make her happy and found a job. She lived in a Jekyll-and-Hyde limbo between the attractive man she loved and had married and a monster who drifted into alcohol and drugs that changed his personality. She told herself that he was sick and did not mean to hurt her, but for the first time she began to be afraid of him.

He sank further into drink and drugs, becoming increasingly violent and regularly beating her. He would be fine for a couple of weeks, and then it would happen again. He would pressure her to tell him about her boyfriends before him, and if he thought she was lying, he would slap her. By that time she was working, and sometimes he would keep her up all night slapping her. She would be unable to go into work in any event, because she would have two black eyes.

They left the Vogue Hotel and moved in with a friend of Gamble's from Ontario and his girlfriend. Gamble's drinking increased and so did Janise's beatings, but after each one he would be so sorry and beg her to forgive him. He promised to stop drinking Canadian Club. He got a job working construction and they saved enough to buy an airline ticket for his best friend to fly out from Ontario. Gamble was doing speed once in while, but Janise didn't recognize the symptoms because she had never done it herself.

He stopped drinking Canadian Club, as he promised, and switched to rum, and things went well for a while. They moved out to Richmond with the couple and another of Gamble's friends, John Morrison, who was nicknamed "O.J." Gamble started to go out more and more often, and then even rum would make him change. Janise was so afraid of him by then that she never asked much about what he did. When he was good, he would phone her regularly and tell her where he was and what time he would be home. If he wasn't drinking, he was good to her.

The first time Janise and Gamble met Tracie Perry, someone who would later be part of the Calgary drama, was when O.J. was taking her out. On 10 October 1975, Gamble and O.J. pulled a break-and-enter at 1680 South East Marine Drive, the premises of Alex Cristal Tool Town Ltd. They were arrested, taken into custody, and charged with breaking and entering with intent to commit an indictable offence, plus possession of housebreaking instruments: a glass cutter, wood chisel, and claw hammer. Gamble, who was charged as both John Frederick Gamble and John Frederick Koster, phoned Janise from the police station and told her to get him out, "for sure." Janise was able to get together $500, which was enough to get him released on bail. But O.J. couldn't get bail. He asked Janise to look after Tracie for him, and Tracie moved in with the Gambles. Thereafter, if they got into an argument and Gamble beat Janise, he made Tracie stay and watch, although he never hit her.

The worst beating Janise got was when they were still living in Richmond. Gamble had met another man from Ontario, Dominic (Nick) Molinaro, and his girlfriend, Cathy Lidster. Gamble had been partying for about three days and had gotten into a fight with Al, the person with whom they had been living, and had half wrecked the place. He threw out Nick and Cathy, who were there at the time, and as Janise was giving them a ride home, yelled at her, "Don't come back." But he had told her on previous occasions that even when he said this, she had damn well better come back, so she did.

By the time she returned, he was crazed. He seemed to think she was a man. He kicked her in the head at least ten times, punched her, threw several big wooden planters at her, and strangled her with the telephone cord. He made Tracie watch, but again didn't touch her. Gamble told her to take Janise to Nick's, and Tracie phoned a taxi. Then, when they tried to go, he accused Janise of running out on him and reminded her of the "little nerves." She and Tracie fled down the stairs to the waiting cab. Gamble came after them and ran his knife down the side of Janise's face, just enough to draw blood.

At the Molinaros' apartment, the three did their best to clean Janise up. After they put her to bed, Gamble arrived at the house. He said that if Janise thought that what he had done to her was bad, she should wait to see what he was going to do to her in the morning. He took her wedding ring and $20 and left. Later he phoned her and said she should take anything she wanted from the apartment. The next day she went to the hospital where she was treated for two cracked ribs, a fractured arm, a chipped tooth, and further damage to her face. Gamble had come over as she was on the way to Emergency. He looked at her face and started to cry and said he would get her the money to go home. He said he understood.

That night she went over to their apartment with Nick and Cathy and another of their friends. Gamble said he knew that she would have to leave him and that he wouldn't beg her to stay after what he had done to her – but if he could straighten up, would she take him back? He started to cry and say, "Why, why, why and why couldn't I help myself?" Janise too broke down and told him she would never leave him. She would help him, but he had to give up drinking.

Gamble agreed, and they moved in with Nick and Cathy. For almost two months things were fine. Gamble started drinking again, but he stuck to beer and seemed okay on that. Then he changed to vodka and seemed all right on that as well. In December he, Janise, Nick, and Cathy all moved, Janise and Gamble, with Tracie Perry, to an apartment at 718 58th Street East near Fraser, and Nick and Cathy to another place in Richmond. Janise was on Unemployment Insurance, taking her secretarial course. Everything was calm until about two weeks before Christmas. Gamble got into an argument with Nick and came home with two bottles of vodka.

Janise, Tracie, and Gamble were sitting at the kitchen table when Gamble suddenly brought up the subject of the man Janise had been dating before him. He accused her of all sorts of lies, and when she wouldn't admit he was right, punched her in the face. Finally she agreed with him just so he would stop hitting her. He punched her again and went to bed. When Janise told him what had happened the next day, he stopped drinking vodka and started on tequila. He was all right on that until Christmas Day. They had been at a party on Christmas Eve next door to where Nick and Cathy lived and got home at 2:00 A.M. Gamble passed out and they were awakened by the phone at 4:00 A.M. It was Janise's mother, calling to wish them Merry Christmas, obviously getting the time difference from eastern Canada confused. They got up, everyone still drunk, and opened their Christmas presents. Gamble had a few beers while Janise cooked them bacon and eggs. Cathy phoned later to say that she and Nick would be over around 1:30 P.M. on their way to Christmas dinner somewhere else. They went back to bed and got up again at noon.

They had a bottle of tequila, a bottle of rum, and two cases of beer in the apartment and had bought a bottle of rye for Cathy and Nick. Gamble and Nick got really drunk, and Nick said that he didn't want to go out to dinner. He wanted to stay with them. They finished off all the booze and decided to go over to Cathy and Nick's place at 430 Number 5 Road in Richmond where there was some Southern Comfort and a bottle of vodka. They would spend the night there. They were all having a ball, taking pictures, and telling jokes, when they again ran out of liquor. Gamble's mood changed, and he said he was going out to find more booze. He may have argued with Nick, perhaps about Gamble's treatment of Janise and one or more of the photographs taken during the party. In any event, he left abruptly, with a knife he had asked Janise to buy him for Christmas.

Janise was in the washroom, and when she came out, he was gone. She went to look for him, but it was late and pouring rain and she couldn't find him. She and Tracie waited at 430 Number 5 Road for him, while Cathy and Nick went over to where they all used to live on Rees Road, to see if he might have gone there. There were break-ins at two vacant houses that evening, and a set of false front teeth found at one of them was later identified as Gamble's.

Approximately an hour later, a call came from the Richmond General Hospital to say that Gamble had been cut up, that they needed his British Columbia medical insurance number, and that someone should come to get him. Janise went to the hospital, but by that time Gamble had left. She returned to Nick and Cathy's, but he wasn't there either. When she phoned home, Gamble answered. He was screaming that she'd better not return or he would kill her. He said he had wrecked all her Christmas presents, just like she had wrecked his Christmas by not being there when he needed her. Then he hung up. Janise phoned back, but the line was busy. She phoned again and got no answer.

What had happened was that about 10:00 P.M., Gary William Reelie, a clerk at a government of British Columbia Liquor Store, had left the freeway and was driving north on Number 5 Road with his girlfriend when he saw a man standing beside the road, bleeding, both hands held over his head. After passing him, Reelie stopped, backed up, and asked the man, whom he later identified in court as John Gamble, what had happened. Gamble said he had been hit by a car. The bleeding was caused by lacerations and a large gouge on his forearms. Reelie got him into the car to drive him to the Richmond General Hospital. This took about twenty minutes, since he did not know Richmond well and did not know where the hospital was located.

Gamble was upset and, to take his mind off his injuries, Reelie talked a bit of football with him. At a four-way stop sign, Reelie got out of his car and found a driver who knew where the hospital was and offered to lead the way. By the time Reelie got back to his car, Gamble had moved over to the driver's seat and was saying he didn't want anything to do with the police. He pulled himself out of the vehicle and tried to run across the street, getting about ten feet before he collapsed. Reelie and the other driver went after him and assured him that the police were not coming. Gamble settled down a bit, and they drove him to the hospital.

On arrival at the hospital, Gamble was violent and swearing. The emergency room orderly, Walter Lozinsky, tried to calm him down while taking him to a room in the emergency ward. He got Gamble to lie down on a stretcher, even though he was still cursing. After a few seconds Gamble asked for a cigarette. Lozinsky said that he couldn't smoke in the emergency room as there was oxygen in there. Gamble jumped off the stretcher, saying he would show Lozinsky what he had. He reached his right hand to a sheath he wore on his belt and pulled out a knife. Opening it, he showed it to Lozinsky and yelled, "Now, do you see any blood on this knife?"

Lozinsky, his back to the wall, replied, "No, I can't see any blood on it." Gamble asked again whether he saw any blood, and Lozinsky said there was none. Reelie, who was still there, yelled at Gamble to put the knife away and grabbed his arm. Gamble put the knife away. Lozinsky shut off the oxygen and gave Gamble a cigarette, which seemed to calm him and make him more cooperative.

A doctor arrived after fifteen minutes to treat the wounds, which were serious and deep. Gamble was in such a drunken state that he seemed impervious to pain. After the doctor had cleaned his arm and was about to put freezing into it before doing the stitches, Lozinsky was astonished to see Gamble stick his finger into one of the wounds and twist it around, apparently feeling nothing. The doctor put in the stitches without anaesthetic. Lozinsky couldn't say what was wrong with Gamble, other than that he behaved as if he were drunk, although he wasn't staggering around. He was extremely emotional. The police were called, mainly because he was using such foul language and was so agitated. Inexplicably, Lozinsky did not mention to the police the incident with the knife. He apparently thought Gamble had shown him the knife because he believed Lozinsky thought he had inflicted the wounds on himself and was showing him the knife to demonstrate that there was no blood on it.

RCMP constable Gary Thomas Tidsbury had arrived about 10:35 P.M. in response to the 10:30 call from the hospital asking for assistance regarding a subject in the emergency ward. Gamble, still being attended by the orderly, was sitting in a small room. Tidsbury was accompanied by a uniformed member of the RCMP, and when Gamble saw them, he became hostile. He jumped up and ordered the uniformed officer to leave, as there was no need for the police. It was Christmastime, he insisted, and he didn't need police assistance. Tidsbury told the uniformed officer to go back to the car while he remained in the hospital. Gamble calmed down considerably, was cooperative with the orderly, and was treated with the stitches to both arms.

After the treatment, Tidsbury and Gamble spoke for a while, and someone called for a taxi. Because it was Christmas, the despatcher said, it would be a long wait. Tidsbury offered to give Gamble a ride home. His eyes were bloodshot, he had no front teeth, and had a strong smell of liquor on his breath, but he was steady on his feet and could carry on a logical conversation. Tidsbury had not seen a knife in Gamble's possession or he would have seized it as a precaution. He drove Gamble to his residence at 718 East 58th Avenue in Vancouver, dropping him off at approximately 11:10 P.M. On his way back to Richmond, he noticed his overcoat was missing from the front seat of the car, so he turned around and went back to Gamble's apartment.

Approaching the back door, he saw that a window had been broken. There was glass on the floor, and his coat was on a kitchen chair. Gamble was talking on the phone, but he came to the door and let him in. He carried on with his telephone conversation, which seemed normal and friendly, making arrangements to go and visit the person on the other end. When Tidsbury asked him about the broken glass, he said he didn't have his key and that had been the only way he could get in. Tidsbury recovered his coat, which Gamble had obviously taken by mistake when he got out of the car.

Gamble then asked him for a ride back to Richmond. He didn't know why he had asked to be taken to Vancouver in the first place, he said, when his wife and friends were in Richmond – although he had been quite clear at the hospital that he wanted to go to the Vancouver apartment. Tidsbury obliged and, after calling ahead to see if it was all right to bring Gamble there, dropped him off at 377 Rees Road at about 11:50 P.M.

Gamble got out and took a couple of steps towards the rear of the car when he observed someone coming out of the driveway of 377 Rees Road. He reversed his direction and headed in the direction of the driveway of 381 Rees Road. Tidsbury left the scene. In the meantime, Cathy Lidster had called Janise to tell her to come, since Gamble was on his way. As Cathy was in the midst of the call, she saw Gamble get out of the cruiser.

Nick and Cathy had been at the window, watching for Gamble. When the police car dropped him off, Nick said he would go down to meet him. A few minutes later, they had not returned. Cathy heard a bang or thump against the door and went downstairs to see what it was. Michael Bureyko, the neighbour at 381 Rees, had also heard the bang on the door and when he went outside, he saw Gamble and Nick fighting, both throwing punches no more than five steps from his door. Moments before, he had seen the police car going away and caught a glimpse of Gamble walking up the driveway. Though Gamble ordinarily wore glasses, he was not wearing them now, Bureyko observed.

Nick had Gamble in a headlock. Bureyko said, "Hold it, you guys, this is my place. Calm down." They stopped fighting, and Gamble said to Nick, "Let me go." Both stood up, glaring at each other, but nothing else happened while Bureyko stood there for a minute or so and Cathy came down.

Cathy had been talking with Janise on the telephone and said to her, "My old man is fighting with your old man," and then went downstairs. When she opened the door, she saw Gamble's coat on the ground and Gamble looking at Nick like he was ready to kill him. Gamble had a mean look on his face, seemed extremely angry, and had his arms out like he was ready to fight. Someone closed the door and told her to come inside, but Cathy turned and ran back outside. The two men were no longer there. She ran around the backyards of 377 and 381 Rees calling for Nick, and heard him call her name from the front of 377. She found him lying on the floor just inside the landing.

Gamble was running up and down the stairs, still with the knife in his hands, looking "just like nuts, absolutely nuts." There was a white sheet with blood on it over Nick. She pulled it off and opened his shirt to see a stab wound over his heart. His eyes were rolling back in his head, twitching, and he was barely breathing. She screamed at Gamble, "What happened, what did you do to him?"

Gamble said, "I stabbed him, I killed him, I didn't mean to, it was an accident." He kept saying he didn't mean to do it. She thought he might be trying to stop the bleeding, but she was afraid he was hurting Nick. She pushed him against the closet and then he got up and said, "I'll kill you, too." She ran screaming to Bureyko's home, saying, "Nick's dead! Nick's dead!" Bureyko called the police, and when she got back to 377 Rees, the police were there.

It had taken twenty minutes for Janise to get a taxi, and it was probably forty minutes after Cathy had called before she arrived. By that time the police were on the scene. She saw Gamble inside the house. "I looked in the door, and as I looked over there, I seen John. He looked like the wild man from Borneo." He was talking incoherently, saying, "They got him, they got him, they got him." Gamble said he had been hit by a car and that somebody had attacked Nick. He was completely hysterical.

On his way to the police station Tidsbury overheard a radio transmission that made him hurry to the station to learn the particulars. He got the details, such as they were, and was back at Rees Road by about 12:00 A.M., by now December 26th. He first went to number 381 and then to 377, where Gamble and Janise were sitting on a chesterfield in the living room. A number of uniformed RCMP members were also present. Gamble and Janise were upset and crying and asked him several questions. Tidsbury advised Gamble that he was under arrest at this time for investigation of assault causing bodily harm. He gave him the standard police caution and told two other officers, at about 12:15 or 12:20 A.M., to escort him to the Richmond police station. Once another officer arrived and was charged with the security of the scene, Tidsbury took Janise and Tracie Perry back to the Richmond detachment office, turned them over to the staff sergeant, then went upstairs and began interviewing witnesses.

The police had put Gamble in handcuffs before putting him in the back of the police car. Janise, in shock, tried to tell her friend Cathy that Gamble did not kill Nick. Cathy, with everyone standing around covered with blood, said, "He did so!" She felt furious with Janise – after all the beatings he had given her and the way he had treated her, what made her think he wasn't capable of murder? Janise and Tracie stayed at the police station for five hours. There they learned that Nick had been pronounced dead on arrival at the hospital. Finally they went back to their apartment and found the back window broken by Gamble.

At 1:05 A.M., Tidsbury went to pick up Gamble from the booking cell area of the Richmond Detachment and take him to the staff sergeant's office for an interview. During the forty or forty-five minutes between arrival at the station and the questioning, Gamble had fallen asleep or passed out in his chair and had to be wakened up. He was very upset, and his immediate concern was what had happened to Nick Molinaro. In the interview room Tidsbury repeated the police caution given at the time of his arrest, but this time told him he was under investigation for murder. He told him that Nick had been pronounced dead on arrival at the Richmond General Hospital.

Gamble began to cry and said he didn't believe it, that Tidsbury was lying to him. He pounded on the wall and desk. Tidsbury let him sit there for ten or fifteen minutes, during which Gamble kept talking to himself. "No Nick, you can't be dead," he said. Tidsbury was lying. He refused to accept that his friend had died.

Tidsbury kept him in the room for an hour and fifteen minutes. He told him that he had seen him get out of the car and meet someone in the driveway and asked if he had had any conversation or an argument or a fight with whoever it was. Gamble said that they had had an argument, but he could not remember what it was about. He said it was probably concerning their "chicks," and he was concerned where his chick was and where Nick's was. When Tidsbury asked if there was a fight after the argument, Gamble denied it.

The next thing he could remember was Molinaro stumbling across the front yard of 377 Rees to the doorway and following him and seeing him lying just inside the doorway. He checked him and saw "the puke" coming from his mouth. Someone named Jim Mathison came down the stairs, and Gamble said he had said something like "He's dead" or "He's hurt." Gamble tried to assist by administering mouth-to-mouth resuscitation. When that failed, he ran upstairs, he said, to call an ambulance. In fact, he had been crafty enough to take the knife sheath off his belt and hide it in a vent in the kitchen, get rid of the knife, and make sure his fingerprints were on a bottle of beer in the kitchen – all to support the idea that someone else might have killed Molinaro. The sheath and the knife were later found by the police, and there was a clear fingerprint from Gamble's right hand on the knife.

Tidsbury wanted to fill in the time lapse between when he had dropped Gamble off and when Gamble recalled seeing Molinaro lying in the doorway. Gamble said he could not remember anything. Tidsbury took him back over the events of the evening to refresh his memory, starting when he had met him at the hospital. Gamble said he could not remember what had happened. He did not recall having a fight with Molinaro. Tidsbury told him that witnesses had seen them fighting in front of 381 Rees, but Gamble denied it – they weren't fighting, they had a small argument – a misunderstanding, not an argument. Nick had probably been stabbed prior to his arrival at the scene, he said. Tidsbury advised him that he had seen Nick standing in the driveway with his hands in his pockets, standing erect, which would have been impossible if he had been stabbed in the chest. Gamble then agreed that Nick was probably uninjured when he arrived, but he could not recollect anything other than the fact that they had had a small argument. He continued to say how Nick had helped him and what good friends they had been. Towards the end of the conversation, Gamble began crying violently, saying he had probably lost his wife now as a result of this. He said he could not remember what happened, but if he could, he would tell Tidsbury. Tidsbury decided to return him to the cellblock area.

At 2:56 A.M., Gamble provided a breathalyser sample that produced a blood alcohol reading of .13. This sample had limited utility in demonstrating what his condition would have been three hours earlier. At 8:20 A.M. he was further interviewed by another officer. In the afternoon the police arranged for a lawyer to visit him and then took him before a judge to have the charges read to him. He was remanded to December 29th. After the hearing he grabbed Tidsbury's arm. "Gary, I just want you to know it was an accident," he said. "I didn't mean to kill him. It's not the fact I killed him that's bothering me, but why. There was just no reason. If he had screwed my wife or done something to me, I could handle it, but what's freaking me out is there was just no reason. Hell, he was my best friend."

A laconic report appeared in the *Vancouver Province* on 27 December 1975:

Murder Charged in Knife Death

John Frederick Gamble, 22, of Vancouver was charged Friday with murder punishable by life imprisonment in the Christmas

Day stabbing in Richmond of Dominic Molinaro, 21.

Richmond RCMP were called to a fight at a Rees Road home late Thursday, and found Molinaro with stab wounds to his chest. He was dead on arrival at Richmond General Hospital.

During the next week the RCMP let Gamble make telephone calls at all times of the day and night. He maintained that he remembered nothing. He cried and begged and pleaded for Janise to help him. He said he was sick, that he needed help, that he wanted help. He would see a psychiatrist, go to Alcoholics Anonymous, straighten out. He would kill himself if she left him and he could never make it without her. Then he said that if she did leave, he would survive in jail on hate and get out and find her and use those little nerves.

Janise was now working as a skip tracer for CCC Collection Agency, a job she got in December, from which she cleared $105 per week. She tried to arrange for bail. Gamble had to see a bail supervisor, join AA, and go to a psychiatrist. He promised her that he would do all of this. His preliminary inquiry was six weeks later on 11 February 1976 in the Provincial Court of British Columbia Criminal Division in Richmond, presided over by Judge T.L. Steele.

It seemed clear that Gamble was practically insane but certainly very drunk that night, and it appeared that the charges would be reduced to manslaughter and he would be sentenced to four years in prison. Gamble said he would take a course in butchering while in the penitentiary and that he would straighten out.

WILLIAM JOHN NICHOLS

William John Nichols was born in New Westminster, British Columbia, in January 1949, son of a truck driver and his wife. When his father was at home, he was often drunk and occasionally violent and had little interest in looking after his son and three daughters. Befriended by a neighbour, the boy was sexually abused and became an angry loner, joining the navy at age sixteen. After three years he left the navy and married a pregnant woman, but the marriage did not last and he was left alone. He took up drugs in earnest: hash, LSD, and speed. He became a licensed practical nurse and worked in a local hospital in Victoria. Off duty he committed burglaries, robbing a few stores and a bank. But he worked alone and kept these activities to himself. He was not caught.

By this time living with another single mother, he decided that prospects might be better in Ontario. They moved to Toronto and later to Brantford, where Nichols applied for a job with the police department and registered with Canada Manpower, expressing interest in electrical engineering. He was accepted at the Conastoga College of Applied Arts and Technology in Waterloo. Before moving to Waterloo, he learned from the Brantford police that he had passed his first screening. At the end of 1969, now twenty-five, he began to hang out and party with a hard crowd, not unlike the people he knew in British Columbia. To make ends meet for this lifestyle, he again turned to burglary. In the course of his electrical engineering studies he learned enough to make bombs, and he and a friend took it up as a business, concentrating powerful explosives into small plastic cassette-like cases. Most of their orders, Nichols would say later, came from Quebec. They tried to branch out and use their bombs for extortion, but one of the intended victims notified the police, who raided the apartment and found several bombs and the related assembly equipment and supplies. Nichols was arrested for extortion, tried, convicted, sentenced to two years less a day, and sent to the Guelph Reformatory. His violent attitude caused sufficient problems to warrant a transfer to the maximum-security Millbrook facility.

There he met Gamble, a younger (at eighteen), but equally violent inmate. They bonded and watched each other's backs, a potentially lethal combination that easily managed the intimidation of prison life. His sentence completed in 1972, Nichols was bussed back to British Columbia, where he took up the relationship with his woman partner and tried to assume a normal life with a variety of jobs. One of them, running a health spa, was very good. But reform did not take, and he was soon back to heavy drinking, drug use, and petty crime. He seemed to know that something was wrong and even sought treatment at a local mental hospital on two occasions, as well as hypnotherapy, to no avail. After police arrived early one morning to search his home, finding nothing, he left his family in Victoria and returned to the mainland. He got a job as a practical nurse in New Westminster at the Royal Columbian Hospital.

On 11 October 1975, while loitering in Vancouver's Stanley Park, hoping to score some drugs, Nichols amused himself by shooting at seagulls with his pellet gun. On his way back to the city he asked a total stranger, James Selfe, for the time, and as Selfe looked at his watch, Nichols shot him in the eye, robbed him, and continued uptown. On Davie Street he pulled the same gun on the doorman of a bar. The police were called, and Nichols was put in Okalla to await trial for attempted murder, robbery, and two charges relating to possession of a weapon. The shooting victim lost his eye.

While in Okalla awaiting trial for murder, Gamble had originally been placed in the same cell as his friend O.J., who had received an eighteen-month sentence after pleading guilty to the break-and-enter in which he had participated that fall with Gamble and another man. Then there was a change of cellmates, and Gamble was reunited with William John Nichols.

From the moment of Nichols's arrival on the scene, Gamble's attitude changed dramatically. He had been resigning himself to jail, knew what the sentence was likely to be (which would probably take into account time already served), and was anticipating learning a trade. But once Nichols came his way, Gamble's only thought became to somehow get out on bail. Nichols managed to raise bail and once he was out, came around to see Janise on several evenings. He told her Gamble said to check up on her and to see about getting him bail. Tracie Perry, formerly O.J.'s girlfriend, was still living with Janise, and Nichols began spending time with Tracie.

Gamble was convicted of the break-and-entry charges on 6 January 1976 in the British Columbia Provincial Court and sentenced to eighteen months on each count, to be served concurrently. Incredibly, despite this conviction and the seriousness of the pending murder charge, on 1 March 1976, he was again released, on the paltry bail of $1,000, by Justice Lloyd MacKenzie, a judge of the Supreme Court of British Columbia. Janise had put up $500, and Nichols raised the balance. In less than two weeks Gamble would be dead, after a series of violent crimes committed in both British Columbia and Alberta.

GETTING OUT OF BRITISH COLUMBIA

In the days after Gamble's release, Nichols moved in with him and Janise and Tracie. Out of the confines of Okalla, the two men decided to join some others to participate in a Brinks truck robbery in Toronto.

To raise money for the trip east, they planned to rob a house. Janise recalled the precursor to their departure: "We were lying in bed and we were just talking and he was telling me, like, 'Jannie, this place just isn't any good for me.'"

On 10 March Janise had been allowed to leave work early. She had things to do, including getting her income-tax return filled out. She got home about 2:00 P.M. to find Tracie there as usual. They were having a drink when Gamble, Nichols, and a friend she knew only as "Ian" came in. The men went out again and Gamble and Nichols returned later, sometime after 3:30.

Suddenly things were chaotic. Gamble announced they were leaving. He began making strange requests, such as asking Janise to burn their photograph album. He told her, "Just grab what you need. We've got to go fast. Don't ask any questions." He would explain things in the car, he said. They had only one suitcase between them, so they threw some clothes into green garbage bags and piled into a rented car. After stopping to get back a $150 deposit they had put down on some rings, they headed east towards Hope.

Nineteen-year-old Tracie thought the idea of the cross-country trip was exciting and begged to come along. Nichols told her she didn't know what she was getting into, but finally he agreed. Neither of the women knew the two men had guns. They had concealed them when they threw the garbage bags into the trunk. On the highway Gamble told Janise that the robbery they had just carried out had been successful, but that he had thought he might have lost his glasses, so they had gone back. He had been observed by the owner of the house, or someone who might have been the owner, and he was afraid that he might be identified. He didn't want to be put back in jail for another armed robbery, so he had to run.

Janise asked him why he had done it, and he implied that he was going to be paid for helping to steal the guns or was going to get paid when the guns were sold. She never saw any of the guns and thought Ian had kept them. Even when they stopped for the night, she saw nothing, since the only bag they brought into the motel was a small plastic Shoppers Drug Mart bag with toothpaste, shampoo, and other essentials.

Both Gamble and Nichols were now in violation of their bail conditions. The RCMP seemed to be sufficiently aware of their departure that they had called Cathy Lidster, the prime witness to Molinaro's murder, then living back in Oshawa, Ontario, to warn her that they thought Gamble was heading that way. By this time Janise had concluded that she would have to get back home in order to leave Gamble and that she would need the protection of her family to do so. So, from her perspective, Gamble's sudden decision that they leave British Columbia and head back east was not all bad.

CHAPTER 3

ROBBERY AND SHOOTOUT

On 11 March the four reached Calgary, by now in a different rented car. Nichols had ditched the Pinto at Penticton in the Okanagan Valley and rented a white over tan four-door 1974 Pontiac LeMans. Nichols remembered listening to the Queen song "We Are the Champions." Janise remembered it as Queen's "Bohemian Rhapsody," which Gamble kept saying was "his song." They spent the night in the Bow River Motel. Gamble was edgy and irritable and got into an argument with Janise. He beat her up, knocking her unconscious.

The next day they did some shopping that included buying suitcases, purchased at the Eaton's branch in Calgary. Someone, probably Janise, bought a large paper envelope. It seems that they had decided to take the 3:45 P.M. train from Calgary to Medicine Hat that afternoon.

ROBBERY

The idea of holding up a bank in Calgary, according to Nichols in an interview given to the *Vancouver Sun*, was Gamble's. He suggested it to Nichols the morning of 12 March. Nichols said he did not think it was a good idea, but Gamble was excited by the prospect. Nichols said he thought they should get to Toronto and do the Brinks job, but Gamble insisted, so he gave in and agreed.

After lunch in Calgary, and presumably on their way to the train station, the men said they wanted to cash a cheque, so they drove up, with Nichols at the wheel, to the rear of the Inglewood Credit Union at 1328–9th Avenue South East. Apparently Nichols had a couple of cheques from his lawyer, so this did not seem to the women to be anything out of the ordinary. The men went into the credit union, which was neither big nor particularly busy. There were four tellers, one of whom was occupied with a customer, and no guards. Although the men had long hair, they appeared reasonably well groomed, wearing the leisure suits that were common garb in that period, and did not appear threatening. This changed abruptly when Gamble pushed a note, written on an envelope, towards the teller. The note said, "I have a gun. Keep calm and don't do anything foolish. Put all the money in this container. Don't sound alarm please." Both Nichols and Gamble showed their guns but did not draw them. The teller gave them $1,631, which Gamble put in his pocket. He took back the envelope as well, and the two walked out of the credit union. The teller reported to her manager that she had been robbed. The police were called and arrived shortly thereafter.

The next portion of what happened has a number of important contradictions. Both Janise and Tracie swore they were unaware of the plan. In an affidavit that Janise would later swear, she stated:

> At about 1:00 o'clock P.M. on March 12, 1976, while we were at the Holiday Inn in Calgary, someone, either John or Billy, made a comment about robbing a bank. I said they were crazy and they told me they were only joking. There was no further discussion about it. Later that day, Billy said he had a cheque to cash and we went to the Inglewood Credit Union. The car was parked behind the Credit Union. John Gamble and Billy Nichols left the car. Shortly afterwards, Tracie Perry also left the car. I was in the back seat but moved into the front seat so that I could adjust the radio. I did not leave the car. I did not know that a robbery was taking place.

Tracie got out of the car to buy Aspirin. Janise insisted that she never left the car but climbed from the back seat into the front to get a different station on the radio and stayed there. But at the trial there was evidence presented by a Crown witness that Janise had been seen in front of the credit union, walking back and forth. The Crown's later theory would be that she was the "lookout" in the robbery.

When the men came back from the credit union, they got in the back seat, Nichols on the driver's side and Gamble on the passenger's. Gamble said, "Drive," and Janise knew something was wrong. She stepped on the gas, spun the wheels, and started to drive away. Then Nichols shouted at her to stop so that Tracie could get in, on the passenger side in the front. Janise drove away as fast as possible, but she was not a good driver so she was only going thirty-five or forty miles an hour as she crossed the Calgary Zoo bridge to Memorial Drive and turned left on the street to go west. She was not aware that they were being chased, although she knew that they had to get out of there in a hurry. No one mentioned that there had been a robbery. Then Nichols said that he was going to drive. Gamble said no. Very soon thereafter, Nichols repeated that he was going to drive, and this time Gamble said okay. Janise was still not aware there was anyone behind them.

As soon as Nichols and Gamble had left the credit union, an alarm had sounded and the police reported the robbery on their radio system. The message was heard by Staff Sergeant Keith Harrison, driving an unmarked police car. Harrison responded to the call and believed he had identified the suspects' car, which he began to follow. In Nichols's interview with the *Vancouver Sun*, he said that Harrison actually spoke to them as they came out of the Credit Union, asking what they thought they were doing. They either ignored him or gave some smart-ass reply and continued walking to their car. After all, he was just some guy in a suit driving a Chevelle.

Harrison had just turned forty on 9 February. He had been a member of the Calgary Police Service since 15 August 1960, starting as a constable in the Patrol Division before transferring to the Traffic Division in November 1964, where he stayed until October 1970, when he was appointed as a detective. Later transferred to the Training Section at Mount Royal College, he returned in May 1975 to the Detective Division and was promoted to the rank of detective sergeant. On 1 February 1976 he was promoted to staff sergeant. He was very active in sports and a well-known baseball pitcher in the Calgary Commercial A league. He and his wife, Patricia Louise, had two teenaged children. Harrison was well liked and respected by his colleagues and in the community. This was not his lucky day.

The first part of his bad luck was that, because of a loose "feed fuse" that simply needed to have been properly connected – a matter of a few seconds' work, and which should have been tested before he went on his eight hour tour of duty at 10:00 A.M., he could receive messages on his radio but could not transmit. He had not reported any malfunction and perhaps was not aware of the problem. Radio checks are meant to be part of the routine when each police car books on duty, but there was no record of whether or not Harrison had performed the check. No one knows what, if anything, he may have tried to communicate in the few minutes that would remain of his conscious life once he started to follow the suspects.

Nichols and Gamble became aware that a car was following them and concluded that it must be the police, although the vehicle was unmarked, the occupant wasn't in uniform, and there was nothing in the speed or conduct of the driving of either car that would have been characterized as pursuit. Nichols told Janise to turn left on an orange light. She did. The car followed them, turning on what was by then a red light, which confirmed their suspicions: it must be a cop. In the back seat Nichols and Gamble discussed what to do. One thing was certain: Janise was not a very good driver and Nichols wanted to take over. The other – in their minds – was that it might be better to deal with the police now rather than wait for there to be ten cops later – an idea that was idiotic at best. Nichols told Janise to pull over in the area of the 1000 block of Memorial Drive, so he could take the wheel. Nichols got out of the back into the front, and Janise flipped over the seat into the back beside Gamble.

While they were stopped, Harrison pulled in behind them and, possibly believing that backup was on its way, decided to act. He had almost certainly reported on his defective radio that he was following the suspects from the robbery and assumed that help could not be far behind (although he may have been surprised to have had no acknowledgment of his attempted calls for backup or to hear calls to other police cars). He got out of his car with his weapon drawn and shouted, "Get out of the car, put your hands up!" Janise was not sure exactly what was said, but thought it might have been "Police!" or something like that.

Nichols, already out of the car, put his gun on the roof of the car between his hands. Janise heard several shouts for them to get out of the car. Gamble then began to get out on the passenger's side and, as he did so, tossed a revolver either into Janise's lap or into the snow at the side of the road – no one will ever know for certain exactly what happened, other than that the revolver was found at the side of the road. There was never anyone who claimed to have seen Janise with a gun. There were no fingerprints on the gun that was found, and it had not been fired. There was no evidence that Janise had any idea how to use a gun, let alone that she would have been prepared to do so against a police officer. The guns used in the course of the events had only been obtained the day before as a result of the robbery in Vancouver. The alternatives are that Janise was never in possession of a weapon at any time; that Gamble himself tossed the gun to the ground, intending to indicate that he had surrendered, while still having the additional gun in his belt; that, if the gun had been inside the car, it had fallen on the road as Janise scrambled to obey the order to get out; that she had the gun in her hands to bring it out of the car as part of the surrender; or that she came out of the car with the gun, fully intending to use it against the police officer.

To this day the Calgary police are convinced that, although no one ever saw her with a gun, Janise had a gun when she came out of the car and that if she had not, Harrison would still be alive, even though both Nichols and Gamble were still armed. When Gamble was out of the car, he was facing Janise with his hands on the roof but with a Luger tucked into his belt. At this point both men had their hands on the roof of the car, assuming "the position." The police officer was still screaming at the women to get out of the car.

Janise looked at Gamble, and he was looking directly at her and nodded. She assumed that he meant it was all over and so got out of the right rear door, the same door from which Gamble had got out. Nichols had dropped his head, as if to say something. Janise recalled much later that she heard something like "Waste the prick," but did not know which of the men might have said it. As she got out of the car, she ended up on the ground and the shooting began. She must have been knocked out for a second, because the next thing she knew, the car was backing over her leg and she was screaming. Then the car started to drive away and she thought she was going to be left behind. She jumped up and Gamble pulled her through the window of the right rear door as they were driving away. He told her to shut up and lie on the floor. She and Tracie did just that.

Inexplicably, Harrison had come around the open door of his car, weapon in hand, and begun to walk towards Nichols and Gamble, still shouting for the occupants to get out of the car. His language was more graphically described by Nichols later as "Get out of the car! Get out of the fucking car!" Given the level of tension, this is probably not far from what was actually said. As Janise and Tracie were in the process of complying, it appears as if the movement, which would have included Janise's exit from the back seat with or without the gun, startled Harrison. Why this was the case is uncertain, since he must have known there were others in the car, as the two men had both got out and he was still ordering the others out. In any event he suddenly turned and moved back to his own car, leaving Nichols with a gun between his hands and Gamble with a gun in his belt.

The next few seconds will probably always remain unclear. Some of the evidence suggests that Harrison may have fired a warning shot to cover his retreat, and some suggests that Nichols and Gamble began the shooting. Seven or eight shots were exchanged between the three men. One shot, possibly a ricochet, grazed Gamble in the forehead, knocking off his glasses, but another struck Harrison, probably when he left the cover of the door of his car and moved to get behind the rear of the vehicle. He was struck from behind, in the abdomen, tearing both the aorta and vena cava. He immediately collapsed and died three hours later in hospital as doctors tried desperately to save his life. The bullet that caused the death was later identified as one fired from Nichols's gun.

During the exchange, Janise was lying, screaming, on the side of the road, partially under the car. The gun she may have had in her hands had fallen by the roadside and was later recovered by the police. It had not been fired, and there were no recognizable fingerprints on it. When the shooting finished, the men jumped back in the car and, in their panic, Nichols backed the car over Janise's leg. He then put the car in forward and ran over it again. Gamble pulled her into the car. There was a high-speed chase through the streets of Calgary, with the perpetrators' car outrunning the police when the pursuer, whose vehicle apparently had a governor that would not allow it to exceed fifty miles per hour, stopped to pick up the paper envelope (the holdup note) thrown from the fleeing car.

Almost thirty years later the shootout is still used as a situation analysis by police forces, including the Royal Canadian Mounted Police, as part of the basic training provided to officers regarding exposure to risk. They are taught not to expose their bodies in such situations any more than absolutely necessary, to keep themselves behind the frame of the car, not just the door, and not even to put their feet on the pavement until they have fully assessed the situation. Harrison would, by the time he came up behind them, have known from the radio dispatches that the men were armed and had committed an armed robbery. He would have seen Nichols put his gun on the roof of the car within easy reach. Why he stepped out of his car in the first place and why he then left the protection, limited as it was, of the car door, we will never know. Why he did not seem to be aware of the fact that there were more than two people in the car, when he knew that two men had robbed the credit union and he had seen the change of drivers occur, thus establishing that there were at least three people in the car, remains a mystery.

All might still have gone well for Harrison but for the fact that he suddenly lost control of the situation by turning back to his own car. He may have fired a warning shot to try to keep the initiative. He may not. For Nichols and Gamble, however, it was their only chance, and they took it, with the eventual tragic results.

Nichols later agreed to be interviewed by the Vancouver police and the RCMP regarding the incident, after he had been convicted and was serving his life sentence. Both police forces wanted to help their officers understand what could lead to shooting situations and why they must be so careful when that possibility existed. Nichols was very candid and said that moving too quickly in such situations could lead to chaos.

WHO SAW WHAT?

Eyewitness reports of crisis situations have long been recognized as potentially unreliable. Criminal trials are filled with conflicting and contradictory accounts of the same situation, even when there is no particular interest in the outcome of a legal proceeding that may have led to uncertainty of result. Judicial and legislative tests have been established to try to ensure that persons are not convicted of crimes, except in circumstances when guilt has been established beyond a reasonable doubt. Yet even with such a high burden of proof, there have been many cases in which convictions have resulted from such evidence, which have later been reversed in the face of subsequently obtained and more reliable evidence. The accounts that would come forth during the trial of Nichols and Janise Gamble for the murder of Sergeant Harrison demonstrate the point all too clearly.

John Hunter was driving his Toyota in a westerly direction on Memorial Drive. He came to a stop behind Harrison's car. His recollection is of Harrison standing in the "v" formed by his open front door. He saw two men get out of the car in front of Harrison's, the driver first and then the other, and start to walk towards Harrison's car. Hunter looked away as he decided whether he could get around the stopped cars. When he looked back, Harrison had moved out from his car with his gun drawn, and the two men had their hands on the roof of their own car. Hunter looked away again for a split second and then saw Harrison shaking his gun as if giving an order to someone else in the car. There was a movement in the back seat of the lead car, and a shot was fired. The moment this happened Hunter ducked down across the front seat and saw nothing more until the shooting stopped. He heard seven or eight shots.

John Cox, driving a cab for the Killarney taxi company, was in the group of cars on Memorial Drive, on his way to the General Hospital to pick up a fare. He stopped two or three cars behind Harrison's car and was thus further away than Hunter. By the time Cox arrived, Harrison was between the front of his car and the lead car. The shooting started. Harrison ducked behind his door, got up and took a shot, and was hit when he rushed to the back of his car to get the full frame as protection. Cox saw the car in front of Harrison's with the driver's door open and the passenger out. He identified Nichols as the man that he saw get out of the driver's side of the lead car and do some shooting. He said it was Nichols who drove the lead car away from the scene.

Another taxi driver, William John McKay, was driving the other way on Memorial Drive on his way to the airport. Arriving late he heard one gunshot and saw the lead car drive off.

Joan Armstead was also driving west on Memorial Drive and stopped behind the Toyota driven by Hunter. She heard shooting and saw some people crouched down on the passenger side of the lead car. There was more shooting and they ran and got into the car and drove off. Shots had come from both cars. She saw the man from the second car go from the driver's side to the trunk of the car, and that was where he fell.

There were three other witnesses to the shooting. One was Edward Murray Zimmerman, also driving west on Memorial Drive when the four cars in front of him suddenly stopped. A man emerged from the second car, whom he later identified from a photograph as Sergeant Harrison. Zimmerman got out of his car. He saw two men get out of the lead car. He was able to identify Nichols as the man on the driver's side and Gamble, from a photograph, as the man on the passenger side. He saw Harrison take two strides towards Nichols and gesture with his left hand. The two men immediately put their hands on their car. Harrison took three more strides and suddenly turned to run back to his car. He ran behind the car door. Nichols ran around to the front of the lead car to the passenger side to join Gamble. Nichols opened fire, aiming at Harrison and his car. He fired three shots. Zimmerman saw three bursts of flame from Nichols's gun. Immediately after, two shots came from Gamble. For some reason, possibly in a panicky search for cover, Zimmerman moved towards the median before moving back to his car. He saw Harrison crouched down with his right hand over the right rear fender with his gun in his hand. He saw a third person at the scene on the passenger side of the lead car. Zimmerman then started to move towards the car in front of his, at which point two police constables arrived. Thereafter he helped with the traffic control.

Constables Greenwood and Lanny Fritz were the first other police officers on the scene. They had received a radio message in their police van and were heading east on Memorial Drive to the Zoo bridge, which the suspects had already crossed, to set up a roadblock. They saw Harrison, apparently at the rear of his car, holding his gun in both hands, pointed at the lead car. They saw his hand jolt, but they were still going east and it took them another fifty to seventy yards to get turned around and come up behind the group of parked cars, forty or fifty feet behind Harrison's car. Constable Greenwood saw a male with dirty blond hair waving a gun around, so he drew his own and went for cover. He saw this male, whom he later identified as Gamble, leaning over a person in a snowbank and heard female screams. As he started creeping up the embankment, the lead car sped away and he saw Sergeant Harrison lying at the rear of his vehicle. He went to try to render assistance to Harrison.

Constable Fritz saw the detective at the back of his car near the trunk, with both arms extended and his revolver pointed at the Le-Mans. There were two people at least running around the front of the LeMans, both male and female persons, and they seemed to be in a hurry. He pulled in behind Harrison's vehicle and said that Harrison had rolled under it and was lying with his head towards them.

He remembered a male person on the passenger side of the LeMans holding a revolver with both arms extended, pointed in their direction. He saw the men drop or put away their weapons, pick up a female at the passenger side, and all dive in and drive off. He gave chase, but lost the trail.

Tracie Perry, in the front passenger seat of the car, said that as they were proceeding along Memorial Drive, Nichols had said he wanted to drive, so Janise stopped the car and they changed places. There was a car behind them, and a man got out of it with a gun, screaming at them to get out. They started to get out, Nichols on the driver's side and Gamble on the passenger's. Janise was just about out, as was Tracie, when there was a shot. Tracie went down on the floor of the car and stayed there. When Nichols had got out, she heard a clunk on the roof. When she heard a shot, she looked up and Nichols had a gun in his hand and was shooting at the man who had ordered them out of the car. She saw Janise fall to the ground.

These events would prove critical for both prosecution and defence in the murder charges to be laid later. The Crown wanted to fix Janise with possession of a gun at the time of the shootout. There was a gun found at the scene, unfired, with none of her fingerprints on it. It was near Gamble's glasses, which fell off or were knocked off when he had been grazed by one of the five bullets fired by Harrison in the exchange. There were no eyewitnesses who could testify that they had seen Janise with a gun.

As to Nichols, his eventual defence, however unappetizing, would be a combination of self-defence and provocation. The theory would be that they had already surrendered to Harrison when Harrison began shooting at them and that Nichols's action in returning the fire amounted to no more than simply protecting himself against this excessive force. For that theory to have the slightest chance, it would be necessary to show, or suggest, that Harrison, not one or other of the fugitives, had fired first. But all that would surface only months later.

The four were in flight now in earnest. The downward spiral of events became even more inexorable. Nichols and Gamble knew they had shot a police officer, even though they did not know then that Harrison would die of his wounds. With both already charged with serious crimes in Vancouver and having jumped bail, their awareness that the police would not rest until they had caught them added to the pressure. The chase eased slightly when the initial pursuit broke off as the officer stopped to pick up what proved to be the envelope on which they had written the holdup note.

Their vehicle was visibly damaged, with the rear windows almost blasted out. They did not know the area and soon were lost. They headed east on Memorial Drive and north to the Thunderbird Restaurant at 104 Meridian Road s.e. Nichols parked behind the restaurant and went in to check whether the coast was sufficiently clear. He returned to get the others, and they ordered coffee and soft drinks. Nichols then went to the back of the restaurant to get the owner, Rahim Kassam Jivraj. Pulling out his gun, he pointed it at Jivraj and said he would kill him. Jivraj asked what had happened and Nichols asked if he had heard about the accident on the radio. Jivraj had not. Nichols said that Jivraj should do what he said and that he was taking him as a hostage. He told him that he had killed a policeman. He brought Jivraj to the front, where he saw his wife, Laila, with Gamble, who was pointing a gun at her.

Nichols asked if they had a car. They did not. The fugitives decided to call a taxi. Shortly thereafter, they went to the back and with the Jivrajs got into the cab that had arrived following their call. Rahim Jivraj was in the back with Gamble, Janise, and Tracie. Nichols put Laila Jivraj next to the cab driver and got into the front seat beside her.

The cab driver asked where they wanted to go and Nichols said, "the Bay." The driver asked which one. Nichols said he did not know the area well, so the driver should just drive two or three miles to the suburbs where they would go to visit a friend who would tell him where. Mrs Jivraj, while looking straight ahead, kept nudging the driver. He thought she looked scared and sensed something was wrong. He said he had to stop for gas, which he did not need. He got out at a self-service station with the keys. Nichols got out as well and told him to get back in the car. When he refused, Nichols took the keys from him and drove the cab away. The cab driver told the service station operator to call the police.

Nichols knew that word would soon be out, so they began to look for another car. They used one of the oldest tricks in the book to get Diane Perry to stop. Gamble pointed out the window of the taxi at her car tire and she thought he meant it was flat. She stopped and got out, only to be met by Gamble with his gun out, who said, "You stupid bitch, do what we say, or we will kill you." They asked her where her house was, but, even threatened with the gun, she refused to tell them.

By then there was a police car on their tail, and the pursuit was joined. In the crowded car with seven people, including the three hostages, options were shrinking dramatically. Followed so closely by the police and with no chance of escape, Nichols and Gamble were desperate. In any police pursuit scenario, almost all advantage rests with the pursuers. The pressure is on the fugitives, and sooner or later they will make a mistake. This is all the more true when it is clear that they are lost and have no idea where they are going. The police have only to stay in contact and wait for the mistake to occur.

Nichols and Gamble started to talk about breaking into a house. Nichols spotted some children in a window and drove the car onto the lawn, getting out of the car holding one of the female hostages, Mrs Jivraj, by the neck with a gun to her head. The occupants of the home, Elaine Ingram and two of her children, Michelle and Tammy, had sufficient presence of mind, or terror, to get out the back door and run to a neighbouring home. Gamble took Diane Perry, and screaming, "Back off! Back off!" at the police who had followed them, broke through the front door of the house, just as the terrified occupants fled out the back. Janise stayed in the car until Gamble, now inside the house, shouted at her to join them. She got out and went into the house.

The finale was to be staged in the modest split-level home of David and Elaine Ingram at 6540 22nd Avenue N.E., in Calgary's northeast section of Pineridge. Within minutes the police were on the scene in large numbers. Inside the house Gamble and Nichols put furniture and mattresses against the doors and windows and smashed a few windows to show they meant business. Janise and Tracie were ordered to guard and then tie up the hostages. The situation was tense and highly unstable. The fugitives were trapped with no possibility of escape, but they were armed and they had three hostages.

AVOIDING DISASTER

The tension was not limited to the criminals, although they were the most likely to make the first mistake if the situation unravelled. The police were highly agitated as well. One of their own had been shot, although they did not yet know that the wound was mortal. As the hostage crisis began, Harrison was undergoing emergency surgery to try to save his life. They knew that there were innocent hostages and that the criminals were not only armed but willing to use their weapons. The police had to be extremely careful not to precipitate any action such as storming the house that would increase the risk to the hostages or that would put police at additional risk. The situation was at least contained inside the house. In the meantime, police sealed off the area, began to evacuate people from neighbouring houses, and established a temporary command centre. But they were powerless to prevent the huge gathering of media, there to witness and record whatever drama unfolded, and could only keep them out of the secured area.

For the media it was a made-in-heaven event, all the more so since, once the situation settled down, Nichols and Gamble were quite willing to talk. Ralph Klein, now the recently retired premier of Alberta but then a reporter, was the first to call the house. He was so surprised to get Gamble on the phone that he did not know what to ask him. Even the neighbours cooperated with the media. One, Rutfy Tidalgo and his wife, Estrella, opened up their home for reporters and provided coffee and meals. Tidalgo was a former police officer in Manila and they had only been in the home for a month.

The Calgary police had had an unhappy experience in a somewhat similar situation in southeast Calgary less than sixteen months before on 20 December 1974. It had ended very badly when a standoff had got out of control, leaving one officer dead and five wounded. It was referred to in the department as Black Friday. No one wanted a repeat of that outcome.

Calgary Police Inspector Ernie Reimer remembered the 1974 disaster. It was a mess. The individual involved, Philippe Gagnon, had been released under mandatory supervision regulations after being jailed at Drumheller, Alberta, for rape. Parole officials received reports that he was a danger to the community even before his release. Gagnon was a notorious glue-sniffer, who by December was completely out of his mind. He had gone to a store for more glue, but the salesclerk refused to sell it to him. When he stormed out, saying that he would come back and kill her, she called the police. Two officers answered the call and came to Gagnon's home, a sort of garage with an old-fashioned mechanic's grease-pit.

The two police officers ordered Gagnon to come out, whereupon he shot at them with a .22 rifle. One officer, Tom Dick, was grazed across the forehead without breaking the skin, and the other, Harvey Gregor-ish, by then getting out of the scene ASAP, was hit in the rear end. Fortunately the bullet hit his wallet, causing only pecuniary damage.

The two officers called for backup and an ambulance. Additional men soon surrounded the place. One, Boyd Davidson, was behind a garage nearby and was shot through the wooden siding he thought would shield him. He died on the spot. Gagnon, whom they thought had only a .22, had a much more powerful 30.06 hunting rifle, which had been overlooked or was thought to be out of action. Another police officer, Nick Graham, stood up from behind his car to put a shotgun blast through the window so they could flush Gagnon out by firing in tear gas. As Graham was ducking back, he was struck in the forehead by a shot that came through both car window panes before hitting him. Fortunately the bullet had flattened out sufficiently so he was not killed. Another officer, Kit Sylvestre, was hit in the throat and would have bled to death except that a paramedic was on hand and held the carotid artery closed.

Gagnon's respiratory system had been so destroyed by the glue he sniffed that he seemed to be completely unaffected by the tear gas fired into the garage by the police. Eventually they had to use an armoured military vehicle to knock down the garage wall and force him out into the open. They could not hit him with their own fire because of the railway ties around the edge of the pit where he was hiding. Gagnon came out, firing. He was killed in a hail of bullets.

At that time Calgary police did not have a tactical team and had no training in what to do in such situations. There was no standard operating procedure; it was more or less left with the detectives to do whatever was necessary with their guns. Nobody had really taken charge of the situation. Police Chief Brian Sawyer vowed that something like that would never happen again in Calgary, especially in a situation involving hostages.

The fugitives barricaded in the Ingram residence were not going to go anywhere without police involvement. The more important problem was to get the hostages out safely. The police were determined to be fully disciplined. One of the lessons learned from the 1974 shootout was to have a strongly organized reaction and a systematic approach to the situation. The place where the emergency was located was cordoned off and the immediate area was cleared. Highly specialized experts were brought in. To avoid confusion, it was important not to have too many people on the scene. With a smaller unit at work, quick changes in tactics were possible. The difficulty was that type of thing never happened as anticipated, so plans had to be flexible.

The new TACT (Tactical Armed Combat Team) teams were armed with shotguns, rapid-fire rifles, tear gas guns, periscopes and body armour. While there were initially some fourteen officers around the perimeter and two of the three five-man TACT teams were on location, the second team stood down late in the evening. This was not because the situation had cooled down but because the sergeant in charge, Gerry Beefers, knew that they would likely have to make an entry into the house and wanted his team to be as rested as possible. The four constables were Don Ogg and Jack Davies, entry, John Barnes, tear gas, and Dwight Mayor, sniper.

The key was to allow the situation to cool down from the initial tension, especially inside where the hostages were held. At this point – only about seventy minutes after the time of the robbery – the police had no idea who they were dealing with. Were they simply panicked amateurs? Were they hardened criminals? Psychopaths? Drugged out? What the police did know, however, was that they were armed and dangerous, willing to shoot a police officer and to take hostages. Contact had to be made to help establish the nature of the abductors, what they wanted, and how police should conduct the negotiations. At the same time, they had to be ready to react swiftly if things got out of control.

One piece of luck was that there were no guns in the Ingram household – unlike numerous homes in the area, which boasts many hunters and firearms enthusiasts. One local resident told the *Calgary Herald* that he broke down his own collection of rifles, dispersed the parts through the house, and hid his considerable supply of ammunition in case the gunmen reached his home, so that the weapons "wouldn't be turned on an officer out there."

Inside the Ingram house, Nichols and Gamble knew by now that their only chance was to try to negotiate their way out of the situation, using the hostages as bargaining chips. It would be up to them to initiate the process. And they would have to do so quickly, in case the police might be considering other options.

CHAPTER 4

INITIAL CONTACTS AND OPENING NEGOTIATIONS

Gamble and Nichols started the negotiating process within minutes of taking possession of the house. They knew they had to start at once, so the initiative didn't shift to the police. At 4:27 P.M. on 12 March 1976, Gamble called 911. The call was recorded, as are all 911 calls. Although Gamble, obviously very agitated and unstable, made the original call, Nichols took over the discussions shortly after.

> OPERATOR: Emergency is coming, sir.
> GAMBLE: Hello.
> OPERATOR: Police Emergency.
> GAMBLE: Yeah, cops?
> OPERATOR: Yep.
> GAMBLE: Okay, ah, what's the address here? What's the address? Hey!
> OPERATOR: Okay, man.
> GAMBLE: It's nine-eleven.
> OPERATOR: Hello. Hello. Hello.
> GAMBLE: We're at 65th and 26th, man, you've got it on your fucking records now, right?
> COATES: (*Inspector Sid Coates of the Calgary Police Department*)

Hello. Hello, Coates here.

GAMBLE: Hello!

COATES: Hello.

GAMBLE: You gonna fuckin' talk to me, man, or am I goin' to start wastin' bodies?

COATES: No, listen, we'll talk to you. Don't get excited now.

GAMBLE: Well, motherfucker, I'm going to get excited, man, 'cause I got dick to lose, you got this?

COATES: Yeah.

GAMBLE: And you're gonna do what you're fuckin' told.

COATES: Right, that's right.

GAMBLE: Now in two minutes' time I'm gonna fire two rounds out this fuckin' window to show you that I mean business, you got it?

COATES: Yeah, we got it.

GAMBLE: Get on your fuckin' mikes, man, and listen to this, all right?

COATES: (*in background*) Tell them he's going to fire two shots out the window, but don't be alarmed.

Coates put out an immediate call for Detective Joe Hautzinger, who had experience in hostage situations, to come into headquarters. He knew that Hautzinger's services would be needed if the situation developed.

Once Gamble had made his call and initial threats, Nichols took over to say that they wanted to negotiate. He said they knew they had shot a cop, and there were going to be a lot more people "wasted" if the police didn't "fuckin' do what they said." Coates said he was listening and that they should go ahead.

Nichols told him to radio Vancouver, to tell the Vancouver police that his name was Nichols and that he was on bail from Okalla for attempted murder and armed robbery. The name of the other man was John Gamble, who was up for Murder One, from Vancouver. They were to ask the Vancouver police about a break and enter and robbery two days before.

At this point Nichols was beginning a campaign of disinformation designed to convince the police that they were far more heavily armed than they really were. In fact they had only two handguns, Gamble's Luger and Nichols's .38. The reason Nichols wanted the police to check with Vancouver was that, among the weapons taken during the break-in before they left, there were some automatic weapons and am-munition. Although they did not have these with them, they had to try to get the police to think they did. Nichols hoped that the Van-couver police would confirm that weapons of this type had been stolen during the break-in, to lend credibility to their claim that they had the weapons in Calgary. This seemed to assume that none of the police in pursuit would have noticed that they had nothing of that size. Nichols claimed to have an M-16, an M-1, a 9-millimetre Luger, two .38s, and some three thousand rounds of ammunition. They were therefore going to do it their way. "We have fuck-all to lose, baby. Okay?" Nichols said. Coates assured him that the police did not want anyone else hurt. Nichols said that if someone got hurt it would be the fault of the police. Coates again assured him it would not be be-cause of the police.

Then Nichols wanted assurances there would be no news leaks. Coates said that would be tough, because the media monitored every-thing. Nichols did not want their names to be made public. The idea that their identities could be kept from the media was unrealistic. In fact, Nichols had already called Diane Perry's husband, David Perry, at her request, to say that she was being held as a hostage. He in turn called the police emergency service to say that he had just got a call that "somebody's got my goddamn wife." He said the men told him they were escaped convicts from Vancouver and that they had his wife and six other people. The officer said they knew and that they had the house surrounded. Perry wanted to know why the police had not phoned him. The police operator, no doubt rolling his eyes, said they had not had time. Nor, of course, had they any idea who was in the house.

In the meantime the call between Nichols and Coates continued, neither of them aware that Perry had called the police. Nichols told Coates they had five hostages. (Tracie and Janise were originally posi-tioned as additional hostages.) He threatened to "blow their fuckin' brains out." He told Coates to stay on the line and then came back to say that they were going to send a girl, whom he said was a diabetic, out to get some medicine from the car. Coates said he would need to tell the police on the scene to stay back while she came out and went back in. Nichols said he and Gamble would have their guns trained on her, and "if I so much as see a cop, I'm going to blow her brains out." He then put a gun to the head of the terrified Diane Perry and forced her to talk to the police. It was an ugly scene, intended to terrorize the victim and intimidate the police.

PERRY: Help me, please. I …
COATES: Yeah, okay.
PERRY: Do as you're told, please.
COATES: Yeah, we'll help ya.
PERRY: No, they haven't hurt us.
COATES: They haven't hurt you, hey?
PERRY: Yes, yes.
COATES: Now everything's okay?
PERRY: I'm scared. I want my … Yes.
COATES: Okay. Are you the lady that's going to go out and pick up your insulin?

Nichols took back the phone and told Coates that Diane Perry was not the diabetic. Coates wanted a description of who would be coming out. Nichols said she was Pakistani and had on a blue polka-dot outfit. Coates was to call back once the police on the scene had been alerted. This was done, and Laila Jivraj came out, got a purse and coat from the car, and returned to the house without incident.

Once the initial call had come in, the police had been making the standard efforts to trace it. This was no longer necessary, since they now knew the address of the house and Nichols had given them the phone number. They made arrangements for the trunk line to stay open and to drop the lock on the line so that it would be possible to call the number. There was no problem with direct calls to the police. The key was to get permission to record the calls involving third parties, which required judicial authorization. This was obtained for thirty-six hours, beginning at 7:30 P.M. However, the wiretap ended up being a matter of frustration, since the evidence gathered that way was later ruled inadmissible at the trial.

GETTING THE HOSTAGES OUT ALIVE

Once the situation involved hostages, the police's primary objective was to get them out alive. A hostage situation would only be measured as a success if every one of them was rescued. The police developed a plan, which they stuck to from beginning to end, and they operated as a team, seamlessly, with no rivalries or turf wars.

The officer with the most experience in such matters was Ernie

Reimer, who had joined the Calgary force in February 1954. He had done the usual series of duties, on patrol for three or four years, traffic (including motorcycle) for five years, canine for about two years, before getting into the Criminal Investigation Division, covering major crimes including robberies and homicides until 1973. He became a detective sergeant in robbery and homicide. He then did some research and put together a program package for training in subjects such as interrogation – how to get all the information and facts from witnesses – and taught at the Canadian Police College and RCMP Depot Division (the basic training depot for all RCMP members in Regina).

Reimer then took a course in hostage techniques from Harvey Schlossberg, a detective and psychologist in New York. Schlossberg was the psychologist for street crime in New York and had written a textbook called *Psychologist with a Gun*. He was fond of saying about criminals that "They only hear it if they say it." Reimer did a year of researching terrorist activities with specific application to policing concepts and was sent to England for a course on terrorism. In 1976, before the time of the hostage-taking, he was appointed staff inspector in charge of training. In January 1977 he would become superintendent in charge of investigations; in 1978, deputy chief of police; and chief of police when Brian Sawyer retired in 1984. He was chief of police during the 1988 Calgary Olympic Winter Games. After serving as chief in Calgary, he went to Regina in May 1990 as chief of police there and in September 1994 retired to Calgary.

As it happened, Reimer was at Calgary police headquarters when the call from Gamble came in. He stayed to direct and participate in the crisis. He made an immediate request for Joe Hautzinger to come in as well, since Hautzinger too had experience in hostage situations. In fact, the experiences of the two went beyond the professional involvement, since each of them had at one time also been hostages themselves.

SECOND CONTACT

The captors re-established contact with the police at 4:55 P.M. By this time Hautzinger had arrived at police headquarters to take over the telephone negotiations. Once he had introduced himself, Nichols told him they wanted the helicopter that was buzzing around the area removed or they would "blow that fucker sky high" with the M-16 he said they had. Hautzinger said it should be easy to get the chopper away from the area. It was not clear at that time whether it was a police helicopter or one operated by a media outlet.

Hautzinger tried to see if some rules of engagement could be established. He also knew that it was important to get the fugitives talking. He said he was a bit worried about the calls the men were making, including the one to Diane Perry's husband, who was now calling in to the police. They shouldn't be doing anything to shake things up and make it impossible for the police to stop interceding, Hautzinger said.

Nichols said that Diane Perry had wanted her husband to know, that they were trying to be "decent" about the situation. He then tried to add another element that would show they meant business with the hostages, that they were desperate and would not be taken alive. He wanted to know if the police had been in contact with the Vancouver police. If they had, he said, they would know their position: that they were not going to be taken alive and would kill as many people as they felt necessary. Hautzinger said he understood and that they all understood that the people in the house had done nothing to deserve dying.

Nichols then asked about the policeman they had shot. At this point Harrison was undergoing emergency surgery, and his condition could hardly have been more serious. The police, however, deliberately withheld this information so that the men would not feel even more cornered and therefore be more likely to do something rash involving the hostages. The police strategy was to do their best to downplay the seriousness of the situation. Hautzinger said Harrison was holding his own, that it had been "kind of a low shot" that had not hit any of his vital organs but that he was hurting and had "scared the hell out of the bunch of us."

Nichols said it was just too bad that Harrison was there where he had been, that it was too bad they had taken the road that they had, but there they were. He said he was glad Harrison wasn't dead and hoped Hautzinger was not lying to him about that.

Hautzinger now began the tentative process of trying to discover what they were dealing with. At this stage police knew virtually nothing about the individuals involved, although Nichols had given them his and Gamble's names and one of the hostages, Diane Perry, had been identified. Police needed to know what the captors wanted and what they had in mind. Was it a standard trade-hostages-for-money-and-escape scenario, or was it something different? Such a situation has many of the elements of contract bridge: each player can see his own hand but not those of the others, and through the bidding process, which may involve genuine signals and deliberate misdirection, or conventions not always equally understood, must reach some conclusion as to where all the cards are located and develop a strategy for the game. Hautzinger asked Nichols where they stood and what the final outcome would be. What did they want?

Nichols said they wanted to get out. They had some money from the credit union and asked if the police were prepared to give them more. Hautzinger said that anything was possible. He was in no position to give guarantees, but he would try anything to get the people out of there. Nichols then asked if they could get a plane. Hautzinger said not to make him promise to do something he couldn't deliver. Nichols said they hadn't decided whether to choose a plane, car, train, or other means of transportation – even a boat – to which Hautzinger retorted, "Well, boats are tough around here, pal. Well, first of all, we gotta have water."

Nichols alternated between threats and wheedling, trying to explain that their idea had been to get away from the charges in Vancouver, and they had to do an armed robbery to get to where they wanted to go, "so that we could start living like decent human beings, packing lunch bags, the whole bit." He did not mention the proposed Brinks job in Toronto. He told Hautzinger they didn't know yet where they wanted to go.

Later they made their monetary demands, showing in the process that they had little imagination and limited expectations. Nichols asked Gamble how much they needed. One hundred thousand dollars, Gamble said. Nichols asked Hautzinger whether he thought it was too much. Hautzinger said only that it seemed possible.

Then Gamble got on the line. "Tell him, hey, excuse me, tell that fucking fat man, take it cool, step by fucking step. Okay, you got that, copper?" Nichols repeated the "step by step," adding, "not too fast."

This was Hautzinger's first hands-on sense of Gamble and his high degree of instability. He told Nichols he did not know how jumpy his partner was but that he should calm him down, because if he got jumpy and did something wrong, there could be trouble. Nichols said that Gamble was very edgy and that if the least thing went wrong, he would start pulling the trigger, but that he was keeping Gamble down and everything was fine. Hautzinger made it clear that there was some risk to the captors if Gamble were to step over the edge, that there were some young guys out there on the street as well.

Putting the money together proved not to be too difficult. The police gave receipts to the Bank of Montreal for it, promising to return the money if it was not required. Two rifle-toting detectives brought it to police headquarters. They did not need to disclose this information to the captors at the beginning of the siege, since it was a card they could play later if matters became tense and they needed something new to show their good faith. They played the difficulty card, saying that money in the amount Nichols and Gamble wanted had to be obtained from the bank vaults, which were locked up for the weekend, even though the banks were still open on the Friday night. Nichols never seemed to figure out the inconsistency in that position – that the banks were still open, dealing in cash, which would also have to be put away for the weekend, but that somehow the vaults were already locked.

Shortly after the conversation regarding Gamble and his excitable state, Nichols made the first demand for drugs. This would be the beginning of a long negotiation and the eventual end game. He said he could keep Gamble cool with some heroin – a very troubling request. Hautzinger immediately said he would be lying if he said he could do that. Nichols said he didn't use it himself, that he would be cool. But Gamble was ranting in the background, "Fuckin' operator, the fuckin' badges, fuckin' do it, you fuckin' goop."

Hautzinger said he would try, but he had to be perfectly honest, it would be very "heavy." He was also worried about the Cloud Nine effect if Gamble got the heroin. Nichols tried to assure him that Gamble did not "do" that much, just enough to keep him down. He would watch Gamble closely. As for himself, "I can't stand the fuckin' thought of heroin. It's dirty, stinking, fuckin' slime, it's fuckin' skunch." If Gamble needed it, he needed it, but he would not let him use too much.

Hautzinger said he would see what he could do and then call back. Nichols said they would need two outfits so that the heroin could be injected and that they would mix it and first try it on one of the hostages, in case there was a "hot cap." They didn't have any idea yet about transportation but would let Hautzinger know. They were in no hurry.

The helicopter was still in the area, Nichols reminded Hautzinger, and again threatened to blow it out with the M-1 or M-16, even though it was only an observation helicopter. Hautzinger agreed to get it out of the area.

The objectives on both ends of the telephone conversation were obvious. The police wanted to calm the situation as much as possible, since tensions were very high and the chances of things going wrong were at their highest. Any additional pressure on Nichols and Gamble might push them into precipitous action, endangering the hostages. The police had to defuse the pressure as best they could, with almost no information regarding the condition of anyone in the house. For their part, the captors were concerned to provide disinformation regarding their status and the weapons they possessed. They exaggerated their weaponry and the amount of ammunition on hand and had to make it clear to the police who surrounded them that they were ready to kill hostages if any attempt was made to storm the house.

Hautzinger called back to report on the apparent difficulty the police were having in getting the money Nichols and Gamble demanded, but assured Nichols they were working on it. He also said that the request for heroin was not going to work. Someone from the drug detail of the department had been in and would not authorize the use of any of the heroin the department might have picked up on the street, so he was going to have to say no to the demand. Nichols immediately asked for some Demerol, after checking with Gamble to see if that would be okay. He wanted a thirty-pack of disposables, with 25g needles. All Hautzinger had to do was drive to a hospital and pick it up. Nichols also wanted something to drink – the people in the house were getting thirsty. He asked if Hautzinger wanted to talk to one of the hostages. Then he put Gamble on the phone.

NICHOLS: Then here's my partner.
HAUTZINGER: Yeah, okay.
GAMBLE: Are you gonna get the broad?
HAUTZINGER: I'm sorry?
GAMBLE: Talk to a chick.
HAUTZINGER: I can't hear ya.
GAMBLE: How're you doing? What's your name?
HAUTZINGER: My name's Hautzinger. Joe.
GAMBLE: Joe?
HAUTZINGER: Yep.
GAMBLE: Okay, Joe. Yeah, look we're gonna try and be as manly about this as possible, right?
HAUTZINGER: Sounds fair.
GAMBLE: Okay? But like I want ta tell ya somethin' right now, man, right? You got all your fuckin' punks outside, and you're gonna probably bring in a lot more, I can dig it. Ah, it's all

fuckin' procedure, man, and you gotta protect everybody. I can dig it. Now I want that fucking junk, man. Okay? I want that fucking junk, bad, man. Okay?

HAUTZINGER: Well, I want the people –

GAMBLE: Now.

HAUTZINGER: – Safe, and, you know, real bad, so we're gonna try hard …

GAMBLE: Hey, baby, if you wanna have 'em safe, man, well, like the name of the game, man, is make a patch, right?

HAUTZINGER: Seems fair.

GAMBLE: Right, you patch with me, man, I'm gonna patch with you, right?

HAUTZINGER: Uh-hum.

GAMBLE: You don't fuckin' patch with me, motherfucker, like, ah, if worse comes to worse, I'll just blow these fuckers away and I'll blow myself away 'cause I ain't going behind fuckin' bars again, dig it?

HAUTZINGER: Well, can you –

GAMBLE: You dig it, you're scared the fuck of shit of me, man, right?

HAUTZINGER: Yeah, can I –

GAMBLE: Okay, now, listen to me. You get that fuckin' stuff, I'm gonna tell you somethin' else right now. If there's one fuckin' shot come through this fuckin' window, you fuckin' turkey, heh-heh-heh, there's gonna be one ear comin' right out behind it, have you got it? One fuckin' ear. Okay?

HAUTZINGER: Well, ya, ya gotta realize that there's no way we want that to happen, okay? We would do anything to keep that from happening.

GAMBLE: Hey, baby, you do it.

HAUTZINGER: Ah, but you gotta buy our situation a little bit too here, John.

GAMBLE: Okay.

HAUTZINGER: And here's what I'm, is, what I want you to understand.

GAMBLE: All right.

HAUTZINGER: I'm in the spot of wanting those people out of there just as bad as you want out of town, okay?

GAMBLE: Right.

HAUTZINGER: So …

GAMBLE: No, not out of town, sweetheart. The country.

HAUTZINGER: Okay, anywhere, that, but what I'm getting at is that, ah, you know, you gotta start somewhere, and town is where you're at, so, ah, if I say the wrong thing, don't hold me, you know …

GAMBLE: Right.

HAUTZINGER: Don't, don't nail me to it, just because of that. But I, what I want you to understand is that, it's, it's gotta be, well it's gotta be cool. We, we can't just jump at things. Ah, you know it and I know it and, ah …

GAMBLE: Hey, we'll take it …

HAUTZINGER: Understand that I want it done as definitely as you do, but I gotta take my time about it.

GAMBLE: Okay, baby, we'll take it step by step, man …

HAUTZINGER: Yeah, yeah.

GAMBLE: But don't take too many fuckin' steps, or I'll blow your fuckin' kneecap. Hey?

HAUTZINGER: Well, you don't, you don't want it and I don't want it, because …

GAMBLE: Okay.

HAUTZINGER: Both got an end to meet.

GAMBLE: Okay, so your name's Joe.

HAUTZINGER: Yeah.

GAMBLE: Okay, I'll be expecting to hear from you, man. Don't be too long with the fucking dope …

HAUTZINGER: Okay, I got a little problem.

GAMBLE: If I don't have the dope, I'm gonna fuckin', like, I'm really hyper, right?

HAUTZINGER: Yeah.

GAMBLE: I just have to have somethin' to calm me down, mother, and don't give me no fuckin' hot caps, man, because I'm gonna try it on some of these people.

HAUTZINGER: Well, is it possible to get a hot cap of Demerol?

GAMBLE: What?

HAUTZINGER: Is it possible to get a …

GAMBLE: Well, man, you fuckers can load anything.

HAUTZINGER: Oh, I see what you mean, but no …

GAMBLE: Tight?

HAUTZINGER: I want you to understand somethin'. I'm a, I'm a flatfoot, a gumboot. I wouldn't know junk if it came from my soup.

GAMBLE: Okay, well I, I'll leave that to your, ah, maybe to your class –

HAUTZINGER: Yeah.

GAMBLE: Boys in the laboratory, okay?

HAUTZINGER: Okay. They're being –

GAMBLE: You fix one fucking joint, man, just one, and it's game over.

HAUTZINGER: It'd be kind of a dumb move.

GAMBLE: Because like I'm gonna end up in the grave anyway, right? I mean let's, ah, let's face facts.

HAUTZINGER: You've kind of got –

GAMBLE: But let's try and make it nice.

HAUTZINGER: Okay, listen, your partner, Bill.

GAMBLE: Yeah, what about him?

HAUTZINGER: Told me to get ahold of Vancouver, find out who you are and what you're up to, okay? I tried.

GAMBLE: Hey, what did you find out about the machine gun?

HAUTZINGER: I tried. Ah, I'm sorta halfway in between. There's a lot of Gambles and Nichols out there. What are your full names?

GAMBLE: Okay, John.

HAUTZINGER: Yeah.

GAMBLE: Thomas.

HAUTZINGER: Yeah.

GAMBLE: Frederick.

HAUTZINGER: Yep.

GAMBLE: Gamble. That's me.

HAUTZINGER: Okay, that's where I went wrong. Hang on a second, I blew it, I'm backwards here. John Tom Frederick.

GAMBLE: Okay?

HAUTZINGER: Just a minute.

GAMBLE: Billy! What's your full name? William Nichols.

HAUTZINGER: Uh-hum.

GAMBLE: And, ah, the hostages' names are, what's your name, baby? Diane Perry.

HAUTZINGER: Uh-hum.

GAMBLE: What's the other name? Get the other name. Laila

(*phonetic*). Who? Who? Paso (*phonetic*), and her old man, man, it's her husband, okay?

HAUTZINGER: What's his name?

GAMBLE: Paso, or some fucking thing.

HAUTZINGER: What's his first name?

GAMBLE: What's his first name? Clayland (*phonetic*).

UNKNOWN MALE: Paso. Clayland (*phonetic*) They're the owner of a restaurant, the Thunderbird Restaurant.

GAMBLE: Yeah, they, they ran, they working at the Thunderbird Restaurant, man, that's how we shook your cops.

HAUTZINGER: Uh-hum.

GAMBLE: Okay?

HAUTZINGER: Uh-hum.

GAMBLE: Now there's, ah, you know, like ah, like man, like, ah, let's get some action, hey?

HAUTZINGER: Well, okay, now –

GAMBLE: I was tellin' ya, I just want to put one point across to ya, and listen to me good, okay?

HAUTZINGER: Yeah, I'm here.

GAMBLE: Then I'm gonna shut up and I'll give you to my partner, man.

HAUTZINGER: Well, okay, I, before you go I got somethin' that I gotta point out to ya, though. But go ahead, I want to hear what you're gonna say.

GAMBLE: One shot comes through those fuckin' windows …

HAUTZINGER: Yeah.

GAMBLE: Right? And, ah, one of them's gonna come out.

HAUTZINGER: Well, let me guarantee you this, first of all, and, ah, John. Ah, I take it your first name is John?

GAMBLE: Yeah.

HAUTZINGER: With all those first names, it's hard to tell. Listen, there's no way I want that. There's no way I'm going to allow that –

GAMBLE: Well, baby –

HAUTZINGER: Give out any kind of a, a, any kind of order, but you got to realize one thing: don't shake up the boat there and those guys out there ain't gonna shake it up on the other side either.

GAMBLE: Well …

HAUTZINGER: Here's my biggest problem right now, John.
GAMBLE: Okay.
HAUTZINGER: The, the junk goin' in, really, it's going to be hard for me to do, and here's what I want you to hear it out now, hear my whole side of this thing, and try to pretend that you got, you know, you got the same problem I got. Let's say for a moment that I get it for ya, let's say I'm able to.
GAMBLE: Okay.
HAUTZINGER: One thing goes wrong after that ...
GAMBLE: Yeah.
HAUTZINGER: Man, I might just as well ...
GAMBLE: Well, you fuck!
HAUTZINGER: Like killed everybody.
GAMBLE: Look, you fuck, you get it and get it now. (*in background*) Talk to the fuck man. Fuck 'em. He's trying to fuckin' ... us.

Nichols got back on the line. He wanted the Demerol to be delivered within twenty minutes, in a police car with one officer in it – a female officer. Hautzinger refused, and Nichols said any cop would do and that the officer was to come to the front door with the drugs, drop it in through the broken window, and leave at once. Hautzinger was concerned with what might happen if the authorities refused to provide the Demerol. He did not want anything to go wrong and was anxious that there should be some way to iron things out. Nichols said he was going to bring Diane Perry to the phone, but that Hautzinger was not to ask her anything about the interior of the house, about guns or about anything other than her well-being, or there would be trouble. Hautzinger said he did not want any trouble and that Nichols knew this.

NICHOLS: Here, here's Mrs Perry.
HAUTZINGER: Right.
PERRY: Hello.
HAUTZINGER: Hello. How are ya?
PERRY: Scared.
HAUTZINGER: Yeah, you – you probably are supposed to be. How's everybody else making out?
PERRY: We're all scared.

HAUTZINGER: Yeah, well, listen now. First of all, ah, the best I can say is hang in there. Ah, there's absolutely no way that we want any harm to come to ya.
PERRY: Yes.
HAUTZINGER: We're going to try everything in our power to, to cooperate with the people that are there. Our biggest problem.
PERRY: Yes, please do.
HAUTZINGER: Pardon.
PERRY: Please cooperate with them.
HAUTZINGER: Oh yes, we're going to, but now, Mrs Perry, our biggest problem right now is they're making some demands that are very hard for us to go along with right now, because it's hard to get our hands on the things they're asking for.
NICHOLS: (*coming back on the phone*) Okay, that's good.

Hautzinger went back to the difficulties in getting the drugs Nichols had demanded and what might happen if he did get them and turned them over to the captors. Nichols was running short of patience, in all likelihood because he knew it was not that difficult to get Demerol. He told Hautzinger that he was wasting time. He had only fifteen minutes to have the police car in front of the house, and Nichols wasn't going to sit on the phone talking to him all day. Hautzinger told him that he would do anything that was possible, but that if Nichols made it impossible for him, it would be Nichols who made it go wrong, whereas he wanted nothing more than for it to go right. If he wanted it to go sour, all he would do was just say "no" and that would be it. He wanted to try, but he could not do it in fifteen minutes. There was not even a hospital within fifteen minutes of where they were holed up. Nichols, who knew nothing about Calgary, said there was one within ten minutes, but Hautzinger said there wasn't. They countered back and forth until Hautzinger said he would do it as fast as he could, and Nichols said all right. If he couldn't get the stuff, Hautzinger said, he would call back. Nichols warned him about Gamble: "Do you remember how Johnny is? When he talks, talk goes along with action. He don't say useless words, okay?"

Nichols tried some good captor–bad captor talk with Hautzinger, beginning with the presence of the tactical units in the area, which he referred to as "SWAT guys." He wanted to know what they were doing in all the windows, and Hautzinger said they had to get the people out of the other houses because they did not want anyone else getting hurt.

Nichols wanted them pulled back, "'Cause Johnny gets uptight. He sees a cop and then he's going to do somethin' wrong." Nichols, did not want that, he said, and he was sure Hautzinger did not want that. "Johnny don't want that, but he's the type that goes ahead anyway." Then he tried to get some alcohol.

> NICHOLS: And I want a bottle of Canadian Club, or rye of any type, okay?
> HAUTZINGER: That's bad …
> NICHOLS: That's mine.
> HAUTZINGER: Really bad.
> NICHOLS: I'd like a drink.
> HAUTZINGER: Really, really bad. I know you do, but we got to keep the heads really clean clear, huh?
> NICHOLS: Like hey, listen, I, my head is the one that I'm worrying about. I'm not going to do anythin' stupid. You just do that, okay?
> HAUTZINGER: Yeah, yeah, but you see what happens if it gets a little thick with some booze?
> NICHOLS: No, no, no.
> HAUTZINGER: Huh, you're talking about a life –
> NICHOLS: Hold it! Hold it! No! No! No, Johnny! Okay.
> HAUTZINGER: What happened?
> NICHOLS: He was going to blow a fuckin' head off.
> HAUTZINGER: What's wrong? Whose head?
> NICHOLS: He's uptight. One of the hostages.
> HAUTZINGER: Yeah, well.
> NICHOLS: Now he's fuckin' uptight.
> HAUTZINGER: You see what –
> NICHOLS: Johnny, stay cool.
> HAUTZINGER: What I'm tryin' to say –
> GAMBLE: (*in background*) Hang up on the fuckin' goop! Let's get some action.
> NICHOLS: Okay. Okay. You go ahead …

Even the captors knew that getting some heroin was probably out of the question, and it was Nichols who suggested Demerol instead, almost immediately after Hautzinger's initial reluctance to consider it. But it was progress, giving them something in exchange for something else. While arrangements for the Demerol were being made, the captors continued to use the phone, and Hautzinger was unable to reach them. He had to wait until Nichols called back later. Nichols explained, "People want to talk to their husbands." Hautzinger told him that the Demerol was on its way to the station and that it would soon be there, along with a doctor, and that it seemed to be a "go." Nichols said they needed some cigarettes for one of the hostages, a carton of Players filter. He complained again about the swat team, and Hautzinger said he had been too busy getting things organized with the doctor and had not done anything about it. He gave the impression that the doctor had been making things difficult. But he assured Nichols that nobody would be making any move towards the house until he said so. Meanwhile Gamble ranted in the background, "One for the fucker in one shot, okay, I have … You were the one who … no more fuckin' shots fired, hey, but if one of them fuckin' stupid pricks out there fuckin' try and take us tonight, there'll be a bullet in their fuckin' heads."

Nichols spoke about arrangements with the hostages for the night, since it was obvious that no one would be leaving the house before the next day. He said there were three bedrooms and that there would be a hostage in each, with a gun in each, referring again to the m-16 they supposedly had. Hautzinger said there was no way anyone would try to make a forcible entry during the night, and Nichols said he was going to try to take his word for that. Gamble shouted, "You fire off two shots, sweetheart, we'll have about twenty-two off to your one, motherfucker!"

Nichols asked again whether the police had checked with Vancouver and found out about the weapons. Hautzinger said they had and that the weapons had been obtained on a break and enter. Nichols said that the police knew they were not fucking around, and Hautzinger replied that they had to know that to begin with, since they had obviously not shot a spit wad at Harrison. Nichols asked if they knew what he had been hit with, and Hautzinger said he did not know, that he had enough on his mind without bugging any doctors. He had his hands full where he was.

The captors were constantly trying to indicate that they had more weapons and ammunition than they actually possessed, and Nichols tried to provide as much disinformation as possible, making sure Hautzinger heard it. "Hey, Johnny. Ah, don't forget that, those two clips down beside Jannie there. Well, the one of them that have only got about twelve or fourteen rounds left in it because I fired off, I don't know, ten, fifteen shots when we came across the … So fill it up, make sure there's the full thirty." He then asked Hautzinger, "What the fuck is that chopper doing back?"

Hautzinger revealed his annoyance with the media – "Everybody wants to be a hero" – and their interference with police activities in complicated situations. The police efforts throughout the hostage scene were complicated by the media presence and their direct contacts with the suspects. All the radio stations had monitors on the police radios and got their hot news that way. Many reporters called the house and spoke directly with Gamble and Nichols. One of the first to make contact was Ralph Klein, then a radio journalist. He was so surprised to get through that he had practically no idea of what to ask them. Hautzinger said the helicopter was probably one of the news outfits. Nichols said again he was worried about their names getting out, and Hautzinger assured him that it would not be through the police.

By now it was obvious that, although both men were extremely dangerous, Nichols could, to some degree, be reasoned with. Gamble, however, was at the very edge of violence and extreme action. The police had still no idea of what the two men would do. Were they dealing with a scenario in which one captor might have a genuine difference in outlook and approach from the other? Or were Nichols and Gamble using something like the good cop–bad cop routine used by police in certain situations? Every time matters began to drag, Gamble would start ranting, but this could have either been an act or the actions of someone very unstable.

The police concluded that the men would probably have more compunction about harming Diane Perry than the other two hostages, but the degree of difference was too narrow to gauge at that point. The negotiations would have to continue. Fatigue and eventual acceptance of the inevitable by the suspects needed to be allowed to develop.

In the meantime, the police had the cash demanded by the captors, in case that scenario might have to be played out to assure the safety of the hostages. That action would later be criticized by the Calgary mayor Rod Sykes.

Both sides, each with misgivings and concerns, settled in for a siege.

CHAPTER 5

HOSTAGE SIEGE

The first few hours of any hostage situation are always the most nerve-wracking, as both sides feel their way. The negotiators, Inspector Ernie Reimer and detectives Joe Hautzinger and Doug Green, were at Calgary police headquarters, well removed from the scene of the crisis, working their way into the confidence of the captors. "There are several different types of people who take hostages," Reimer observed. "The first task for the police is to identify what type is involved." Hostages are often, but not always, taken simply as a means of trying to ensure escape. That was certainly what Nichols and Gamble had first hoped and the position they first took when contact was established with the police.

The initial contacts had to some extent calmed the situation to the point that there seemed to be no immediate likelihood of unilateral action from either quarter. The captors had made their demands for money and some sort of free passage (to be determined), as well as for drugs, ostensibly to calm Gamble, who seemed to be the more agitated of the two perpetrators. There was no immediate prospect of quick resolution, and both sides appeared ready to let the solution develop as time went on. The police objective would be to delay, delay, delay and to give as little as possible in return for the most concessions possible.

They had to be careful, however, to build a relationship that gave them credibility and to gauge the maximum amount of delay that would keep the two men from acting precipitously. Nichols appeared to be someone with whom they could reason, although by no means unwilling to resort to violence if pushed into a corner. Gamble was mercurial and by far the more unbalanced, clearly on the edge of self-destruction and willing, in the process, to kill the hostages. There was a delicate balance to be maintained as the passage of time would, they hoped, leech some of the tension from the situation. They had to make haste, but ever so slowly, all the while building a relationship of credibility.

The drugs were obviously a much greater problem than the money. Providing the criminals with heroin was clearly not an option, and even they seemed to understand that position. It was Nichols who suggested Demerol when the police resisted the idea of heroin. Both he and the police seemed to know that something would have to be provided to calm Gamble down. The question was what this should be and in what quantities. A three or four day supply of anything had to be out of the question. And, whenever the police gave something, they had to get something in return.

While that aspect was beginning to play itself out, it was important to keep in regular touch with the situation, to be in a position to gauge the emotional temperament of the captors. With some understanding that Demerol would be provided, although always looking for some excuse that would lead to a bit more delay, Hautzinger called the house. Gamble answered the phone.

GAMBLE: Yeah.

HAUTZINGER: Hello. Who have I got?

GAMBLE: John.

HAUTZINGER: What happened?

GAMBLE: What do you mean, what happened?

HAUTZINGER: Well, it took a long time to come to the phone. You scared the hell out of me.

GAMBLE: Well, I ain't in no fuckin' hurry.

HAUTZINGER: Okay, well as long as that's all. Listen, ah, it seems to be go on the Demerol. Just, ah, you know, hang in there and she's on the way.

GAMBLE: Yeah, how long?

HAUTZINGER: Well, ah, here again, ah, in all honesty, as soon as we can possibly hustle our ass out there. It's just a matter of, of picking it up and getting out there with it.

GAMBLE: Now, okay, you listen, man. Like I can see your boys all over the fuckin' place, right? Don't play no fuckin' games with me.

HAUTZINGER: Well, we, like I said, we're not terribly smart, but we're not stupid enough to do something like that.

GAMBLE: Looks to be fuckin' smart, Joe, don't play no games with me, man.

HAUTZINGER: Man, this is no game. It sure isn't to me, John. I don't know about you, but it don't feel like any game to me. Ah, I don't know how to, express how I feel about this, but I know that you want things to go smooth, and you know bloody well I do, so let's just –

GAMBLE: Okay, what about the gr– what about the money?

HAUTZINGER: The money is just a matter of, ah, of, of getting a, a bank, ah, to go along with us. As I told Bill, ah, two hours earlier, no big sweat.

GAMBLE: Yeah, okay.

HAUTZINGER: Right now, it's a matter of getting managers from home and, ah, and coordinate it with the alarm people, and, ah, you know, so we can get these vaults open, those things we were talking about.

GAMBLE: Okay, well, you're a Dick Tracy fella, I can dig it, yeah.

HAUTZINGER: Well, you, you know as much about these vaults as I do. They just, ah, they close up on us at a certain time. The front end of the bank's still–

GAMBLE: Okay, lookit, ah, once we get the Demerol and the, ah, booze, and the stuff, right, then we're gonna negotiate, ah, transportation, okay?

HAUTZINGER: Sounds fair.

GAMBLE: All right, do you want to speak ta Bill?

HAUTZINGER: It's up to you. Ah, either one.

GAMBLE: Hey, Bill, have you got anything you wanna say to this fuckin' turk? Hold on.

For the two men in the house, the biggest fear was that the police might decide to force the issue and enter the premises. It was one of the reasons why they continually exaggerated the extent of their weapons and ammunition. All they had were the two handguns and a small amount of ammunition, nothing that would enable them to resist a well-planned attack by the police. They knew that the police, if they decided to come in, would have no hesitation in killing them, whether or not they had harmed the hostages. One of their own had been shot and, although the fugitives did not know it at the time, killed. They could not expect to be handled with kid gloves. Nichols complained again about the police in the neighbouring houses. Hautzinger asked him what he expected, but that they were not moving in on them. Then Nichols complained about an airplane in the area. Hautzinger said it was not a police plane and that a plane would have been no use to them in any event.

Nichols asked about Harrison, and Hautzinger lied, saying he was hanging in there. He asked Nichols how things had gone wrong and what had happened. Nichols said that Harrison had pulled into the alley behind them when they came out of the credit union. Hautzinger asked what Harrison had been hit with, and Nichols, also dissembling, said it could have been a 9mm, .38, or .45 calibre, that they had fired all three. There had of course never been a .45 calibre weapon, and only two guns had been fired. Hautzinger said he wanted to know how much damage there might be from the bullet, and Nichols said they were hollow point, which would cause far more damage than steel jacketed bullets.

Keeping him talking, Hautzinger asked Nichols why they had picked that particular credit union – "a little, shit little jerkwater place like that?" Nichols said they needed enough money to keep travelling, "to get the fuck out of here." Hautzinger started to ask about their background when Nichols said the helicopter was back. It was exactly the sort of distraction they did not need, and Hautzinger said, "Oh, fuck!" He knew it was not the police helicopter. "Now, okay," he said, "just, are you sure it's the same one? There's a goddamn news company in town, the radio station, that could be nosing …"

As the men in the house tried to look for any markings on the chopper, Hautzinger said that the dispatcher had reported that the police helicopter was sitting down in a field away from the area. The crisis passed, and Hautzinger resumed his questions.

Nichols described the pending charges in Vancouver and said they were out on bail. He said that they hadn't left Vancouver to come to Calgary to do all this. Although they had planned on doing an armed robbery, they hadn't intended on anyone getting hurt. They wanted to get out of the country and go somewhere to settle down with their girl-friends and pack a lunch every day and live a happy, normal life. But, if need be, they were fully prepared to go all the way.

Hautzinger asked how many were involved. Nichols said there were four of them, referring to the two women as "girlfriends." "Now they're scared shitless. They didn't expect none of this. They didn't know what we had planned." He refused to give Janise and Tracie's names because they did not want their parents to know. Hautzinger said he was worried about the girls getting "jumpy" and wanted Nichols to be sure to keep them as cool as he could, because if they blew it, it would all go sour and a lot of work would go down the tube. Nichols said that was why they wanted the Demerol; he was a nurse and knew what he was doing with it. He invited Hautzinger to check with Promotion College in Victoria. How was it coming? Hautzinger said generally fair and interjected that he'd just got word on Harrison and that he was not too bad. Hautzinger continued the effort not to paint the criminals into a corner from which they might decide that there was no possibility of escape. They had enough experience on the wrong side of the law to know that, if Harrison died, their chances of getting away would be non-existent.

Hautzinger played along with their hope of getting away and living happily ever after. He also continued the tactics of delay. In his next call to Nichols he pursued that strategy, this time by haggling over the dosages of the drugs and the amount to be provided. He blamed the doctor for the questions and wanted again to know how much was re-quired. Nichols said to send 20 cc, but Hautzinger insisted that the doctor wanted to know what strength and how much Gamble took on a regular basis. Nichols got impatient and asked to speak to the doctor directly. Hautzinger said that the doctor was on a different line, so Nichols said the doctor should call him directly. Hautzinger agreed. He called back later, ostensibly to see how things had gone with the doctor. Obviously, the doctor had been told not to call before there was another conversation between the two men and the police. The tactic now was to convince Nichols that the police were doing their best and that they would help break the logjam.

Hautzinger pretended to be surprised that the doctor had not called. He said he would get onto it at once, that the doctor was "a bit of an ignorant bastard." Nichols told him to hurry, and to have the doctor call Hautzinger after Nichols had spoken with him. He said that things were getting awfully tight. He also wanted to speak to the leader of the SWAT team, to warn them what would happen if they tried to enter the house. Hautzinger said he would try, but that unless the men in the house started it, the police were not coming near them.

The next conversations involved Ernie Reimer for the first time. Reimer took up the Demerol discussions. The captors wanted to use the media to get their story out and were much more comfortable dealing that way than they were with the police. The police, for their part, needed to continue to get as much reliable information as possible. Jim Knowler, a reporter from the *Calgary Herald* and a friend of Don McNeill, had come to police headquarters once the hostage situation had developed. The police thought that he could be trusted. Knowler had already been in touch with the captors by phone. He had called the house at 9:33 P.M. He was willing to meet with them as part of getting their story, but the police, unsurprisingly, were unwilling to take the risk of putting a further hostage in their hands. Knowler called back at 10:46 P.M., with Reimer alongside. In his discussions with Hautzinger, Nichols had said he would release a hostage if Knowler would come to the house.

It was a lengthy but inconsequential chat, since it was obvious that the police would never let Knowler enter the house. He told the captors that perhaps he could combine the interview with delivery of the drugs they wanted. He wondered if, after the interview, once they had told him their story, they might be prepared to give up the hostages and come in. Nichols wanted to know who was the top criminal lawyer in Calgary. Knowler said there were two or three, but he did not know who was the top.

Then he said Reimer wouldn't let him come to the house. Nichols threatened to shoot one of the hostages and demanded to speak to Reimer. Reimer wanted to know how they could talk to Knowler where he would be safe. In the midst of the conversation, already tense because of the most recent threat to kill a hostage, the men claimed there was someone on the roof. Reimer said he would get on the radio and investigate, but that the police were under orders to stay back. They were concerned with the safety of the hostages and were not going to move in on them. The police were going to try to talk them out.

Reimer was adamant but not confrontational about refusing to allow Knowler to come to the house. If they sent him with the drugs, what would they get? Nichols said they would get a hostage, the newsman, and a true story. Then they would start negotiating and they would want a lawyer. Reimer asked if Knowler could talk to them from

next door. They had hostages and maybe they wanted another one. He
said that Nichols seemed like a trustworthy soul and would keep his
word, but there were other people involved. Nichols said that they had
done an armed robbery, they had bad records, they had shot a cop, but
that when they gave their word, "we give our fuckin' word." Reimer
said he was not just dealing with Nichols but a group: him, Gamble
and Jenny (presumably Janise/Jannie), and who else? He was trying to
find out how many were involved. How many hostages did they have?
Nichols said four. Reimer thought there were only three. Nichols said
three women and one man. Reimer knew about the Jivrajs and Diane
Perry. Who was the other one? Nichols referred to Tracie Perry, but
said the two women were not related.

  Reimer asked if Gamble was hurt. Nichols said he was uptight because he needed the drugs, and whether he was hurt or not was neither here nor there. Reimer asked why Nichols wouldn't tell him.
Nichols replied that the only person there who was hurt "was hurt because they got run over by the car." Reimer told Nichols three times
that their backgrounds were not that good and that this was why he
did not want to send in Knowler and why the police were sitting back.
He asked Nichols to think of another way. Nichols said he already had:
he was going to blow away a hostage and throw him out the window.
Reimer asked him why he would want to do that to someone else, to
which Nichols said Reimer would then understand they were deadly
serious. Reimer said he knew they were serious, that they were desperate, but why would they kill a person unnecessarily? Then maybe they
would get a newsman in there, Nichols said. Reimer said he would talk
to the newsman again, but how could he get him to put his life on the
line? Nichols said he had been talking all night already. "I know I've
been talking all night," Reimer said. "That's my job."

  The conversation then went back to the drugs, the cigarettes, and
Knowler. Reimer asked what they would get for this deal. Nichols said
one hostage. Reimer asked for four, Nichols said no. Then three?
Nichols said that Hautzinger had asked them to show their good faith.
They'd talked it over and they said, okay, one hostage. Reimer knew
that was what had been agreed, so he backed off and said they would
go one step at a time. The police would throw the drugs out in front
of the house, and Nichols and Gamble would give up a hostage. The
drugs would be traded for one hostage. Nichols still wanted a newsman, but Reimer said the drugs and the hostage would be the first step.

That would be to show good faith, and then they could talk about somebody else. They would send in the drugs and cigarettes in a bag with cotton to pad the needles, and throw them as close to the front door as possible. The captors would send out a hostage for them. There would be no tricks or gimmicks, and Reimer guaranteed it on his word. Nichols asked who he was, and Reimer said he was a staff inspector, not the chief, who was not there. Nichols said he was the big man, and Reimer replied no, but he was getting up there, which was not what Nichols had meant – it was that Reimer held the word. Reimer confirmed, "I hold the word."

The deal would be that the hostage would come out to get the bag and take it into the house, and the captors would then release the hostage. Nichols thought the hostage was from Africa. Then he asked how far they would be from getting a newsman. Reimer said they would have then established some credibility, and he would talk to Knowler. The first step was the drugs and cigarettes.

They settled on one carton of Players Filter, and even that was a bargain. Nichols asked for a carton or two, and Reimer asked if he was trying to break the police department. Things would be on their way in a matter of minutes, he said. Nichols was still nervous about what action the police might make, and Reimer wanted assurance that they would not try to shoot the officer who would be throwing the bag. Nichols said they were not interested in killing people, and the fact that the police officer had been shot was not in their minds at all. Reimer asked him what they would do if the hostage just kept going when he went out for the bag; he did not want Nichols to welch on the deal if the hostage decided to break and run. When he insisted on knowing, Nichols told Reimer they would shoot the hostage. Reimer said he didn't think that was very good, and why didn't they send someone else, someone they could trust? Nichols thought that the male hostage would be all right, and it was left at that.

This step dealt with, the next was to cut back on the amount of the Demerol to be provided. As if it were a last-moment change, Reimer said there would only be a couple of vials of the drug. He did not know how many. When the captors had talked earlier with Hautzinger, the discussions had been for a box of ten or twelve vials. Now Reimer suggested three or four, and Nichols agreed with four. The package would be there shortly, Reimer said. Then he called back to say they only had a package of cigarettes at the station and had to go out to buy the carton; he would phone when the package was about to arrive. He called five minutes later to say that it was almost there and that the Safeway bag would be thrown as close to the front door as the police officer could manage. He also said that there were only two vials of Demerol and that the doctor had refused to release more than two. Nichols said they could manage on two vials for the night. He gave his word that they would not shoot at the policemen and said he would call once they got the bag.

The bag was thrown, and Rahim Jivraj picked it up, brought it in the house, and left as had been agreed. At 11:41 P.M., Nichols called police headquarters.

> OPERATOR: Operator.
> NICHOLS: Emergency call. 264-7949.
> OPERATOR: 264-
> NICHOLS: 7949.
> OPERATOR: And your number please?
> NICHOLS: Uh, look, this is the police that I'm trying to get through. Could you connect it, please?
> OPERATOR: I'm sorry but I'll still need to have the details on the call. Can I have your number, please?
> NICHOLS: I don't know this fuckin' number.
> OPERATOR: I'm sorry, I can't help you then. It should be listed on your telephone.
> NICHOLS: Lady, have you been listening to the radio? We're holding hostages here, and someone is going to die unless you do this.
> OPERATOR: What is the number you are calling from?
> NICHOLS: I don't know.
> OPERATOR: Okay, what number do you want?
> NICHOLS: 264-7949.
> OPERATOR: And what happens when you dial?
> NICHOLS: I can't see to dial.

The impasse was overcome, and Reimer picked up the phone. It turned out to be the second major tension spike in the siege. Nichols said the contents of the package had been smashed, and there was now no Demerol. The story was that when the officer, Alex Penner, had thrown the package containing the cigarettes and drugs onto the doorstep, the vials of Demerol were broken. The vials had not just been broken but smashed into tiny pieces. This seemed an unlikely outcome from throwing a light bag that contained only a carton of cigarettes and the drugs, none of which weighed a great deal. Nichols and Gamble thought that they had been tricked, that they had given up a hostage for nothing, and became extremely agitated. Nichols seemed on the verge of violence.

> NICHOLS: Fuck it. Let's just dust these fuckin' motherfuckers. Let's just blow their fuckin' cocksuckin' brains out. Maybe then they'll fuckin' understand. Get that fuckin' hostage out here, I'm going to dust one right fuckin' now.
> REIMER: Bill.
> NICHOLS: Right so he can hear it. I'm gonna let you listen to something, buddy.
> REIMER: Bill, I –
> NICHOLS: You fuckin' listen to this. (*To Gamble:*) You just get me a hostage out here. (*To Reimer:*) I'm gonna let you hear this fuckin' –
> REIMER: The doctor's on the line. Now, do you want a couple more?
> DOCTOR: Come on, now. Come on. Ah, we've sent –
> NICHOLS: What do you mean, do I want a couple more? I'm not sittin' here all fuckin' night.
> DOCTOR: Come on, now. We'll, ah, we'll get it up to you quickly.
> NICHOLS: How long?
> DOCTOR: Well, as quick as we can get it there.
> NICHOLS: Yeah, yeah, as quick as we can do it. As quick as we can do it. Okay –
> DOCTOR: What happened was that –

Diane Perry was brought to the phone with a gun at her head.

> NICHOLS: Sit down. Sit. Now, do you understand what this is pointed at your head? Do you?
> REIMER: Bill, do you want two vials?
> PERRY: Yes. (*sobbing*) A gun.
> REIMER: We're gonna get the stuff. It's on it's way.

PERRY: Please help me.

NICHOLS: You hear that? Now, I'm ready to dust her.

REIMER: Bill, I told you it's on its way.

NICHOLS: How long?

REIMER: As soon as we can get it up there. We kept our word the first time.

NICHOLS: Now you have someone bring it right up to the door and set it inside and everything will be fine. There's no one's gonna get fuckin' blown away for bringin' it here.

REIMER: Okay, well, it'll get there and just, don't hurt anybody.

NICHOLS: I could've blown that fuckin' cop away if I wanted, you know.

REIMER: Pardon?

NICHOLS: That cop that brought it here?

REIMER: Yeah?

NICHOLS: I could've blown him away. I had him right in my sights.

REIMER: I know.

NICHOLS: Now, I didn't. We let one go. To show – get her back in the bedroom for now. Do you understand?

REIMER: I understand.

NICHOLS: Okay. Are they on their way?

REIMER: So did we. What are you blamin' me for?

NICHOLS: Are they on their way?

REIMER: They're on the way.

NICHOLS: Okay.

The drugs arrived shortly, and the two men took partial hits to calm them down and keep the situation from getting tense again. It was the first time the police had been set back in their relationship with the captors, and they had to show their good faith. Not long thereafter the police decided they were not getting the right advice from their psychologists.

At 2:15 A.M. Nichols placed a call to Doug Green, who had come on duty to replace Reimer. It was during this call that the police disclosed to the captors that Harrison had died. This was interesting timing, especially since they had not initiated the call and it was Nichols once again who asked about the officer. The police knew that the Demerol had arrived and had probably been used, which would calm the captors to some degree. Likely the police knew they wouldn't be able to keep the news from becoming public and the captors would discover the information had been withheld from them.

NICHOLS: Yeah. How's that cop doin'?
GREEN: Well, he didn't make it, Bill.
NICHOLS: Johnnie?
GREEN: Pardon?
NICHOLS: The cop died.
GREEN: Yeah. I want to be perfectly honest with you. I don't want to deceive you in any way. That's, that's the story.
NICHOLS: Sorry about that.
GREEN: Well, nothin' we can do about it now. He was just too badly injured. He couldn't come out of it.
NICHOLS: Yeah. What kind of a slug?
GREEN: I don't know, uh, Bill. I've no idea. That hasn't been determined yet.
NICHOLS: When did he die?
GREEN: Well, I'm, I don't even have the time. I just received word not too long ago that he was, he was gone, but, ah –
NICHOLS: Well –
GREEN: I gathered it was some time before I heard about it, but that's in the past now. We have to think about the future. Nothin' we can do about it. We can't bring him back
NICHOLS: Ah, right.

Now there had been a murder: the killing of a police officer in the course of his duty. Nichols still wanted to get out of the country, but they had no plan. Green brought up the subject of the hostages, saying he was sure the men did not want to hurt them. Nichols said that would only happen as a result of action by the police. Green told him he knew that Nichols did not want to do that, and Nichols replied that it was not what he wanted but what he would do.

NICHOLS: Okay? Now, listen, Doug. I'm not, it's like you said, I'm going to be straightforward. I don't give a fuck if I'm dead in two minutes or, ah, two years or two decades. Okay? Because there's fuck all left here. This world is, uh, sort of fuckin' turned black all of a sudden, you know.

GREEN: Well, if you feel that way, why would you even consider taking any other innocent people with you? Like those poor hostages there. I mean those, those women, they're perfectly innocent. They've done absolutely nothing to you. Why on earth would you even think of doing them harm?

NICHOLS: Well ...

GREEN: You know, it just doesn't make sense.

NICHOLS: It's the only crutch we've got right now.

GREEN: Well ...

NICHOLS: Okay? For our sakes. Right?

GREEN: Don't you feel that it's gone far enough? Why compound it? Why make it any worse than it really is?

NICHOLS: Heh, look, you're not going to talk me out of this. Okay, Doug?

GREEN: Well, I'd like you to think about it, and be sensible about it. You know, as rational as, as you can be at this point.

According to Green, Jim Knowler, who had by then left the police station, was making arrangements to find a lawyer who would talk to them in the morning. Nichols asked Green who were the top lawyers in town. Green said he didn't know, but that some might well refuse to become involved with them. He brought up the subject of capital punishment, reminding Nichols of the situation and that there was not going to be any death penalty. Nichols said that was too bad, that it would be better if there were. He was going to choose death over jail – that was all there was to it. This was dangerous psychological ground, and Green tried to inject some calm by saying it was something that he did not have to be in a hurry to decide and that it needed careful consideration. Nichols said he had done that, he had twenty-seven years of careful consideration, or else he would not have pulled the trigger the previous afternoon. Green said that was on the spur of the moment, something that happened, the gun in his hand and a reflex action. He wouldn't want to compound this by doing anything to the innocent people who were not after him and had nothing to do with the situation. Nichols refused to give any commitment not to hurt the hostages, other than to say they were fine as long as no one tried anything.

Green again tried to reassure the two men that they no longer had to worry about a death penalty. As everyone knew, there had been no executions in Canada for several years, and there was been considerable public discussion about removing the death penalty. On 24 February a bill had already been introduced in parliament to abolish the death penalty, although it had not yet been enacted. For all practical purposes, its eventual enactment was a foregone conclusion, since it was a bill proposed by the federal Liberal government in power and, apart from some pockets in western Canada, it enjoyed widespread public support. Strictly speaking, however, the applicable law of the day was that killing a police officer acting in the course of his duties was still a capital offence punishable by death. The fact that Harrison's murder had been committed during this interim period would later assume a significance of which none of the parties to the negotiations could possibly have been aware.

> GREEN: You know, ah, with the legislation as it exists today, there's no way that you have to fear for any kind of capital punishment. Ah …
> NICHOLS: Heh –
> GREEN: You know –
> NICHOLS: Jail is bad. That's why we left Vancouver. Because we didn't want to do anymore time.
> GREEN: Well, I think that's something that you could adjust to. Three months, is, you know –
> NICHOLS: Johnnie?
> GREEN: That isn't really –
> NICHOLS: He says … you can adjust to.
> GREEN: – giving yourself much of a chance. Pardon?
> NICHOLS: You don't adjust to jail.
> GREEN: Thousands of people do.
> NICHOLS: Yeah. A lot of dead men walking around in there.
> GREEN: Well, there's a lot of useful productive ones too when they get out.

With the death of Harrison confirmed, Nichols and Gamble knew that they were not going to be able to walk out of the situation, no matter what they might choose to do with the hostages. They began to discuss their options, which were few and bleak – from being killed by the police to at best serving long prison sentences, assuming the death sentence for killing a police officer in the course of his duties was to be commuted. They now began to consider extending the demands to trade the hostages for enough drugs to kill themselves rather than be taken into custody. Their plan was to say that they needed the drugs to calm down and some time to resign themselves to the prospect of arrest and imprisonment. As a condition for the release of the hostages, they would try to make a deal to get the two women out from under any possible charges.

At 3:11 A.M. on Saturday morning Nichols placed a call to John Short of the Canadian Press and eventually talked with Barry Nelson. He gave them everyone's names and said he wanted all charges against the women dropped. The women had done nothing wrong. They had no guns. They did not go into the credit union. They had committed no crime except to be with the men. The men wanted the best lawyer in the city to negotiate the charges for them. Knowler called at 3:38 A.M., and Nichols repeated that they wanted the charges against the girls dropped and gave him Janise's name. But over the next six hours, something happened that changed the approach taken by the criminals regarding amnesty for the two women.

Another call came in at 9:51 A.M., this time from CKXL News. Nichols said the girls were holding up pretty well, considering what they had been dropped into. They'd had no idea anything like this was going to come down. The robbing of the credit union was bad enough for them – blew their minds. Now that a policeman had been killed and hostages taken, how would they be expected to take it? They were upset. The reporter asked Nichols what he could see ahead, and Nichols said one alternative was "lots of fuckin' bars," and the other was one big granite block – a headstone.

It was here that some of the wheels of the men's plan began to fall off. There was no doubt that Tracie Perry was free of any involvement in the robbery and shoot-out, although she had played some part in the hostage-taking aspects. But she was small potatoes in the overall picture. The problem began when, after the general lines had been agreed upon, Janise said she did not want to leave Gamble and that if he intended to commit suicide, so would she. The men wouldn't hear of this, but she insisted, and eventually they said she could do what she wanted. It also meant that they would have to alter some aspects of the story they had been telling the police and the media. They had to make it appear that three persons were involved in the robbery and shooting, so that the police would be satisfied that all the innocent people were safe. The early calls had clearly been aimed at getting both women out. For the first time, some six hours after the call with Knowler, the men began to differentiate between Janise and Tracie. Partway through the call with CKXL, Nichols changed his position, after initially asking for amnesty for both women, to say that the complete amnesty was to be for Tracie, that the only thing she did wrong was to love him and come with him. He added nothing about Janise, but there was now a difference between the two – one that would remain and become ever wider.

CHAPTER 6

END GAME

Why did Janise insist on staying with Gamble and decide, apparently, to share his fate? It may have been the obsessive relationship that had developed between them. It may have been that she was devastated by the most recent events and could see no future, as she indicated in a program aired years later on CBC's *the fifth estate*:

> At one point, yes, I was. Like you have to understand. You sit in a house for forty-eight hours with people that you have nothing against, that someone's just pulled off the street and told them that their life's in jeopardy unless they get what they want. You go through ten months with a man that – I just, I just had enough. I just couldn't take it any more. Like I didn't … what did I have? You know, like you base your whole life on somebody, and you try and you try and you try. And then all of a sudden all the trying, all the love and everything, isn't enough. And without him what did I have? When you've based all that time on him. I couldn't let him die alone. He'd always been alone.

Or perhaps, as the police concluded, Janise had guilty knowledge of her role in the events and decided to take the same way out as her husband. This decision, which confirmed some of the evidence the police had obtained through their wiretaps as to the role Janise might have played in the robbery and subsequent events, would lead to the withdrawal of any offer of amnesty for Janise. It was eventually offered only to Tracie Perry. It is difficult to imagine that a small-town girl, who had never owned a gun, who probably only knew that the men had guns when she saw them in Calgary, who was terrified by the fact of the robbery and being stopped by the police, could have been transformed in the few seconds by the side of the road into someone who would emerge from the car armed and with the intention of shooting an armed police officer. On the other hand, there were statements made in some of the wire-tapped conversations and observations by some of the hostages that were troubling and could explain why the police came to the conclusions they did.

During the evening, Janise made a call to her mother in Peterborough.

MOTHER: Hello, Janise?

JANISE: Yeah.

MOTHER: It's not true what I'm hearing on the radio, is it?

JANISE: Yeah, it is.

MOTHER: Oh, god, Janise. Where are you?

JANISE: I'm right here.

MOTHER: Where?

JANISE: With John.

MOTHER: Oh, Janise.

JANISE: Please, Mom. Mom, don't cry.

MOTHER: Why are you with him?

JANISE: Because I have to be with him.

MOTHER: Oh, Janise.

JANISE: I can't live without him. I can't. Do you love me, Mom?

MOTHER: More than anything on earth.

JANISE: You want me to be happy, don't you?

MOTHER: I want you alive.

JANISE: Do you want me to be happy?

MOTHER: Yes, I want you to be happy, but I want you alive.

As part of their exit strategy, Nichols and Gamble decided it was important not to let the police know they didn't intend to come out of the house alive, in case police intervened before the drugs had had their desired effect. It is at least consistent with this strategy that for the same reason they then had to make it appear that Janise was staying because she was involved. This might account for the series of statements made by Nichols and Gamble over the course of several hours. It seems far more likely that the statements the men made were part of this plan than to imagine they were public-spirited individuals trying to set the record straight for posterity by revealing that Janise had been part of the robbery and part of the shooting of Harrison.

JIM HOGAN

Jim Hogan was a former football player for the British Columbia Lions who had become a criminal lawyer following his career as a professional athlete. In the course of his practice, he had participated in two hostage negotiations during disturbances in the British Columbia penitentiary system. He had been Gamble's lawyer and had acted in his application for bail. He had also heard of Nichols. When he learned of the Calgary shooting and hostage situation, he contacted the Vancouver police to see if he could be of any help. He felt badly that he had been responsible for getting Gamble out, and he knew that both men were dangerous. The Vancouver police got in touch with the Calgary authorities to advise them that there might be someone available who knew Gamble and had some experience with hostage sieges. The Calgary police agreed this could be useful, although they were somewhat reluctant to have the situation further confused with lawyers on the scene. All the media attention was bad enough.

By early Saturday morning it was agreed that Hogan should place a call to the Ingram home to see what he might be able to accomplish. He called at 10:33 A.M., from Vancouver police headquarters, after discussions with both police authorities as to the situation, the outstanding demands, and an assessment of the mental state of the two men. Nichols answered, and then Gamble came on the line. Hogan did not beat around the bush. They had got themselves into a bit of a mess, he said. Not a bit of a mess, Gamble said, a big one.

Hogan asked if there was anything he could do. Gamble was not sure there was anything. They had made a few demands, which Hogan knew, like amnesties, hits of heroin, and a little time. Gamble said he had to trust someone, and he couldn't trust anyone in Calgary. The police were "all jam picks tryin' to pull the shooter act." He said that he had wanted some Demerol the previous night because "my leg's really fuckin' racked up, right?" This was a complete fabrication, since the only person with an injured leg was Janise. He said the police had come across with the Demerol and that they had been discussing the matter all night and they could not ask for amnesty for Janise. He said that was because "she had a bit of knowledge of what happened." He was not going to go into details now. But Tracie "knows fuck all," he said, and should go free. So the deal would be that if the heroin was delivered and they found a good lawyer, Tracie and the two hostages would come out, and then they would start negotiations through their lawyer for the amount of time. Hogan was not sure what he meant, and Gamble said that because of all the sharpshooters, he was afraid to walk out the door and wanted to be protected. He wanted to have something on paper.

Hogan said he would go back to the police with the requests, but he wasn't sure why they were saying that Janise was in on it, or why she should stay in the house too, because it was quite likely that the police only wanted the two of them. He was unable to speak definitely because he had not talked to anyone about it, but he was prepared to come to Calgary, although he did not think it would be easy to get the fifty hits of heroin the men wanted. Was there not something else besides heroin? Would they be satisfied with a heroin substitute? Gamble said they wanted heroin and wanted such large amounts because they were pretty good users. Hogan was suspicious and asked whether they were planning to OD. Gamble, who did not want anyone to suspect the real purpose of the dosage said, "I got a Luger sittin' in my hand, Jimmy."

"In other words, you could blow your head off if you wanted to, eh?" Hogan said. Gamble replied that he could blow anyone's head off if he wanted to. "If I want to do myself in, man, I just, all I got to do is pull the trigger." This seemed to satisfy Hogan, and he went back to the matter of coming to Calgary and trying to get the heroin and amnesty for one or both of the women.

The point was to make it clear that they wouldn't see him until he had the "stuff" in his hands and a promise of amnesty. Then, once they had him in their sights, they would let the hostages go and he would walk in with it, because they could blow him up if they wanted. He was wondering what they meant by wanting some time before they gave themselves up. He was prepared to make sure that they did not get the shit kicked out of them, that they got put into a jail, that they were put properly before a court and so forth without getting wiped out. In order to get at them, the police would have to wipe him out first.

Gamble told Nichols that Hogan thought he might be able "to bring both the broads" and gave him the phone. Hogan explained to Nichols what he had told Gamble, and Nichols agreed that it was fine and they would let the others go when they had him in their sights. Now, he asked, how long did they want to straighten out their heads? Hogan again said he was prepared to put himself between them and the marksmen outside the house. Nichols agreed that they were worried about getting plucked off. Then he implicated Janise:

> NICHOLS: Okay. Jim? Janise's prints are all over one of the guns.
> HOGAN: Right. Now don't say … I don't want to hear any more about it. Okay?
> NICHOLS: Okay.
> HOGAN: 'Cause I don't know where these teleph – I'm talking from the Vancouver City Police Department.
> NICHOLS: Okay, well, she doesn't –
> HOGAN: And I don't know whether your line is touched or or not, but I don't want to deal with any issue in the case.
> NICHOLS: Okay, well, she doesn't want to come out until John comes out. She wants to come out at the same time. She doesn't want to leave him.
> HOGAN: Well, okay.
> NICHOLS: But Tracie does. Tra– … I want to send Tracie out. I want her safe. Okay?
> HOGAN: Okay. Uh, let, let me say this. I'm just thinking as we're talking. Um, why do you want the heroin? Obviously you're all buggered up. Uh, see, the heroin, I figure, is probably our biggest problem, okay?
> NICHOLS: Yeah.

Hogan was concerned about the prospects of amnesty for both Tracie and Janise and continued to try to work that agenda.

> HOGAN: Now, if you got, if you get an amnesty situation for one of the girls or maybe even both, I don't care what the facts are,

but if I can get it for both – 'cause I think that probably they
want you two guys, you know, you're their number-one prizes.
NICHOLS: Yeah.
HOGAN: Now, if I can, if I can get you the amnesty, and I'll re-
place the two hostages with myself and then I'll walk out with
you and make sure that nothing happens. Now, it, does that, it –
and I may be able to get your heroin, but if I can't, I'll get you a
supplement of uh, probably Demerol or something like that.
NICHOLS: Okay, not Demerol. We did …
HOGAN: What do you want in its place?
NICHOLS: We had some last night and that …
HOGAN: Eh?
NICHOLS: We did some Demerol last night and it was bad.
HOGAN: Shit, eh? Okay, what else is there?
NICHOLS: Uh–
HOGAN: 'Cause, see–
NICHOLS: – you can't get heroin.
HOGAN: Well, I, I don't know whether I can or not, see. I don't
wanna say I can or I can't.

Nichols was ready to give his word that if Hogan came with the
drugs, he would let the hostages go and be willing to walk out of the
house behind Hogan as long as they were not going to be shot. Gamble was not willing to commit himself to coming out in an hour with
Hogan carrying all the weapons. Hogan said he would not go into the
house without a guarantee from the police that there would be no
shooting if he started walking out the door. Gamble said he was moving too fast, that he was willing to stay a week, if he had to. Hogan said
he did not want to come from Vancouver unless the two men were
going to take him seriously. Gamble said it was too fast for him.

Well, what did Gamble want, then? He wanted the two "bundles"
and "no set time on me to come out." Hogan said he wanted to know
how long he had to stay in the house and pointed out that this seemed
to be a "decent request" on his part. Gamble said twenty-four hours.
Hogan said that meant he would have to stay in the house for that
long. Gamble replied, "Maximum of twenty-four hours and it's all
over. That way, man, like, ah, that way I've got myself psyched into
doing twenty years, maybe. Do you understand?" He wanted Hogan's
word that they were not going to get shot on the way out.

"Listen, I ain't comin' out there to get shot, you know. I'd just as soon go skiing today as do what I'm doing," Hogan said.

Gamble then agreed and said to Nichols, "The man's got a point like, uh, he don't want to get shot either." He asked Hogan if he would still represent him and Janise, and Hogan gave him his word that he would. He would have to get a call to the Alberta bar before he could do so, but thought he could do that. He would talk to the police and get back to them. Then he tried once again to deal with the matter of Janise.

HOGAN: And Janise doesn't want to leave, eh?
GAMBLE: Eh?
HOGAN: Janise won't leave if I get her a promised amnesty?
GAMBLE: No. No. No, she's staying with me. She, when we all go, she comes with us.
HOGAN: Okay.
GAMBLE: Okay?
HOGAN: Good. I'll get back to you.
GAMBLE: Okay. Bye, Jim.
HOGAN: Bye.

After conferring with the Calgary police, Hogan called back at 11:13 A.M. He was coming to Calgary. He was still having some hassle on the heroin but thought he could solve it. The police were concerned about his going into the house, but he figured he could solve that as well once he got there. The first flight he could get was at 1:10 that afternoon, which would put him in Calgary around 3:00 P.M. He told them to take it easy until he got there.

He added that he had also been talking to a friend of his, Al Connelly, the head doctor for the Narcotic Addiction Foundation, who had come up with a suggestion in case he could not get the heroin. It was a new substitute called Dilaudid. Nichols said he had heard of it and that it was as good as heroin.

As promised, Hogan caught the 1:10 flight from Vancouver. The police set about gathering the substitute drugs to take the place of the heroin demanded by the captors. They also continued their investigation of the robbery and shooting and interviewed Rahim Jivraj, the hostage who had been released. By the time Hogan had arrived in Calgary, the atmosphere regarding Janise had changed dramatically. The

Calgary police were now convinced she had played a role in the robbery and shooting. There was no question that they intended to charge her if she came out of the house. Hogan continued to try to get amnesty for both women, but it was out of the question for Janise.

Events at the hostage scene now entered their penultimate stage. The deal was that the hostages would be exchanged in return for the drugs and the police would take no further action until noon the following day. Ernie Reimer, concerned that Nichols and Gamble would continue to trust the police to live up to their side of the bargain, went on television to announce the deal. He thought that Nichols would probably walk out but that Gamble would likely put a gun to his own head. These were, however, secondary considerations. The principal objective was to secure the release of the hostages.

In the interim, however, Gamble appeared to have changed his mind about allowing Janise to remain with them until the end. He probably did not tell her of his decision until Hogan arrived on the scene.

On the fringes of the hostage action was a young Calgary lawyer, Webster Macdonald, Jr., who at the time had a criminal law practice. He had been in a bar with Doug Keller on the Friday afternoon when the call came in about the hostages and the standoff. It seemed to Keller that there might be a need for a lawyer, so he invited Macdonald to stick around with them. Over the course of the siege, Macdonald had some conversations with Nichols and Gamble and agreed to explore what kind of arrangements might be made on their behalf.

When Hogan arrived from Vancouver, he and Macdonald got together and agreed that there might be some value in both of them going to meet with the captors. They were on their way to the house with the drugs when Macdonald changed his mind. He said to Hogan that he had two young children and that, while the two gunmen might know Hogan, they did not know him.

At 6:15 on Saturday evening the police allowed Hogan to enter the house. He seemed to have the confidence of the two gunmen and had the necessary experience to deal with such situations. It was by no means a sure thing that events would play out as everyone hoped, but it seemed to be the best of a series of otherwise unappetizing alternatives. There were clearly further negotiations to be undertaken, especially with respect to Tracie Perry and Janise, to get them out as well.

Hogan approached the house carrying a package and two cartons of soft drinks. Everything was barricaded up in preparation for an assault. It was "dark as hell," he said, but the hostages were "pretty cool." After he had been there for a few minutes, "had a Coke, had a chat, things started to calm down and we had a pretty good discussion." The eventual price for the release of the hostages was some methadone, amnesty from prosecution for Tracie Perry, and no police action until noon on Sunday. After thirty-five minutes inside, watched by police marksmen, Hogan left the house and moved back down to the street where the police waited, to report on the discussions.

Moments later he returned to the house and waited outside. Nichols appeared at the door shortly thereafter followed by the two women hostages, who moved slowly past Hogan, down the sidewalk, and across the street to the sanctuary of the waiting police officers.

Then Tracie and Janise appeared. Nichols embraced Tracie for some moments before she left. Janise reached the end of the sidewalk, hesitated, and started to turn back. Hogan and Tracie forcibly escorted her to the street, where the police took them both into custody. Janise said later that one of the police officers told her, "You better hope we find him [Gamble] alive, or you're gonna do his time." No one from the police ever acknowledged that this had been said.

Tracie Perry would later testify that Gamble had pushed Janise out of the house, saying that she was too young to die and had a full life ahead of her. He also assured her, no doubt to encourage her to leave, that he would not commit suicide, despite their previous plan to do precisely that. The three would-be suicides had signed a letter written by Nichols to try to protect Tracie:

> To whom it may concern:
> This is to state that Tracy Perry had no knowledge of partaking in any criminal activities.
> She stuck with me through love and had no other motives.
> [signed] W.J. Nichols
> We also approve and stand behind these words.
> [signed] Mr. John Gamble   Mrs. Janise Gamble

Hogan made a final trip to the front door, delivered a package to Nichols, shook hands with him, and left. Gamble, he said, was fully aware that Janise would face a capital murder charge.

Everyone settled down for the night to await the next day, when Nichols and Gamble were, in accordance with the deal that had been struck, to strip to their underwear and come out of the house at noon, unarmed. It was a deal that neither Gamble nor Nichols intended to honour.

SUICIDE SUCCESSFUL AND FAILED

Beginning at dawn, police attempted to contact the two men. When the telephone went unanswered – the jack had been removed from the connection – they used a bullhorn to try to get a response. Hogan, who, as someone known to the two gunmen, could get closer to the house, banged on the garage door. Speculation increased that, instead of using the drugs and the extra time for purposes of calming down and coming to terms with a trial and conviction for their actions, Nichols and Gamble might have attempted suicide.

As the noon deadline drew closer and closer, the police ring around the house was complete and fire trucks were on the scene. It seemed increasingly obvious that the men were not going to answer, even if they were still alive. The police decided to storm the house.

By 1:00 P.M. some fifteen tear-gas pellets had been fired through the windows. No response. After five more minutes, police went in through the garage window and reached the living room. They reported, "Pair down and out … one still breathing." Gamble was dead and Nichols near death.

Perhaps because of vibrations, Gamble's body moved slightly, and the entry team dragged him to the paramedics on the scene. When they said he was dead, his body was taken back to where it had been. Then Nichols's eyes opened slightly and they saw that he was still breathing. He was rushed to the General Hospital, suffering one cardiac arrest in the ambulance and another upon arrival at the emergency ward. His condition was reported as extremely critical and it would be several days before it began to improve. He needed an operation to relieve a blood clot in his left arm, apparently caused by the tourniquet found on his arm when police stormed the house. His kidneys were badly damaged, and he required dialysis to retain renal function.

Hogan also went into the house immediately after the assault by police, to make sure that no shots had been fired and that Gamble had died of an overdose. Hogan had not, it seemed, expected the suicide attempt. When Gamble let Janise leave the house, knowing she would be charged with murder, Hogan said, he "thought there was no way they'd let her bear the charge alone."

A post-mortem later performed under the auspices of the Chief Medical Examiner's office confirmed that Gamble had died of "asphixia due to depression of his breathing mechanism as a result of high levels of the narcotic drug methadone." A scrawled note was found on the scene, written during the night:

> Please try to belive that Nick & I never wanted to hurt anybody.
> They just wouldnt lay off. Janise Gamble & Tracy Perry are
> innocent of all our crime. We picked our own rouet in & out.
>   [signed] John Gamble

The note was never referred to during the trial, and there was no indication that police disclosed its existence to Janise's counsel.

AFTERMATH

As an exercise in police work the entire effort had been an outstanding success. The hostages, in a situation fraught with uncertainty and danger, were all released safely, and the perpetrators were dead or in custody. The elements of a prosecution for the murder of a policeman were in place, and the necessary collection of other evidence was underway. No police officer, other than the unfortunate Keith Harrison, had been put at physical risk. The discipline of the police had been complete, despite the natural desire for revenge against the killers of a fellow officer.

The aftermath also brought an opportunity for hindsight assessment of the operation. Incredibly, the mayor of Calgary, Rod Sykes, was very critical of the police tactics. He stated that "irresponsible" methods were used and that the police had set a risky precedent in supplying drugs to the fugitives and attempting to pay a ransom. "We must not bargain, we must not provide drugs or money," he said. The first concern should be for the community at large, and hostages had to be a second concern.

Sykes's view was rejected outright by the provincial solicitor general, Roy Farran, who stated publicly, "I resent his undermining the confidence of the police, who can feel very proud of what they did. The actions taken were completely in accordance with our pre-planning for hostage incidents." Farran took full responsibility for all legal shortcuts taken in the circumstances and said that police had to be able to act quickly and decisively when lives were at stake. This included using public money to buy drugs without a prescription to appease the gunmen, sealing off streets, ordering helicopter support, and offering Tracie Perry immunity from prosecution, a deal the police made without the agreement of the attorney general's department. The police, Farran said, have to be able to build up an element of trust during negotiations over releasing hostages and be able to demonstrate that they would live up to their side of the bargain. One of the reasons that Ernie Reimer had appeared on the local CTV news to announce the deal was so the captors could watch it live and be confident that it would be honoured.

Police Chief Brian Sawyer, who still had to work with the mayor on a daily basis, simply said he would prefer to handle the mayor's criticisms by dealing with him directly. "We did what we believed was right after weighing the pros and cons of a variety of alternatives open to us. We were conscious at all times of the problems involved, and we were also conscious of the dangers being faced by the hostages." These remarks were made in calmer circumstances, after his initial expression of outrage: "All I hear from the mayor's office is criticism." It would have been interesting to have been a fly on the wall to hear what Sawyer said in private.

There had been no civic messages of condolence to Harrison's family nor to the police department, nor had there been any congratulations to the department for its handling of the situation. "I don't think criticisms without supporting comment do much to enhance the atmosphere and feeling which exists between the mayor's office and this office," Sawyer said. All of the decisions made by the negotiators had his strong endorsement: "Any suggestion that politicians ought to have been involved is totally unwarranted." It is not unusual for political figures to stay out of the way when the situation is tense, only to arrive later to say, with the 20–20 vision of hindsight (plus what they think might help in the next election), what would have been the best action.

Jim Hogan, back in Calgary to help represent Janise, also opposed Sykes's view of the matter. In fact, he would have gone so far as to have given the men the heroin they were demanding – a request the police refused to consider – because of its tranquillizing effect. However, the actual drugs supplied to the men, Demerol and methadone, were "calming" drugs, Hogan said, and when dealing with someone in an excitable situation, "I think you're ahead with such drugs." If a request was made for them, it was "not an unreasonable one to meet." The police had discussed the tranquillizing nature of the drugs and the dosage with the psychiatrists and other experts on the scene. They were also aware that inability to get such drugs had a tendency to increase the risk of violence, and they had no way of knowing the level of dependence that the captors might have had. Hogan put Sykes where he belonged – out of play – with a final observation: "If Mr Sykes says there should be no negotiation with these people, then let him bear the responsibility for the loss of lives that I believe would have occurred."

Mayor Sykes belatedly tried to bail out of the problem he had created by announcing that he would not be looking for any postmortems on the events, and retired from the fray to enjoy the flavour of his shoe polish. He barely escaped censure by the city council by walking out of the council chamber minutes before two motions were presented. Councillors voted unanimously to support the actions of the police in handling the hostage situation. A second motion, to "express regret" over the mayor's criticism, lost on a tie vote. "Although we don't agree with the mayor," Alderman Bob Simpson told the council, "he has the right to speak his will."

One of Sykes's regular critics, Alderman Tom Priddle, also opposed the motion for censure, stating that the mayor "has the perfect right to put his own foot in his own mouth." Later Priddle told reporters, "He knows he was a complete idiot. There's no point in censuring him." At the same session the council voted to endorse the actions of the city commissioners who helped the police collect the $100,000 demanded by the gunmen from two banks in the city. In particular, Chief City Commissioner Denis Coté had agreed to the acquisition of the money, even though he had been subject to severe criticism, presumably from the mayor's office.

IMMUNITY FOR TRACIE PERRY

Almost as soon as the siege was over the matter of immunity for Tracie Perry came under scrutiny. The provincial attorney general, Jim Foster, said police had no authority to offer anyone amnesty or immunity from criminal charges during negotiations with gunmen holding hostages. Answering a question in the legislature, he denied knowledge of the promises made at the scene. He agreed that police at the scene can only make recommendations to the Crown, and that anything further would deprive the civil authorities, whose responsibility is the overall administration of the law, of the control they are required to exercise. Although he sympathized with police officers negotiating in extremely difficult circumstances, he emphasized that their flexibility stopped well short of actually granting legal immunity from charges. He had received, he said, no recommendations for immunity in Perry's case. In the meantime, however, the absence of any charges against her would not necessarily mean a deal had been made but might merely indicate that there was a lack of probative evidence that she had committed a crime. Were the prosecutors to uncover reasonable cause to charge Perry, she would have no immunity unless the director of criminal prosecutions could find extraordinary circumstances to warrant it.

On 17 March, just prior to Janise's second appearance in court, the Calgary chief Crown prosecutor, Paul Chrumka, met with police to review whatever evidence might exist to support charges against Tracie. The police, he was aware, had agreed on the Saturday evening not to press charges against her in exchange for the two female hostages. She was being held as a material witness, and her release from custody was to be determined that day. Chrumka maintained that there was still a possibility she could face charges in the robbery, murder, and kidnapping events over the weekend. "If there is any evidence implicating her with the homicide we do not even consider the prospect of not prosecuting her." Speaking to the *Calgary Herald*, he said that the police had consulted him before granting amnesty to Tracie but that he did not do anything toward granting immunity from charges. "The evidence at that time did not show that she participated in the robbery or had anything to do with the shooting." But "all the evidence" had not yet been considered, and charges could still be laid by his office. Any deal that the police might have made referred only to charges they might have laid and only as a result of evidence they had at that time.

The custody determination was not made until two days later. Judge John Gorman, before whom the matter was argued, was very hesitant, despite the apparent agreement of both Crown and defence counsel that she be released in the care of her parents in Vancouver. Given the wave of criticism levelled against the B.C. judge who had released Gamble on bail, he was concerned that her release might cause "criticism of the bench." On 19 March, however, he ordered her release

to her mother and stepfather in return for a no-deposit $10,000 sure-
ty; Tracie's parents were not required to pay anything at the time but
were told that the amount would be owing if she failed to appear in
the proceedings. The judge accepted the assurances of counsel that the
attorney general was aware of the application for her release and had
no objection to it. Complicating the situation somewhat was the fact
that the attorney general's department was still considering the possibility of charges against Tracie, on the basis that they had had no part
in any agreement with the police.

Speaking later with reporters, Laila Jivraj said, "We had an un-
pleasant experience, but it was as good as possible." They were kept in
the bedroom all the time but were never left alone. Although the men
usually carried guns and the women had knives, they "were very pleasant" and "served us constantly" with food and coffee. The men did not
talk much to the hostages and were concerned with negotiating their
own release.

BUREAUCRACY AT WORK

No one would acknowledge liability for the damage done to the Ingram home. David Ingram himself did not ask the city for anything,
except to pay for accommodation so that the family could get back together. City Hall punted and said it couldn't help because the situation
was not the city's fault. One official adopted the manifestly unhelpful
suggestion that the family sue the "fellows that broke in." Ingram, later
acknowledging that his remark was as stupid as the official's statement,
retorted by asking which fellow would be the best bet: the live one or
the dead one?

The Calgary police rejected the idea of paying for the damage, ob-
serving that the choice of the Ingram house was an act of God, and
pointed the finger at some insurance company. Ingram's householder's
insurance policy did not cover the risk. The Alberta Crimes Compensation Board was authorized by statute to compensate for personal injuries but not for property damage. By 18 March, the solicitor general's
department, according to police chief Brian Sawyer, was considering
the possibility of an *ex gratia* payment to the Ingrams – a payment
made without acknowledgment of any liability to make it or of any
legal requirement to do so. They called for an estimate of the damages.

The community, however, had different standards. Servicemaster sent rug and upholstery cleaners to the house. Ingram was stunned. "They had three crews here – there was a person in every room." They shampooed all the rugs and furniture, took away the drapes, reeking from the fifteen canisters of tear gas that had been fired into the house, cleared away trash and broken dishes, and washed the dirty plates and kitchenware. Elaine Ingram said, "One woman spent nearly all day in the kitchen and then she apologized for not knowing where to put everything."

Western Aluminum Company of Calgary offered to replace the smashed windows for free or at minimal cost. The thirty broken windows were covered with plastic by Denis' Trucking until Western Aluminum Products re-glazed them and replaced the screens and metal frames. Hansen Interior Decorators promised to repaint the walls to get rid of the tear gas odour. Alcan offered to replace siding damaged by bullets and tear gas canisters. Rusco Industries provided a safety door, "just in case."

Ingram's employer, Imperial Oil, which originally offered to pay the whole shot if nothing else came through, paid for meals for the family until they could move back home. Meanwhile they stayed free of charge at the Crossroads Motor Hotel. Employees of Imperial Oil bought four new mattresses to replace those soaked with tear gas. Many other members of the community came forward to offer help. Burns Funds donated $500 to cover out-of-pocket expenses. A neighbour with whom Ingram had had words over his barking dogs came to the door with a cheque in his hand. "We may have our difficulties in day-to-day life, but when something like this happens, we've got to work together."

This show of support was sufficient to cause discomfort at the level of the provincial government, which promised to amend the crimes compensation legislation to cover ruin during combat between police and criminals. The insurance company "reconsidered" its position and eventually came through with a payment to cover some of the damages.

BAIL REGULATIONS

Unsurprisingly in the circumstances, there was great outrage once the identities of Nichols and Gamble were known that two such obviously dangerous men had been let out on bail while facing serious charges,

Gamble for murder and Nichols for armed robbery and attempted murder. Calgary Police Chief Brian Sawyer was quoted as saying that their release was "bloody awful" and wanted to know "what the hell we have to do" to prevent such a thing happening again. Solicitor General Roy Farran demanded, with the support of the provincial cabinet, a federal inquiry into bail regulations that free dangerous men from jail. Writing to the federal minister of justice, Ron Basford (who came from British Columbia, where the two had been released), he stated, "In our opinion, the laws and the legal system which permitted bail for men facing such serious charges are prejudicial to public safety." Speaking with reporters later, Basford said that he wanted no more bail for suspects facing serious charges and that the courts must "err on the side of public safety," not defendants.

In Ottawa, Eldon Wooliams and Harvie André, two Conservative MPs, sitting in opposition, attempted to have the House of Commons consider the issue. But because the unanimous consent to deal with matters not on the Order Paper in a special debate was denied by the Liberal majority, the effort failed. They were left with throwing a little political garbage, designed to get media coverage and show solidarity with Calgarians at home. "I hope that Justice Minister Basford, Solicitor General Warren Allmand and Transport Minister Otto Lang, who originally eased the bail laws, find it difficult to sleep at nights with Staff-Sgt. Keith Harrison's death on their consciences," huffed André. The political opportunism was all the more apparent since there was at the time a bill near passage in the House of Commons with the precise object of establishing restrictive bail for persons accused of violent crimes. Basford said it would be proclaimed in force as quickly as possible after its adoption and he would urge uniform application of the law throughout the country. He proposed that a number of courts be monitored for six to eight months after the law came into force and that further changes be made if they appeared to be warranted.

In British Columbia, Attorney General Garde Gordon asked for a report of the circumstances regarding the release of the two men and was in turn asked by Basford to provide details. The police were generally solid in their opposition to the bail laws. R.B. Kerr, president of the Corrections Branch of the British Columbia Joint Peace Officers Council, went further and said the organization would "like to see somebody take the judge to task for allowing this." Police officers from across the country, in Calgary to attend Harrison's funeral, met to discuss bail reform and changes to the Criminal Code.

THE MEDIA IN CRISIS SITUATIONS

While there is much to be said for the freedom of the press, one of the complicating features of the Nichols and Gamble affair was the media regularly calling the gunmen at the hostage scene. The police were furious for several reasons, one of them being that it made it difficult for the police negotiators to get through on the phone to the criminals. Said Police Chief Sawyer, "While the media has a role to play and a clear-cut requirement to get all the news it can, the primary concern is the police operation. There were occasions when the negotiating team was starting to holler 'obstruction.'" Some of the conversations, questions, and statements bordered on irresponsibility, Sawyer said. He would not reveal the other reason, other than to say later that, since it appeared generally known that police had taped the calls on the phone line, "in that light, any further comment by me is barred by the provisions of the Criminal Code respecting the recording of private conversations."

The recorded calls, especially those with reporters, would later assume an important dimension in the murder trial. Nor would Sawyer comment on why the police did not change the phone number. Hogan commented, "It's not a game. It was a pretty serious situation, and they should have left it to the people doing it." The communications from the police to the house should have been changed from the telephone to something else. With too many people involved, Hogan said, "you get cross messages going, and they are edgy in any event and whatever confidence they have in you is eroded." He was told that someone had phoned the gunmen and told them it was foolish to release their hostages and so give up their bargaining power. "That's a pretty dumb thing." Had he known that was going on, Hogan said, he would have been "a hell of a lot more apprehensive" than he was. This statement, when reported in the newspapers, was accompanied by the observation that Hogan said he did not blame anyone and understood that everyone was trying to get a story. The police, despite the criticism levelled at the reporters by Sawyer during the press conference following the incident and his promise to look into the possible repercussions, decided not to lay charges against anyone from the media. "The press over-participation in one particular aspect of the events … was not such as to warrant any court action being taken by the police," he said.

The bottom line was that the hostages were all recovered safely and the crisis was over. Harrison was dead and buried. Janise was in custody and charged with murder. Nichols had clung to life and was likely to recover to face the same charges as Janise. Gamble was dead and his remains cremated. Janise asked that his ashes be sent to her mother, so that they could be scattered. Her mother flushed them down the toilet.

CHAPTER 7

ON TRIAL FOR MURDER

The machinery of the law moved into action. The police and the Crown prosecutor's office started the detailed work to determine the extent of the evidence. The basic forensic work was in the main routine. That Nichols would be charged with the murder of the police officer was almost self-evident. Witnesses had seen him firing a gun at the victim. The ballistic evidence would show that the bullet that had killed Keith Harrison came from the gun found in Nichols's possession when he was taken into custody.

More difficult was the case against Janise. No one had seen her with a gun. There were no fingerprints on any gun that could prove her possession of one. Statements had been made by Gamble and Nichols that might implicate her, but none had been made by her. The prosecution, however, had seized on some troubling features that, if established in court, might create some problems for her. It was not just anyone who had been killed but a popular Calgary police officer.

Janise's family rallied around and told her to find the best criminal lawyer in Calgary. In the remand centre where she remained until after the trial, she asked who was the best and was told to call Webster Macdonald. He had already been involved during the hostage siege, although Janise did not know him and had not spoken with him during the crisis. His contact had been only with the men, who were handling the negotiations. Some have speculated that when she was advised to contact Webster Macdonald, the person was referring to the father, not the son. Macdonald Jr. had never tried a murder case, whereas Macdonald Sr. was a very experienced criminal lawyer. In the event, however, Janise was represented by the son, who was assisted during the trial by Dale B. Pope. Nichols was represented by R.A. Cairns and J.A. Butlin.

The Information was sworn on 29 April 1976 by G.M. Chekaluck, a Calgary peace officer, and docket number 0146028419-32 was created. The charge was read in the presence of the two accused and their counsel.

PRELIMINARY HEARING

After a few postponements, the preliminary hearing began on 14 June in provincial court. Nichols and Janise were reported as appearing calm as they sat through the first four hours of testimony recounting what had happened at the credit union and in the ensuing getaway and shooting. Although there were eight charges involved, the only one under consideration at the hearing was the capital murder count in relation to the death of Sgt Harrison. Nichols was still in a wheelchair suffering from almost continuous pain, the aftermath of his near-fatal overdose of methadone three months earlier.

The purpose of a preliminary hearing is to establish whether there appears to be enough evidence to commit the accused to trial for the offence. The Crown is required to disclose its evidence to the defence and to satisfy the presiding judge that there is a prima facie case to be answered. The defence is not required to produce evidence but is entitled to cross-examine the Crown's witnesses. Janise was formally represented by Webster McDonald Jr. and Dale Pope, and a junior, Daniel Russell, was physically on hand for the hearing. Nichols was represented by Calgary lawyer William Stilwell. The preliminary hearing process is detailed and painstaking, since a failure to obtain a committal for trial may allow an accused to go free. Thus the Crown had the duty to be certain that sufficient facts were in evidence to convince the judge that a trial was warranted. There would be fifty-eight witnesses and 145 exhibits produced on the occasion. Much of the same evidence would be put before the jury during the later trial of the accused.

The getaway car was traced from British Columbia and identified as the car used by the accused both at the credit union and during the later flight. The pair of policemen in the traffic education van had heard the report of the robbery and were looking for the getaway car when they drove past the gunfight and stopped to aid the lone police-man just as the culprits pulled away. One of the constables testified that he saw Harrison standing behind his car, pointing his gun with both hands as their van approached. Two people were outside the car the police officer faced. "I saw his [Harrison's] hand sort of jolt as the gun went off," the officer testified. "Then a person with long, scraggly sort of dirty-blond hair was waving a gun from side to side."

A man who pulled up behind the police van on Memorial Drive said he saw Harrison walking toward the beige and brown car when two men got out and moved behind it. As Harrison approached, there was "a commotion" in the back seat of the car, "and Harrison made a spin toward his car and ran back to it." He then said he saw one man, whom he identified as Nichols, fire three shots from his gun and the other man, identified as Gamble, fire two shots. A third unidentified person who left the back seat of the car fell as an answering shot from the officer's gun was fired, and "the next time I saw Keith Harrison he was lying on the ground." Evidence produced included Harrison's service revolver and three handguns, one of them the 9 mm Luger thought at the time to have been the death weapon.

Diane Perry described how she came to be involved, driving home from her Friday classes, when she saw Gamble pointing at one of her tires as the cab passed her. "I stopped, thinking there was something wrong with it," she said, when Gamble "came over, pointed a gun at me and opened the door. The rest of the people came out of the taxi and started getting into the seats. I was in the middle." Gamble took over the steering wheel and drove into the nearby Pineridge area. He had no idea where he was going, since no one, except the locals, had any knowledge of Calgary and its suburbs. "There was a police car fol-lowing us," she said. The officers in the car said that the vehicle swerved onto the lawn of 6540 22nd Avenue N.E., and then a man left the car holding a gun to the head of the woman he had in front of him, while another man in the back seat pointed a revolver at the police car. Everyone got out of the car after Gamble, still holding Diane Perry, forced open the locked door of the house.

Perry described her ordeal as a hostage and said that the men start-ed talking about the incident on the first evening of the siege, after they had taken the Demerol supplied by the police. "They were laughing about the police officer being shot. They were also laughing about Janise Gamble being run over." It is not known whether Janise, who was the only person who had been hurt, had been given any of the Demerol, which might have made her somewhat high as well as the men. In the *Calgary Herald*, the headline read, "Accuseds laughed at officer's death." One version had it that Gamble had been grazed in the head and knocked over in the gun battle and that he had fallen on Janise and knocked her over in turn, before Nichols drove over her.

The taxi driver testified to the taking over of his taxi by Nichols and five other persons after the original getaway vehicle, littered with bullet casings and shattered glass, was abandoned outside a northeast area restaurant. He was met at the door of the small café by Nichols, who ordered him to pull around to the back of the building. Then he picked up his passengers, with Nichols and a middle-aged woman who "looked scared" getting into the front seat. He was directed to Memorial Drive. The cabbie told the passengers he needed gas and pulled into a service station at 52nd Street and Memorial Drive. Nichols followed him inside, and then, according to the attendant, said, "Forget the gas. I just shot a cop. Let's get out of here." When the driver balked, Nichols snatched his keys and drove off without him.

Tracie Perry was called as a witness for the Crown. She described how the group had driven from Vancouver to Penticton in the first car they had rented in Vancouver on 11 March, then changed to another, which they brought to Calgary that night. They spent the evening in a motel, where she first noticed a gun in the suitcase she shared with Nichols. When she asked about it, he said that it was being delivered "to a friend."

The next day, after shopping for some new luggage and lunching downtown, "the guys wanted to cash a cheque" before continuing on to Toronto. They drove to the Inglewood Credit Union and pulled up to the back door. She and Janise waited in the car. Then Tracie said she "got out and went toward the store" nearby to get some Aspirin. On the way she discovered that she had some pills in her purse, so she turned back. She arrived at the car to see Janise, and "John and Billy getting in." She said she did not know the two men had just robbed a bank.

As they drove away with Janise at the wheel, "driving normally," there was no mention of a bank robbery. But after they had travelled a few blocks, Nichols insisted on taking over. Tracie had no idea why the plain-clothes officer began to follow them after they left the credit union.

When Nichols wanted to drive, they stopped and she noticed a car stopped behind them. "There was a man pointing a gun at us and screaming 'get out, get out.' John and Billy got out. I heard a clunk on the roof … and the shooting started." She did not know much about the gunfight, because she "went onto the floor" after seeing the lone policeman pointing a revolver at their car and hearing a shot. However, she could see "Billy (Nichols) pull a gun down from the roof of the car and saw him shoot it toward the policeman." After the gunfire ended, "Billy jumped into the car and shouted, 'get in.'" They [the Gambles] got in the back door."

She described speeding towards the back door of a nearby café. Nichols told her to call a cab, "but I couldn't because I was too shaky." Someone else called, and they drank coffee until the taxi arrived. Then "the guys" decided to take the restaurant owners hostage to guarantee safe passage. After leaving the cab driver at the gas station, they drove to the Pineridge area where they tried to change cars. They first pulled up behind a small car but rejected it because a woman and baby were inside. After more driving, they came across a larger one driven by schoolteacher Diane Perry. She was added to the hostage group and they went on to the scene of the later drama. The men gave her and Janise knives "as protection against whatever was going to happen."

Rahim Kassam Jivraj, the owner of the Thunderbird restaurant, said that when a man came into the back of his restaurant with a gun, "I thought he was joking." The man said, "Don't you know I already killed a policeman? I'm serious. You're my hostage." When Jivraj went to the front of the restaurant where his wife was sitting with another gunman, "I realized the matter was serious." He identified the second man from a photograph as Gamble.

His wife, Laila Jivraj, testified that while one man (she called him "Nick") went into the back where her husband was, another man, whom she identified as Gamble, pointed a gun at her and said, "Don't move from here." She said he told her that they had just killed a policeman and could do the same to her. The men asked where they kept their car, and when they were told they did not have one, phoned a cab. They took $250 from the cash register, and Janise took Mrs Jivraj's blue coat to wear. Although unable to identify Janise in the courtroom, she identified her from a photograph. At the siege house, she said, "They laid us on our tummies on the floor and tied our hands and legs with stockings and, I think, bed sheets."

Rahim Jivraj was released in return for the first delivery of cigarettes, drugs, and sandwiches: "So they released me and told me, 'We are not going to harm your wife if police give us what we want.'"

During the hearing that final morning, 25 June, Nichols had to leave after his lawyer explained he was "in the throes of a nervous breakdown." He was brought back briefly that afternoon, still confined to a wheelchair, to hear that he was to stand trial. It was not until 30 June that Judge Thurgood ordered Janise to stand trial as well. Webster Macdonald had argued that there was insufficient evidence to show that Janise "caused or assisted in causing the death of Sgt. Keith Harrison." "Not one of the seven witnesses at the scene of the shooting said Janise Gamble used the gun. The evidence is clear she was not an active participant in the shooting." He also said it was clear that she had not played an active part in the robbery. The Crown prosecutor, Paul Chrumka, said that although Janise did not enter the credit union, her movements in front of the building indicated she was a lookout in the robbery. She also drove the getaway car. He added, "It wasn't until she started to scramble out of the car that the shooting [which killed Keith Harrison] started." Despite the *post hoc ergo propter hoc* (after it, therefore because of it) logic of the latter statement, Judge Thurgood found "ample evidence" to support the charges.

ON TRIAL FOR MURDER

The trial was eventually set down for 22 November 1976 in the Alberta Supreme Court. The charge would be first degree murder, a feature that would come to play an important role in the life of Janise Gamble. Nichols and Janise both pleaded not guilty. The indictment, dated 30 August 1976, stated:

> Janise Marie Gamble and William John Nichols stand charged that they, Calgary in the juridical district of Calgary, on or about the twelfth day of March, AD, 1976 did unlawfully kill Allan Keith Harrison, a police officer acting in the course of his duties, and did thereby commit first degree murder, contrary to the Criminal Code

Below the date there was a reference to section 218(1) of the Criminal Code, and underneath it, "imprisonment for life."

A panel of seventy-two potential jury members was assembled and addressed briefly by Mr Justice M.E. Shannon, to whom conduct of the trial had been assigned. It was his first trial as a judge in a first degree murder case, or what had previously been called "capital" murder. Jury selection was difficult. Before the full jury was selected, the original panel of prospective jurors was exhausted, and there was a rush to collect another panel. The court adjourned for a portion of the morning, and reassembled at 12:00 P.M., at which time the sheriff reported that the bailiff was having difficulty getting jurors off the street in time to be back at noon. They thought that sufficient numbers would be available by 2:00 P.M. and, shortly thereafter, the last of the twelve jury members were selected and sworn. The court then gave them enough time to go to the jury room, go home and make any other arrangements that were necessary in their private and business lives before evidence commenced in the trial.

Originally scheduled for five days, the trial would eventually take nine. The courtroom was crowded with spectators, media, and families of the murdered police officer and the two accused. Extra seats had to be provided, a table arranged for the media, and extra security laid on to maintain order.

In criminal trials, there are often points of law and matters regarding admissibility of evidence that have to be sorted out before the jury is allowed to consider the particular evidence. In some cases, portions of what the prosecution or defence might want to produce as evidence may be ruled inadmissible, with the result that the jury never gets to hear or see it. When such matters are raised, the jury is excluded from the courtroom until the judge hears arguments from the lawyers in a sidebar process referred to as a *voir dire*. Only when the judge has made a ruling is the jury brought back in. This technique is designed to keep the jury from hearing inadmissible evidence that might prejudice their view or assessment of the facts that they are bound to consider when reaching a verdict of guilty or not guilty. At the commencement of this trial, several predictable motions were raised.

Macdonald made a preliminary application to sever one accused from the other and to have separate trials. The indictment had charged them both together. He acknowledged that, based on the jurisprudence, nothing really justifies severance, unless prejudice can be shown if the trial were to proceed in the manner where the accused were charged jointly. He argued that it appeared clear that the defence of Janise Gamble was antagonistic to that of Nichols. He thought that the defence of Nichols might well be an attempt to put the blame for what happened on the day of the murder onto Janise Gamble. There might be, he said, evidence that normally would be inadmissible against Janise Gamble which might be introduced against Nichols, and that evidence would work prejudicially with a jury. He cited in that regard the question of a severe criminal record on the part of Nichols: attempted murder, demands for drug usage (in particular, heroin), comments made about "wasting" cops and "wasting" bodies, guns being applied to people's heads, the general coarseness of the language, the swearing and the abuse, and especially certain statements out of the mouth of Nichols that Janise Gamble had participated in the crime of robbery. He also referred to a confession allegedly made by Nichols, which clearly prejudiced Janise and which would not be admissible against her. It might be admissible against Nichols, but it certainly should not be against Janise.

Chrumka, obviously ready for the application, argued that the evidence indicated a joint venture from the time that the two accused and the deceased, John Gamble, as well as Tracie Perry, decided to leave Vancouver to go to Calgary, that in Calgary the two accused and the deceased Gamble robbed the Credit Union, that after the robbing of the Credit Union Janise's fingerprint was found on the hold-up note, that she drove the getaway car, and that she came out of the car with a gun and lost it. Further, although it had nothing to do with the murder charge, she assisted in robbing the people at the Thunderbird Restaurant shortly thereafter as well as holding the hostages. The Crown's submission was that Janise was an active party throughout and that it would work an injustice if there were to be an order for severance. The Crown had specifically alleged that she was a party to the killing pursuant to the Criminal Code. Chrumka was also concerned because where there were two accused, one could get up, under the protection of the Canada Evidence Act (which allows evidence to be given under oath, but which thereafter may not be used against the person giving the evidence), lie as to his or her involvement, and the other person at a subsequent trial could get up and lie as to his or her involvement, each taking the blame under that protection, without the Crown or society having any recourse.

Mr Justice Shannon ruled that the case involved an indictment and a trial that would involve strong elements of a joint enterprise and a common intention. He was of the view that it was in the best interests of the administration of justice and indeed in the interests of the two accused themselves that they be tried together jointly. He refused the application for severance. Macdonald was left with a position of saying that he understood the law to mean that he could renew the application at any time throughout the stage of the trial depending upon the evidence. The court concurred with that view of the law.

Macdonald also asked that there be a direction that the press not report any potential evidence that might or might not be admissible, particularly if the jury were not to be held over or sequestered. A motion was also made to sequester the jury by the counsel for each of the accused. The Crown had no comment to make on that application. Justice Shannon asked whether there had been a ban on publicity with respect to the case when the preliminary hearing was held. Chrumka advised him that there was no such ban, whereupon Justice Shannon said that he was of the view that in this case the jury should be allowed to separate (to go home at the end of each day) and that he would permit them to do so until such time as they retired to consider their verdict.

At the request of Pope, Justice Shannon drew to the attention of members of the press the provisions of section 576.1 of the Criminal Code, which provided that no information regarding any portion of the trial, at which the jury is not present, shall be published in any newspaper or broadcast before the jury retires to consider its verdict. The defence also drew the attention of the Court to there being no reference to evidence of questionable admissibility by the Crown or the defence counsel in their opening addresses and that this was a matter to which the Crown, in particular, should address its attention. Chrumka merely stated that he had no observations as to the conduct of the defence. It was clear to counsel and the court that the case was going to take the entire week and probably go into the following week.

At this point the jury was called back. Shannon advised them that he had decided to allow them to separate at the end of the hearing each day, but that they had, of course, to report back and be on duty every morning. It was not necessary for him to advise the jury as to the applications or rulings that had not been accepted. He gave them a brief description of the function which they would be performing in the trial:

> You and I together comprise a single Court whose duty it is to hear the evidence and determine the guilt or innocence of the two accused. I must tell you that as a jury it is you and you alone who is responsible for finding the facts as they may be found, weighing the credibility of the evidence of any witness and deciding whether or not you accept the whole or any part of it. It is my function as a judge to preside over the trial, to rule on all questions of law and the admissibility of evidence and to instruct you on the laws: that you and you alone, as I have said, are the judges of the facts and it is you and you alone who determine innocence or guilt. You will reach that conclusion as a result of the evidence you hear and, you will decide it in the light of the law as I give it to you. In the field of the law my function is as absolute as is yours in deciding the facts.

He reminded the jury of the presumption of innocence, that the accused remain innocent through the course of the trial and stay that way, unless and until the jury might find that they are guilty. He advised them that he would charge them later on the subject of reasonable doubt and that if they had heard anything outside the courtroom from any source whatsoever, they were to remove that information from their minds in considering the problem then before them. He warned them of the secrecy of jury deliberations under the Alberta Jury Act, reminded them of the terms of the indictment, and introduced counsel to them.

THE START OF THE TRIAL

The opening statement in a criminal case is made by the Crown. Chrumka began by stating that the evidence would deal with the timespan of the weekend of 12 to 14 March 1976 and that by the conclusion of the trial he would have called some fifty-five witnesses and that there would be approximately 145 exhibits entered. He was careful to indicate that what he was describing was what he anticipated the Crown's evidence to be, but asked them to remember that what he said to them now was in no way evidence but merely a summary of what he anticipated the Crown would be able to prove. Were there to be any variance in what he said at this time and what the evidence would be, he would try to remember that and draw the jury's attention to that at the conclusion of the trial. He then summarized much of the evidence, very little of which, other than perhaps the role of Janise Gamble in the robbery and shooting, was much in dispute. He indicated the expert witnesses he intended to call for purpose of giving opinion evidence. At the conclusion of his address, he requested that all witnesses be excluded and then began to call the evidence.

Murder trials are seldom, if ever, the spectacular performances of which television series are made. In almost every case, there is a careful, painstaking, mundane plodding through the various items of evidence, identifying each connection back to the accused and the events contained in the indictment, establishing the continuity of physical evidence and the fact that it was not tampered with or otherwise altered, and tying into a neat, seamless package every element necessary to establish the offence. Many of the witnesses called in such trials have very marginal roles to play, such as identifying photographs or individuals, accounting for what might otherwise be gaps in the web woven by the Crown. Defence counsel normally have nothing to add or to seek to diminish with respect to the evidence of such witnesses. Their main fodder is the eyewitnesses – whose recollection may be faulty or who may not, for a variety of reasons, be credible, and whose shortcomings can be used to raise a reasonable doubt in the minds of members of a jury – or the expressions of the opinions of expert witnesses, who may not be sufficiently qualified for the purpose or whose opinions have insufficient factual basis to be reliable. That is all defence counsel have to do. They do not have to prove that their clients are innocent, just that, on the basis of a reasonable doubt, they may not be guilty. There is an apocryphal story (which may be only that, since I have never seen it officially reported) of a seasoned defence attorney in a criminal trial who was said to have addressed a jury on the issue of reasonable doubt by saying, "Ladies and gentlemen of the jury, right about now you are probably thinking that my client is probably guilty, and you're probably right. But if that is what you are thinking, it is your duty to acquit him."

One of the other main objectives of any criminal defence is to try to keep prejudicial evidence from being admitted or to raise the possibility of alternate conclusions that may be drawn from the facts described by a particular witness. Unlike civil trials, where many facts are admitted for purposes of shortening the expensive process of a trial and getting at the central issue of the dispute, in most criminal trials virtually nothing is admitted by the defence. In fact, the defence often hopes against hope that the Crown will fail or omit to prove some essential element of the charge and thus give rise to a directed acquittal or a subsequent appeal. Chrumka was much too experienced as a Crown counsel to let anything like that happen in this case.

Our system of criminal justice is based on the presumption of innocence of the accused and the legal duty of the Crown to prove the elements of the crime beyond all reasonable doubt. There is no duty on the part of an accused to say anything whatsoever in his or her defence, and juries are not permitted, as a matter of law, to draw any adverse inference (unlike in civil trials) from the failure of an accused to testify as a witness in the trial. Many accused, no matter how guilty they know they may be, plead not guilty and take their chances that there will be some kind of error. This was obviously the case with Nichols, especially once it was known that his gun had fired the fatal shot. None of the essential facts relating to him were in any doubt. All he had to offer was a barely arguable suggestion of self-defence; and to make it work, he had to sell out Janise, to make her the cause of the shootout. He would be arguing that he had already surrendered and that when Harrison started shooting, he was merely defending himself. That was one of the reasons why Macdonald had tried to have the cases separated.

The Crown's theory, as it related to Janise, was that she was involved from the beginning, as a lookout during the robbery and as the driver of the getaway car. By coming out of the car once it had stopped, she had caused the shootout. She had participated in the subsequent flight and hostage taking and had been identified by the two men as having been involved. That theory had been compelling enough that the court was not willing to split the cases, even though it must have known the psychological, if not legal, impact of what Nichols would say. It was critical for the Crown to place Janise at the scene of the robbery and as part of it, since it was clear that she had been in the car and that she was the person at the wheel when the car left the scene of the robbery. The evidence of the subsequent flight was not in serious dispute, but for the charge of first degree murder to stick, she had to have been shown as involved in the entire plan.

THE CASE AGAINST JANISE GAMBLE

The account that follows does not concentrate on much of the routine evidence that was presented during the trial, such as identifications, causes of death, fingerprints, ballistic evidence, and chain of custody of exhibits and photographic material. All of this was accomplished quite professionally by the Crown, and defence counsel had slim pickings, if any, in cross-examination. Summarized here are those parts of the trial with a direct connection to the charge against Janise Gamble; where the evidence was important, it is considered in more detail.

The Crown's case against Janise had six main elements. First, an eyewitness claimed to have seen her outside the credit union while the robbery was in progress, which would point to her as the lookout and therefore a party to the robbery. Second, she was the driver of the car immediately following the robbery. Third, it was her action at the scene of the shootout that led to the exchange of gunfire and the death of Harrison. Fourth, her fingerprint was found on the envelope used during the robbery. Fifth, she participated fully in the subsequent flight and events, including the robbery at the Thunderbird Restaurant and the tying up and threatening of the hostages. Sixth, one of the hostages would testify that she had her own gun, which was somehow lost or misplaced during the hectic events. Taken together, these elements might be sufficient, if proven, to make her a party to everything that happened and to the offence of first degree murder.

EYEWITNESS IDENTIFICATION OF JANISE AT THE CREDIT UNION

On the morning of 18 March at about eleven o'clock, six days after the robbery and after Janise had already been in custody for five days, the police conducted a lineup of seven women, including Janise and Tracie Perry. Calgary police detectives Lund and Goetjen arranged for the lineup portion of the procedure, and two other detectives brought witnesses in to view the lineup. The other girls in the lineup were from the remand centre. Lund gave each of the girls Janise's red leather coat to try on while the witnesses watched. He testified that he did not speak to any of the persons who were there to view the lineup. Chrumka asked him whether he or anyone in his presence spoke to the persons in the lineup indicating to them what number the accused Janise Gamble would be wearing. His answer to that question, as well as to where she would be standing was, "absolutely not." To the question of whether he indicated how she would be dressed, he answered "no."

The people who came to view the lineup were Sharon Homan, Ann Dredge, and Constable R.G.T. Greenwood. The persons in the lineup were varying sizes from about five foot zero to five foot six, and each tried on the red coat. Because the girls were different sizes, it fitted some better than others. When Macdonald tried to get Lund to say that he agreed that it fitted Janise Gamble best, he said there were two or three it "fit good." When asked whether it didn't fit Janise Gamble the best, he said, "Well, I didn't really pay much attention." Macdonald persisted, saying, "So it fit two or three better than it fit the other four?" "Yes." "Or five?" "Or five, yes." When asked if he understood the coat to be Janise Gamble's coat, Lund's answer was, "I sure did." The next question was, "So it didn't surprise you that it fit her better than the others, did it?" Lund replied, "No question."

Looking at the photograph of the lineup, Macdonald asked whether Lund would agree with him that there appeared to be two or three blonds and the rest were dark-haired girls. His answer was, "There is three anyway, and after looking at the photos, I think there might be a couple more that are pretty blonde. Number 20, Tracie Perry, is blond, number 1, Lorraine Monkman, is blond, number 10, Janise Gamble, was blond at the time. Number 28 was blond." He did, however, acknowledge the other three were darker-haired. Macdonald said, "Definitely [darker], though, aren't they?" Lund answered, "It is hard to tell on here." When challenged by saying, "You were there," he said, "Although their hair doesn't look much darker than Lorraine Monkman's and she was blond, I know her personally." People who came to view the lineup stood across the counter in the viewing office. The girls in the lineup were told to put the coat on in turn and then told to turn in circles, a quarter at a time.

Chrumka did not feel it was necessary to re-examine the witness. This reflected his view that Macdonald had done nothing to impeach the proper conduct of the lineup.

Witness Sharon Lea Homan remembered pulling up in front of the

Inglewood Credit Union on 12 March 1976. She stopped her car in front of the building but not directly in front of it. She was asked what happened when she stopped there: what did she see? She answered, that, "As I stopped I just seen a young girl out in front by the pole out in front of the building. The young girl was just pacing back and forth." When asked if the young girl was in the courtroom today, she said, "Yes," and identified Janise Gamble. The event occurred about ten after three. She described the woman as wearing a brown leather coat and tan or light brown slacks. There was no one with her nor anyone else outside the credit union. After Homan saw the girl pacing there, she parked her car and went into the building. When she entered the building, she saw "there was two fellows at the far left wicket" who were being waited on by teller Henrietta Reed. She was unable to describe the two persons because she did not see their faces, but one was wearing a light blue suit and the other was wearing a green suit; she called these "leisure suits." Both appeared to be about the same height, she guessed about six foot, and one hundred and fifty-five pounds. As to hair colour and style, the length was a little below their collars, and on one of them it was on the dark side and on the other one she thought it was light brown. She did not hear anything being said by either of the two men at the wicket or by Mrs Reed. She did not see where the men went once they left, nor did she go out and look for them afterwards.

She identified the credit union from the photograph and said that her car would have been just in front of the one in the photograph. She would have walked east into the credit union, and she identified a pole in the photograph with a no-stopping sign on it. The accused was pacing back and forth, going four to six feet, and she seemed to be looking down. Homan remembered the incident because it appeared that the girl was waiting for a bus and Homan knew that it was not a bus zone. She double-checked the sign when she pulled up. She did not speak with the girl who was pacing.

Homan was shown the coat supposedly worn by Janise and could not say whether it was or was not the coat she was wearing. When asked again about the style, colour, and type of coat and how it compared to the coat entered in the proceedings, Homan replied she did not remember the coat being like that. She thought the colour would compare, but the coat the girl was wearing didn't seem that long.

Asked whether she subsequently attended the lineup in Calgary, Homan said she did. She had identified Janise Gamble in the lineup.

This was the week following the robbery. She was not told that any specific persons would be in the lineup, nor did the police point or direct her attention to the accused in any way. At the lineup she was asked to observe what went on very carefully as the different girls walked back and forth and tried on coats. After that, she was told that if she could make an identification, she was to mark the numbers down on a piece of paper, which she did. She had written on it "Sharon Homan, 44 Lindale Road, No. 10." When asked who was the person wearing number 10, she said it was Janise Gamble. Asked whether Janise Gamble's appearance today was the same as when she saw her, she said, "No, her hair colouring is different." She recalled the girl's hair as being quite straight.

Macdonald then cross-examined. Homan had not stopped and talked to the girl she saw on the sidewalk. When he suggested that there was no reason to make a mental note about the girl, Homan replied, "Other than the fact she was standing by the pole and I double-checked to make sure it was not a bus zone." That was what had drawn her attention to the person. She admitted at the time she did not make a mental note of it and didn't think too much about it. When asked whether there was any real reason to, she said, "No, other than the fact that she was pacing back and forth." Going back to the coat, she could not really be sure of the exact colour of the coat, nor could she remember it being that long. She did say it was a leather coat and was sure of that.

Macdonald then asked Homan about the preliminary hearing when Chrumka had asked her, "Do you recall what the material might have been, what did it appear to be?" and she had answered, "I don't know sir." She said that she might have been referring to the exact colour. In any event, today she had said it was a brown leather coat, but she was not really sure about the colour and she was not really sure about the length.

There were other questions about whether the collar was up or down, and Homan said it she believed it was down. In the preliminary inquiry, when asked the same question, she said she had never noticed. She did not recall making that answer nor having been asked the question. She had not noticed what Janise had on her feet. The girl was wearing sunglasses, and Homan could not tell the colour of her eyes. When asked how long it took her to cross the sidewalk, she said, possibly forty seconds. Shown the photographs, she identified the sidewalk and estimated that it was about fifteen feet from the curb to the front door of the credit union and said that it would have taken her forty seconds to go fifteen feet. It was a routine day for her. She was on the way to the credit union to make a deposit. She saw a girl standing by what was not a bus stop and was thinking that she might think it was a bus stop (she had not thought too much about it at the time). She did not stop to talk to her. She did not recall whether she had a purse. She could not tell what kind of boots she had on. She could not say that the coat entered in proceedings was the coat.

Asked "What was particular about the young lady that stands out that enables you to make the identification?" she answered, "At the time, it was her hair." She said it was blond at the time, and she just noticed people with long hair, especially when it was clean and shiny. She agreed that a lot of people have long, clean, shiny hair. When asked what there was about this particular head of hair, she said it was the girl herself, but the hair stood out. Macdonald said, "She is a girl with long, clean, shiny hair and you have agreed that there are a lot of girls with long, clean, shiny hair." Homan agreed. "What was it about this girl, is there anything in particular that stands out about her?" Macdonald asked. She answered, "Other than that, no." "Other than her hair there is nothing, the same hair, that a lot of other people have, is that correct?" "Yes sir."

At the lineup there were about ten girls present, Macdonald said. When they were there, did the girls try on more than one coat? "Yes," Homan said. When asked whether the coat showed to her that morning fitted all the girls same, she said she said she never noticed. When asked if she recalled that at the preliminary hearing, when she was first asked if she could identify Mrs Gamble, she had looked right at her and passed her by, Homan answered, "Yes." The reason she gave was that she was not looking for someone wearing glasses. And she said, "Yes, nor the colour of her hair." Pressed with the question, "You did look directly at her and passed her by, didn't you?" she answered, "Yes, I did."

Chrumka re-examined on that point. He only did so because Macdonald had made some progress with his cross-examination, and he did not want to leave the jury with the impression that his witness might not have made a reliable identification. He too went back to the preliminary hearing.

CHRUMKA: My learned friend [Macdonald – this is the customary manner in which lawyers describe their opponents] asked you about the identification that you made at the preliminary after

you were asked to identify her, or to identify the person that
you saw at the bank. You indicated that you didn't see her, is
that correct?

ANSWER: At the preliminary hearing?

CHRUMKA: Yes.

ANSWER: First of all, I didn't see her.

CHRUMKA: Within two questions of that, did you identify her?

ANSWER: I believe I did, yes sir.

CHRUMKA: Were you asked these questions and did you make
these answers at the preliminary hearing: "Is the young girl in
court today? Answer: "No, I don't see her." Question: "Did you
identify that person at a lineup subsequent to this?" Answer: "Yes,
I did, pardon me." Question: "Do you see her?" Answer: "Yes, I
do." Question: "Where is that person?" Answer: "Right over there
with the glasses." Do you recall those questions being asked and
making those answers?

ANSWER: I do.

The next witness was Detective Leslie Herbert Goetjen, a peace officer with the Calgary City Police who was on duty in Calgary on 18
March 1976. He was called to confirm that the lineup had been properly conducted and that no indications that might have influenced the
witnesses had been given as to the identities of any of the women who
appeared. Goetjen had conducted a lineup at that time at the remand
centre of the Calgary City Police Station, at which time the accused
Janise Gamble was in the lineup. The persons for the lineup were
picked by the people from the remand centre. Janise Gamble was given
the option of standing where she wished and choosing the number she
wanted to wear.

A photograph was introduced as one taken when Goetjen was
there. He said that Janise Gamble picked number 10 and stood in the
middle of seven people. Other people in the lineup included Tracie
Perry, who selected number 20, and she also chose where she wanted
to stand. Goetjen was then shown a lineup identification sheet prepared by the remand centre, which had a list of seven people with their
ages, heights, and numbers given. The oldest person in the lineup was
twenty-five and the youngest was eighteen.

There was some confusion in understanding what the lineup sheet
showed for heights and weights and how that compared with what
Goetjen physically saw. He first said that there was a very good line-

up. Questioned further, he was asked that if the girls gave a height of five foot two and a weight of so-and-so, did it appear to be correct, and he answered, "Yes." The lineup sheet was signed by Goetjen, and it was conducted at 11:00 A.M. on 18 March. It included Janise Gamble, aged twenty-one years, five foot two, who selected number 10. Tracie Perry, five foot two and a half, selected number 20 and stood on the extreme left of the lineup, which would be on the extreme right of the picture. Lorraine Monkman, age eighteen, five foot six, was given number 1, Shaun Kirby, age twenty-five, five foot five, number 12, Ewa Motyl, eighteen years old, five feet tall, number 28, Marcia Hanachuk, twenty years old, five foot six, number 17, and Holly Anderson, nineteen years old, five foot six, number 11.

The lineup was viewed by Mrs Homan and Mrs Dredge. Detective Lund handed each girl Janise's coat to put on and walk in front of the length of the lineup and back behind it. Subsequent to that, Homan wrote number 10 down on a piece of paper, which had Goetjen's initials along with Lund's and the date of 18 March 1976. He did not tell Homan or Dredge where the accused or Tracie Perry would be standing in the lineup. He said he had never seen them prior to the lineup. He was asked if there were any other identifications made, namely paper given to him with numbers on them. He replied that, yes, there was a paper with numbers but no ID on it. It was not made clear whether Dredge had been at the lineup as a prospective witness. If she were, she was unable to make an identification or she would have been called as a witness to corroborate Sharon Homan's evidence.

Cross-examined by Macdonald, he said that the girls in the lineup had only tried on one coat. Because of the variation in the girls' heights, Macdonald suggested to Goetjen, the coat would have fitted some better than others. Goetjen replied that it fitted at least three of them very well. With respect to the other four, he was asked if it did not fit too well, and he answered that it didn't miss all that much either. In the lineup there were three girls who were exceptionally blond, some who were obviously not blond, and some who were in between. No one had told Janise Gamble to take number 10.

On this point Macdonald had made little headway. The lineup had been professionally conducted, and Janise had been positively identified as having been outside the credit union, pacing up and down – just the sort of thing a lookout might have been expected to do.

When Tracie Perry had been called as a witness for the Crown, she gave background evidence as to the trip from Vancouver, the rental of the car in Penticton, staying overnight and shopping the next day for suitcases. Nichols had driven to the credit union and she had been in the front seat with him. Janise had still been in the car when she got out to buy Aspirin. She had asked Tracie to get some gum at the same time, while the men had gone in to the credit union, and was not upset when Tracie left the car at that time. When Tracie came back, Janise was in the car and the men were getting in and she drove off in no particular hurry. Tracie had never seen Janise looking for a gun and she only heard about the robbery after they had been barricaded in the house. She also described Gamble's physical abuse of Janise, including how he had forced her to watch as he beat Janise. The jury could have been under no misapprehension as to his brutal treatment of her. She also identified the gun found at the side of the road as belonging to Nichols.

DRIVING THE GETAWAY CAR

Since it was known that Janise was at the wheel initially when the four-some left the area of the credit union and that she stopped the car when Nichols said that he wanted to drive, no serious issue arose on this point. The only question was how Janise happened to be behind the wheel at the time. The evidence of Tracie Perry was that they seemed to be in no hurry and that neither of the men mentioned anything about a bank robbery. Janise was not a good driver, the last sort of person the men would want to be driving the getaway car. By the time the shootout began, she was obviously in the back seat. She had not got out the driver's side door to change places with Nichols, having climbed over the seat into the back.

ACTIONS AT THE SCENE OF THE SHOOTOUT

There is no doubt that, at least by the date of the trial, the police believed that Janise had come out of the back seat of the car with a gun in her hands and that this had destabilized the situation to the point that the shooting began. The only basis for this belief seems to have been the statement made by Nichols to Detective Leslie Herbert Goetjen on 29 April, some six or seven weeks after the events, at the Calgary Hospital, since there was no witness at the scene of the shooting who had seen her with a gun. A pearl-handled gun had been found at the scene near where she had fallen beside the car. It was the largest and heaviest of the guns in their combined possession, although of the same .38 calibre as the others, excepting Gamble's 9 mm Luger and a .22 calibre pistol in one of the suitcases in the car.

Expert evidence was produced to identify the various handguns – the three in the possession of the criminals as well as Harrison's – and to identify the source of the bullets and fragments of bullets that had been recovered. Harrison had fired five shots in the exchange, and his revolver had only one live cartridge remaining. The bullet that killed him had come from the revolver found next to Nichols at the hostage scene, not from Gamble's Luger. On cross-examination, Macdonald elicited the evidence that none of the bullets or cartridges came from the pearl-handled gun, which had not been fired, and that it was the biggest of the guns. The witness acknowledged that it had a larger frame and was slightly heavier than the others. This was important for Janise, since it demonstrated that she had not fired the weapon and that, as the largest and heaviest of the guns, it was unlikely she had carried it around in her purse. No identifiable fingerprints had been found on that gun and thus there was no physical link to Janise. Also, Tracie Perry identified it as Nichols's gun.

FINGERPRINT ON THE HOLDUP NOTE

Detective Robert John Galloway, attached to the Identification Branch of the Calgary police, was called as a witness. He was on duty on 12 March and had gone to the Inglewood Credit Union at 1328 9th Avenue South East at about 4:00 P.M., where he dusted countertops for fingerprints, following which he photographed the interior and exterior of the credit union. He identified seven photographs which he had taken and developed himself. He was then asked if he had been given a particular item by another police officer. The item was a large envelope which, when he received it, was light brown in colour and had something written on it. He had received it from Detective Bechtold at approximately 9:00 P.M. on 12 March, when it was turned over to him in the police station in the Identification Branch. Galloway then took the envelope to the police garage where there was an examination room and treated it with silver nitrate, leaving it for about half an hour. He took it back to the identification office in headquarters and placed it under a heat lamp, also for roughly half an hour, and then left it. He had taken photographs of it prior to treating it with the silver nitrate and identified those two photographs for the court. One photograph showed writing on the envelope; the other photograph of the other side had no writing. Galloway had examined the envelope for fingerprints.

Chrumka then had to establish that Galloway had qualifications to do that type of examination and to express an opinion on it. The difference between ordinary witnesses and expert witnesses is that the former can only testify as to what they have observed or heard, whereas expert witnesses, if properly qualified as experts, are permitted to express an opinion based on the facts they have seen or observed. So, if a witness wishes to express an opinion on fingerprint evidence, for example, for purposes of concluding that a certain fingerprint is that of a particular person, the witness must first establish to the satisfaction of the court that he or she possesses the qualifications to express that opinion. Galloway had joined the Identification Branch in September 1975, spending four months training under Detective Lawrence Hewko, at the end of which time he was permanently attached to the Identification Branch and had worked with fingerprints pretty well daily. Following his initial training, he had done the normal duties in the Identification Branch by himself. Hewko had been with the Identification Branch for some eight years. Galloway had not attended any courses other than the training offered in Calgary, but said he had read the books they were required to read and had done so prior to making the examinations on the fingerprints on the envelope. He said he had done several fingerprint identifications prior to this.

Galloway was then cross-examined by Macdonald with respect to his expertise. This was necessary because it was already known from the preliminary inquiry that Galloway had concluded that Janise's fingerprint had been found on the note. This was an important link in the Crown's theory of the case, namely that she had been in on the robbery from the beginning. Macdonald thus had to try to challenge the qualifications of the expert produced on behalf of the prosecution. There would have been no point in making an issue of Galloway's qualifications during the preliminary inquiry, in case that might simply lead to the Crown using another expert at the trial whose qualifications could not be assailed.

Galloway acknowledged that there was no formal examination involved in becoming an expert in fingerprints. When asked how many books on fingerprinting he had read, he said approximately three, doing some of the reading on city time during his four-month training period and at other times on his own. He was not sure how long Detective Hewko had been involved in that field and acknowledged that he had had some on-the-job training in fingerprinting. He had never been sent back to take the course in Ottawa and had not made up a fingerprint chart since 12 March. Prior to that time he had made five charts only, which had amounted, on average, to less than one chart per month. He had never been qualified to give opinion evidence in court before on the matter of fingerprints. With respect to the books on fingerprinting he had read, he said that they were books put out by the RCMP. One of them was called *The Fingerprint Manual,* and he could not remember either the titles or the authors of the other two.

On re-examination by Chrumka, he indicated that charts were prepared for cases in which a person appeared in court and pleaded "not guilty" and where there was a suitable fingerprint or a latent fingerprint. He had been qualified as an expert in fingerprints in the Provincial Court subsequent to 12 March. Chrumka said that there was a first time for every expert to become an expert, and that Galloway had on-the-job training and dealt with fingerprints daily. Macdonald objected to the qualifications of the witness to give expert evidence notwithstanding that there must always be a first time. The court was, however, satisfied that Galloway was an expert in the field of fingerprinting, and he would be allowed to give opinion evidence as an expert. This would have been a disappointing outcome for Macdonald, since the expertise, assuming it existed, appeared to be marginal and Galloway was unable to identify most of the books he had read as part of his professional training.

Galloway produced a fingerprint chart with Janise Gamble's prints and identified them as those of the accused. They had been taken on 14 March in the city police station in the "mugging room" where prisoners were photographed and fingerprinted and their particulars were taken. Going back to the envelope, Galloway said he found fingerprints on the envelope and found the impression on the envelope that matched that of the rolled impression of Janise Gamble's left middle finger. The print was still visible, and he had taken a photograph of that print and enlarged it. He had done the same thing with the rolled-ink impression on the left middle finger and then enlarged it and charted those two. He thereupon identified the chart and stated that he had charted ten points of identification, giving in the result his opinion that the print was placed there by Janise Gamble.

The envelope did not leave his possession once it came into his possession, and had not been handled by Janise Gamble while it was in his possession.

When asked whether he had examined it for other prints, he said that he had found some which he could identify, but he had not taken the prints of that other person. His access to the prints of this other person were those photofaxed to him from Vancouver, along with a photo with which he could compare them. These had come from the RCMP station in Vancouver to the RCMP station in Calgary where they were picked up. These were copies of John Gamble's fingerprints. He said that he had found five fingerprints of John Gamble on the envelope: left index finger, left little finger, two of the left thumb, and one of the right middle finger. Gamble had not, said Galloway, had access to the envelope once it had come into his (Galloway's) possession, and John Gamble was the person identified in the photograph produced by the Vancouver detective.

On cross-examination, Galloway could not say whether Janise Gamble's fingerprint was placed on the envelope at 2:00 P.M. of 12 March nor at 4:00 P.M. He did not know whether it went on before or after the handwriting was put on the envelope. It was not possible to tell whether the print was put there when someone picked up the envelope or whether the person merely touched it. On re-examination by Chrumka he indicated that from the placement of the fingerprint of Janise Gamble, the palm of the hand would be over the larger part of the envelope. Whatever that may have suggested, Nichols would later say that he thought the handwriting on the envelope had been put there by Gamble, although he had not seen him write the note, and that Janise had bought the envelope while they were shopping on the morning of 12 March.

Evidence was next led regarding the continuity of possession of the envelope. Roger Allan Bechtold, a detective with the Calgary City Police, identified the envelope as having been received from Constable Austin at approximately 4:00 P.M. on 12 March. He had initialled the envelope and indicated the date he received it. He received this at the identification bureau on the main floor of the Calgary City Police station at 316 7th Avenue South East, where it remained in his possession for five hours until 9:00 P.M. on the same evening, when it turned it over directly to Detective Galloway. During the time it was in his possession, neither the accused Janise Gamble nor a person by the name of John Gamble handled it. No one handled it while it was in his possession, and he did not alter it in any way.

There was not much more to be said about the fingerprint. It was there. It would be possible to argue as to the meaning of this and the conclusions that might be drawn from a single print, but once the expert witness was properly qualified and allowed to express an opinion, the technical matching of Janise's fingerprint with those taken while she was in custody was routine and unquestioned.

SUBSEQUENT FLIGHT AND JANISE'S PARTICIPATION

As soon as the judge had ruled to allow evidence of the subsequent flight from the scene of the shooting as part of the evidence that would go to the jury, even though much of it had arguably not much direct connection with the sole charge of first degree murder under consideration in the trial, there was not a great deal that could be said to have been much in favour of Janise, with the possible exception of her relative kindness toward the hostages and to Diane Perry in particular. She was in the car, she had been part of the hostage taking, she had taken the money from the Thunderbird Restaurant cash register, she had helped to tie up the hostages and threaten them with knives. She may well, given Gamble's character and her fear of him, have had little practical alternative in the circumstances, but it was not going to make for a sympathetic hearing.

THE SEARCH FOR THE MISSING GUN

When the next witness was to be Diane Perry, one of the hostages, Macdonald wished to make an application in the absence of the jury. He was concerned that during the course of her evidence Perry would say that she heard John Gamble say to Janise, "Where is your gun, Janise?" His submission was that a statement by a third person as to certain facts repeated by someone else in the witness stand is a classic example of hearsay and is not normally admissible until one gets to the area of "adopted" admissions and whether Janise Gamble could be said, on the evidence, to have adopted that statement as her own. Part of this issue was whether there should be a *voir dire*.

At the preliminary inquiry earlier in the year, the questioning had gone as follows:

> QUESTION: All right. You indicate that you were bound with ny-
> lons and sheets in house. Where did this, in what room did this
> first happen, please?
> ANSWER: In the living room.
> QUESTION: What else was happening in that room at the time?
> ANSWER: Janis Gamble was looking for a gun. Mrs Kassam
> [Laila Rahim Jivraj] was sent out of the house to pick up the
> things that were in the car. I believe Janise Gamble's purse was
> out in the car – because they couldn't find her gun. She thought
> maybe she had left it in her coat.

The narrow point here was that this was not a question of a statement being adopted by the accused but one made by the witness giving her own testimony. The concern was that a jury hearing that
statement might take it as true, even if it was not something that the
accused knew about or accepted as a statement of fact. So it had to be
determined, without the jury present, whether there was any basis to
think that Janise had adopted the facts as they were about to be stated
by the witness. The upshot was that there was a *voir dire* on the question and Diane Perry was sworn and advised that the purpose was to
determine the admissibility of this evidence.

Chrumka established that she had been taken as a hostage to a
house in northeast Calgary and that she had heard conversations between the people who took her hostage. The two accused were among
the people who took her hostage, and for the record she identified
Nichols and Janise. She had heard several conversations between those
two people, and John Gamble and Tracie Perry were involved in them.
There was discussion about a lost gun between Janise and Gamble and
later Nichols. Her recollection was that Janise started looking for a
gun. She told Gamble that she had lost her gun. Nichols later entered
the conversation and was told that the .38 was missing. Janise was looking for it in her coat, which she could not find, and her purse. There
were later conversations when Nichols was talking to the police on the
phone and she thought they asked them to give their names, tell them
who they were. Nichols turned around to both Janise and Gamble and
said, "We might as well tell them who we are because they will have

the fingerprints off the gun anyway." They both agreed that they would tell their names.

It was not clear whether the men meant just the two of them or Janise as well. Even if the disclosure were to include Janise's name, there is no indication that her fingerprints would have been available for any possible examination, so the point was equivocal at best.

Macdonald's cross-examination took Perry back to the evidence at the preliminary hearing, in which there was the following series of questions.

QUESTION: Tell me, who else was talking about that gun?
ANSWER: I think everybody was looking for the gun. I think Bill was in on the conversation.
QUESTION: Is it fair to say that it was clear from the conversation that a gun of some kind had gone missing?
ANSWER: Yes.
QUESTION: And nobody seemed to know where it was?
ANSWER: No.
QUESTION: Again, did Janise Gamble ever use the word "my gun?"
ANSWER: I couldn't say for sure.

Perry was asked whether she was asked those questions and whether she made those answers. She said, "Yes." The series of questions at the preliminary inquiry continued as follows:

QUESTION: So you were sure John Gamble said "… your gun, Janise," but you are not sure whether Janise Gamble ever acknowledged whether it was hers?
ANSWER: Yes, I remember John asking her where her gun was.
QUESTION: You are sure about that?
ANSWER: Yes.
QUESTION: And you are not sure whether Janise said, "It was my gun," is that correct?
ANSWER: Right.
QUESTION: I take it that you are not sure that she used any words that indicated that it was her gun.
ANSWER: I can't remember.
QUESTION: Did you make those answers to those questions?

ANSWER: Yes.

QUESTION: Was it the truth?

ANSWER: Yes.

QUESTION: Yet you have told his lordship this morning that Janise said she had lost her gun.

ANSWER: That was another conversation. When Janise stated she had lost the gun at the scene of the shootout, Bill had run over her leg.

QUESTION: When was that?

ANSWER: That was during the middle of the night at about 3:00 to 4:00 A.M.

QUESTION: The statement where John Gamble said "Where is your gun, Janise?"

ANSWER: Yes.

QUESTION: That occurred as soon as you got in the house, did it not?

ANSWER: Shortly thereafter.

There was some further questioning about the noise and confusion at the time, plus the fact that Perry was lying face down on the carpet, followed by:

QUESTION: When John made that statement, you don't know what she said, do you?

ANSWER: No, I do not.

QUESTION: You weren't watching them?

ANSWER: Pardon me?

QUESTION: You weren't watching them?

ANSWER: I was watching, but I can't remember what she said.

QUESTION: Or did?

ANSWER: No.

There was no further evidence presented on the question of admissibility. Macdonald argued that, with respect to the statement made by Gamble, "Where's your gun, Janise?" there was no evidence on which a jury could reasonably infer that Janise adopted that statement, bearing in mind the situation at the time. The woman had just been taken hostage. There was noise, confusion in the house, she was lying face down on the carpet, she didn't know what Janise did or said when John Gamble said that. It was just a blanket statement not covered by any words, deeds, or gestures by Janise Gamble indicating she adopted this as her own. It was Macdonald's respectful submission that the question should not go to the jury.

Chrumka observed that the question, "Where's your gun, Janise?" was never put by the Crown. He never referred to the question. It was Macdonald who had. What Chrumka had asked was, "Was there any conversation about a gun?" and Perry said, "Yes, they were all looking for the gun." There was a conversation in which Nichols said, "We might as well tell them because our [sic] fingerprints are all on the gun," or, "We might as well give them our names because our prints are on the gun," and they all agreed that they would disclose their names. He submitted that was admissible against Janise and the evidence that Diane Perry gave in chief was all admissible. Whether or not the one statement, "Where is your gun, Janise?" was admissible he didn't know because at the time when the question was asked, it might not be admissible. But if Perry said that, subsequent to that statement being made, Janise started to run around the place looking for a gun, it was admissible then.

Macdonald said Janise ran around and looked for a gun, but it was the question of ownership with which he was having difficulty. The fact that she was looking for a gun, if she was looking for a gun, did not go back to "my" gun. Chrumka said her subsequent conduct or subsequent statements adopted the statement of Gamble, "Where is your gun?" as hers and she said, "I lost my gun at the scene." It was not adopted a split second after it was made, but later on. Adoption could come at any time.

The trial judge noted that there would have to have been a lapse of time of six or seven hours between those conversation and thought that the break in time was too great and that a jury could not reasonably infer from something Janise said six or seven hours later that she had adopted the statement made shortly after they arrived at the house. He was of the view that the proper foundation had not been laid by the Crown for an admission of the question nor the surrounding conversation at that time and warned Chrumka to be careful with his questioning of the witness on that point.

Diane Perry was then sworn as a witness in the case itself. She was a teacher's aide, living in The Properties in White Horn in Northeast Calgary and was driving a 1965 Pontiac north on Sixty-Eight Street between 4:00 and on 4:30 P.M. 12 March. A taxi pulled up beside her. Gamble was in the back seat of the cab and pointed to her tire and she thought she had a flat or something, so she stopped the car and started opening the door. Gamble was immediately beside the car and pointed a gun at her and called her a stupid bitch and said, "We have just killed a policeman and we are taking you hostage." He pushed her over to the middle of the car and got in beside her. Other people started getting into the car. Janise was on the other side of her, and at the time she did not know who was in the back seat of the car. She identified Gamble from the file photo that had been produced as an exhibit. He had a long black gun that looked like the gun that was in another photograph. She identified Janise and Nichols. Chrumka established that Tracie Perry was not related to her. Once they got into the car, Janise told her not to worry – they weren't going to hurt her. Both Janise and Gamble looked at the gas gauge, and saw that the gas tank was just about empty. There was talk about going out of town but when they saw that the gas was so low, they realised they couldn't. Gamble was driving and they drove north. By the time they got to Sixteenth Avenue, there was a police car behind them and there was talk about going to somebody's house and holing up in the house. At the time she thought they were talking about going to her house and she had said she didn't want to go to her house. She said she knew her husband wasn't home.

They had now crossed Sixteenth Avenue and took the first left off Sixteenth Avenue into Pine Ridge and as they were driving down the block they passed one house with the doors open and two houses further down saw a young girl outside a house. Perry thought Gamble said, "This is where we are stopping." The girl immediately ran into the house. Gamble drove up on the lawn. The police car was right behind them at the time. Gamble then dragged Perry out of the car, put a gun to her head, and screamed at the police car to get back or he was going to kill her. Everybody was getting out of the car at the time. They walked up to the door. The door was locked. Gamble kicked in the glass panel beside the door and they entered the house. When they got in there, they were told to lie face down.

Here the judge intervened, following up on his ruling in the *voir dire* to advise Chrumka that it would a good thing to be very careful at that point, since they had just now entered the house and were dealing with the conversations, and he trusted that Chrumka would caution the witness in that regard. Chrumka acknowledged that he understood and told Perry not to relate any conversations she might have had or heard, unless he asked her about them. He said that if there was something said in the house which was said by Janise Gamble, she could relate that, but if there was something just said in her presence, he would ask her not to talk about that until he asked her.

Once they were all inside the house, the girls were told to go to find something to tie the hostages up with. Nichols and Gamble were putting up barricades at the door with beds, putting things in front of windows, that type of thing. Tracie and Janise tied up the hostages with sheets around their feet and pantyhose around their wrists. After they were tied up, Nichols or Gamble, she didn't know which, went to the window and shot out of it to show that they meant business, that they weren't just fooling around, that they had weapons with them. Nichols, she said (actually the initial call had been made by Gamble), phoned the police and told them he wanted to talk to somebody, that they had just shot and killed a policeman and they were now holding hostages and wanted to talk to somebody about the situation.

The hostages were held in the living room for a while and then moved to the first bedroom. Janise Gamble was with them most of the time. Nichols and Gamble were also in and out of the bedroom. Janise was looking out the window. Tracie was in the living room looking out one of the living room windows. Gamble gave Janise the money to count, and there was $1,601, which she knew because she heard Janise tell Gamble that amount. The money was counted in the bedroom an hour or two after they got to the house.

Perry later asked if she could call her husband. Nichols phoned her husband and talked to him. She did not speak with her husband the first time. The hostages were later made comfortable The blankets had been pulled off the beds, as the mattresses were used as the barricades. Perry was untied – her hands were originally tied behind her back – and her hands were re-tied in front. She was a very heavy smoker and was allowed to smoke, which is why they had her hands tied in front. Mr Jivraj was on the other side of the bedroom from her and Laila. Gamble had a knife in his hand while Janise was counting the money, and he kept stabbing at the mattress and saying, "This is a really good knife." It just barely penetrated the mattress. She thought Janise also had a knife at the time.

Nichols was on the phone quite a bit of the time talking to the police, Perry said. Gamble was very high at the time, uptight, ranting, and raving, with a lot of swearing, and she did not know if it was an act. Nichols later came in and said to her, "Don't worry about it, John isn't really like this, but he is just putting on an act for the sake of the police." The ranting and raving was going on when someone was on the telephone. About six o'clock Nichols again phoned her husband. She was not allowed to talk to him at that time either. While they were talking to the police, Nichols and Gamble were making demands for $100,000 and, she believed, for an airplane and many of these types of things that they wanted. The men were afraid to leave the house because they felt they would be shot the minute they walked out. She thought there was also talk – she didn't know whether this was during the phone conversation or just amongst themselves – about an armoured car pulling up to the back or to the front entrance to the house so they could get out of the house that way. This went on for quite a while, a lot of conversation between the police with Nichols on the phone.

Mr Jivraj was released later that night in exchange for Demerol. The conversation had been that, if the police did not give them the Demerol, the fugitives would give them nothing. She thought the Demerol was generally for all of them to calm down. Janise and Tracie were told that they were to stay in the bedroom with the hostages with knives. Gamble's words were, "The knives are to be held at their throats. If anything happens, their throats are to be cut." This threat was never carried through. The girls did come to the bedroom with knives, the Demerol was delivered, and Mr Jivraj was released. She never saw anyone use the Demerol but she believed Janise, Nichols, and Gamble took Demerol. Macdonald objected to this answer, and the court agreed. However, it might have been helpful for Janise if there had been evidence that she had used some of the Demerol and been a bit high on it at the time they were talking about the loss of the gun and her having been run over by the car.

Chrumka then moved on to the conversations among Gamble, Nichols, and Janise. Were any people looking for anything specific in the house? Perry answered they were looking for a gun and that it was Janise who was looking for it. She was looking for a gun in her purse and she was looking for her coat to find a gun that she had had in her possession. Did Perry recall what Janise was saying when she was look-ing for it? Perry answered that Janise was telling her husband that she could not find her .38, but could not recall the exact words Janise used. This was while they were still in the living room, shortly after they got there, perhaps fifteen minutes or half an hour. Janise said she thought it might be in her coat, which she said had been left at the restaurant. Much later, about 4:00 A.M. when they were talking, Janise said she had probably dropped the gun when Nichols had run over her with the car at the scene of the shootout.

QUESTION: All right. Do you recall how the words she used to convey this meaning, how she put it?
ANSWER: In this last conversation?
QUESTION: Yes, how she put it as she was speaking, which she in fact said.
ANSWER: They were laughing about Bill backing over Janise's leg and I don't like to use the language that Janise used to describe what she said.
QUESTION: It may be personally embarrassing to you but it would be very helpful to us if you told us and used the language she used.
ANSWER: She said, "I probably lost it when you ran over my fucking leg."
QUESTION: And what else did she say?
ANSWER: And they laughed about it.

Interestingly, Laila Jivraj, who later testified that she had always been in the presence of Diane Perry while they were hostages, said that she had never heard the girls talking about guns. Both the Jivrajs had been called as witnesses for the Crown, but had little to say about the main events, since they had not been involved until they were taken hostage after the robbery and shooting. They identified the participants, either in court or from photographs, and described the flight, the additional capture of Diane Perry, driving to the house, the break-in, and several photographs of the interior of the restaurant and the house. Neither had seen the girls with any guns. Both agreed that Gamble had appeared to be the most violent and unstable of the captors. It was Nichols who told Laila that her husband would be released for the drugs.

Perry said she had never seen any guns in the possession of Janise Gamble or Tracie Perry. She also said that Nichols was talking to the police when Janise and John were both by the banister of the stairs in the living room and Nichols turned around and said, "We might as well tell them who we are because they have got the gun and they will have the fingerprints all over it and then they will know who we are anyways." John agreed and said, "Yes, tell them." Perry did not know what Janise said.

Macdonald cross-examined and got Perry to repeat some of what she had said in her earlier testimony, that she had said that Janise assured her that things were going to be all right when they came to her car, not to worry, not to be afraid, and this happened as well on other occasions when they were in the house. It was Gamble who told the girls to hold the knives to her throat. She did not know what Janise did with the knife in the bedroom and, in fact, she had lost it but didn't tell anyone she had lost it, entering the room in the dark trying to find it. It was Janise who untied her, and when Gamble found out, he became extremely angry at both her and Janise. The antics and actions of Gamble in particular scared Perry, and she was terrified when she was being dragged out of the car.

As to the gun, Janise had walked in from the kitchen with her purse, looking through her purse. Gamble walked into the room shortly after, and that is when the conversation about the gun started. As she was looking through her purse, Gamble entered the room and Janise said, "I can't find my gun." Nichols later entered and Gamble told Nichols that the .38 was missing.

Perry was confronted with her testimony in the preliminary hearing where she was asked the question, "Again, did Janise Gamble ever use the words, 'my gun'"? Her answer had been "I couldn't say for sure." Perry acknowledged making that answer to the question then. When asked whether it was truthful, she said the conversation was such that it was Janise's gun. Her wording may have been different, but the conversation was that it was her gun that was missing.

QUESTION: Do we take it from that, Mrs. Perry, that from the conversation that you heard in the room, you inferred that it was her gun?
ANSWER: No.
QUESTION: Well, I ask you again the question and answer I put to you just a minute ago: Was that a truthful answer? Did Janise Gamble ever use the word "my gun"? Answer: "I couldn't say for sure." Was that a truthful answer at that time?
ANSWER: Yes.
QUESTION: Do we conclude from that, Mrs. Perry, that you are not sure she used the words "my gun"?
ANSWER: Yes.

QUESTION: This morning on giving your evidence in chief, did you indicate that you can't remember exact words?
ANSWER: Yes.
QUESTION: And that applies to this conversation as well does it?
ANSWER: Yes.
QUESTION: But definitely there was a conversation in that living room that you heard among various people that led you to believe that the .38 had been lost, is that right?
ANSWER: Yes.

This may have weakened the effect of the testimony a bit, but it was certainly clear in Diane Perry's mind that Janise, whatever else may have happened or been said, was involved in the search for a gun that was missing.

NICHOLS'S STATEMENT REGARDING JANISE

Leslie Herbert Goetjen, an officer with the Calgary City Police, was on duty on 29 April several weeks after the events, in the company of another police officer, Detective Snaith. Goetjen was called to introduce a statement allegedly made by Nichols the same day. The two officers had gone to the Foothills Hospital, Nursing Unit 1001, at about 12:15 P.M. Nichols was sitting on the edge of the bed, having just finished his meal.

Chrumka noted that the court might have to determine the admissibility of some evidence and perhaps the jury should be removed. Goetjen would testify that he had asked some questions of Nichols and that Nichols made some answers. This called for a *voir dire* regarding the admissibility of those answers.

In the *voir dire* Goetjen was allowed to refer to notes that he made at the time (not right away, but at the first opportunity he had to do so). Goetjen had gone to the hospital room by himself and he said to Nichols, "Nichols, I am Detective Goetjen of the Calgary City Police. I know you are Bill Nichols, how are you?" to which Nichols had replied, "Hi, and good." Goetjen said, "I am investigating the murder of Police Officer Keith Harrison. You are charged with murder in relation to that death, do you understand that?" To which there was a reply, "Yeah, my lawyer told me." Then Goetjen said, "You know you don't have to tell me anything unless you want to." The reply was, "Yeah, I know that." Then Goetjen said, "What happened, would you like to tell me?" And Nichol's reply was, "It was that damn Janise. I was going to surrender and so was Johnny, but not Janise, she didn't want to get separated from him. That bitch had to come out of the back seat of the car with a gun in her hand. The cop fired first and we all started shooting except her, she lost her gun."

At that time Detective Snaith entered the room and Goetjen said, "Bill, this is Detective Snaith of the Calgary City Police. He is my new partner." They exchanged greetings, and Goetjen said, "Okay, Bill, what happened next?" Nichols replied, "Janise was driving. We thought that guy following us was a cop. Janise can't drive worth a shit so I was going to drive. That's when it started. He came out of his car with his gun out and we knew he was a cop. He fired first. I don't blame him. All hell broke loose then."

Goetjen asked, "How many shots were fired?" Nichols replied, "I don't know, but lots, bullets were going all over hell, I said, 'Let's get out of here,' and Janise and Johnny dove into the car through the back window. I think I backed over her, because her leg was sore. We drove all over the place, lots of cop cars around and we knew we had to get rid of the car."

At that point, the nurse entered the room and had a conversation with Goetjen, nothing in relation to what he was talking about to Nichols. The nurse had brought in a bag and put the property that Nichols had into it, and at that time she complained a bit about the police being there early, as she didn't have Nichols quite ready. After she left, Nichols said, "Johnny died, eh?" and Goetjen said, "Yeah, I went to his funeral." Then he said to Nichols, "How come you made it?" His reply was, "I squirted half the big one down the sink. I didn't want to die. Johnny didn't care, he didn't give a damn. It was his idea to get the hostages. I just went along with it."

Nichols's statement was particularly convenient evidence for the prosecution, especially since there were no identifiable fingerprints on the gun, it had not been fired, and there was no witness, including the police on the scene of the shooting, who had seen Janise with a gun. On a capital murder charge, as the law read on 12 March, Nichols's evidence would have been indispensable, since the Crown would have had to prove that Janise had by her own act caused the death of the police officer.

NICHOLS TAKES THE STAND

After lengthy argument about the admissibility of certain of the Crown's evidence, it came time to present the case for the defence. James Butlin, Nichols's lawyer, said Nichols would take the stand to say that he had grabbed his gun and started shooting only after Harrison had opened fire. Nichols had become filled with remorse after the shooting and could not remember all of the statements he made to the police on 29 April, in which he was reported to have said that he had not wanted to join Gamble in a suicide pact. In that statement as read, he said that he had squirted half a container of methadone down the kitchen sink. The lawyer said this was untrue: "Both attempted to overdose, and Nichols doesn't know why he didn't die."

Nichols gave his evidence on 1 December. His defence was that he shot Harrison in self-defence after Harrison had first shot in his direction. "I was terrified. I grabbed my own gun out of self-preservation. My intention was to surrender." He said that the two women knew nothing about their plans to hold up the credit union and that they waited in the car while they were inside. Janise drove the car away, through the zoo and onto Memorial Drive. There he told her to pull to the side so he could take over the wheel, "because she wasn't a very good driver." The gun concealed in his waistband started to fall out as he got into the driver's seat, "so I grabbed it." At this point, he said, a man who had stepped out of an unmarked car stopped behind theirs yelled, "Drop your gun and put your hands in the air." Nichols said, "I put the gun on the roof of the car and my hands on the side of the car." The man then shouted, "Get out of the car," and fired his gun as Janise moved across the back seat. "I fired six shots back," Nichols said. Then, "I dove into the front seat and John dove in through the shattered right rear window. Johnny grabbed Janise and pulled her back into the car."

He described the negotiations with the police. Letting the first hostage go in return for some Demerol, he said, was "to calm us down." The next day, he said, he handed his gun to Diane Perry and told her, "Here, hold me hostage." He testified, "I told her I was fed up with everything. We were getting phone calls continuously. A reporter told us the policeman was dead. [This is either wrong or out of order. It was clear from the wiretaps that the men first learned of Harrison's death from the police.] There was nothing left and the only alternative was death."

After Jim Hogan had delivered the supply of methadone on Saturday afternoon, and the hostages and the two women left, Nichols mixed the methadone into four small and two large syringes. "I made sure the dosages were even." After that, he said, "We sat on the chesterfield and administered three syringes each."

As to the statements he was alleged to have made to Detective Goetjen, he could not remember a number of them. "I didn't tell him I knew I was being followed by police before the shootout." Under cross-examination by Chrumka, he said he and Gamble assumed the man behind them might be police – "until he fired the first shot." Nichols also specifically said, in relation to Goetjen's assertion that he had stated, "That bitch had to come out of the back seat with a gun in her hand," that "I never saw a gun in Janise's hand."

In his statement to Goetjen, whether admissible or not, he had never said that he had seen Janise with a gun. Standing outside the car with his hands on the roof, it seems highly unlikely that he could possibly have seen what might or might not have been going on in the back seat, nor that he could have seen anything as Janise got out of the car.

Medical evidence was given by Dr J.J. Hartford, a psychiatrist from Waterloo, Ontario, who had treated Nichols in 1971 during his incarceration in Ontario. Hartford characterized him as an impulsive neurotic able to maintain control under stress "only with great difficulty."

JANISE LEADS NO EVIDENCE

Throughout the trial Janise was under heavy sedation, receiving triple doses of drugs: an anti-depressant, an injection for nausea, and a sedative for sleeping. She had been in custody, all applications for bail denied, since 13 March, and apart from infrequent visits from members of her family, had been alone in a strange environment for almost nine months. She was on trial for a murder that it was clear she personally had not committed, in the city where the victim, a well-respected police officer, had been killed. Nichols, who would undoubtedly have said anything in an effort to save his own skin, had apparently decided it would suit his defence for her to have been the cause of the shooting, and that evidence was now in front of the jury. Troubling portions of the evidence linked her with all the key events, starting with the preparations for the robbery to the robbery itself, the getaway, and the hostage-taking. There was pressure on her to take the stand, to tell her story, to create the reasonable doubt that would require a jury to declare her not guilty.

But that pressure was enormous, too much for her to bear. On the morning of the day she was to give her evidence, Macdonald took one look at her and concluded that she could not possibly take the stand. She was shaking, her eyes all but spinning in her head, incoherent. Macdonald said that he could not allow her to give evidence under those circumstances, that "it's not going to happen." The defence called no evidence.

Janise's story was never heard by the jury or the judge. The only unchallenged or uncontradicted evidence against her was her single fingerprint on the holdup note.

CHAPTER 8

LEGAL SUBMISSIONS, CHARGE TO THE JURY, AND VERDICT

Once the evidence was completed, the closing addresses to the jury were fairly brief. The lawyers knew that the jury, after so many days of sitting, would not welcome long harangues from lawyers, especially since they knew they would be getting a lengthy charge from the trial judge. They – particularly the defence lawyers – understood that the jury would already have a good idea of the facts, and they simply wanted to emphasize those most in their favour and create whatever tendencies to a reasonable doubt could be derived from them, as well making sure that the jury did not lose sight of what constituted reasonable doubt.

On Nichols's behalf, Richard Cairns reviewed the evidence, particularly that relating to the shootout, trying to demonstrate that it was likely that Harrison had fired the first shot, as well as emphasizing the actions that would lead to the conclusion that Nichols had surrendered and put down his gun before the shooting started. He admitted that the bullet that killed Harrison came from Nichols's gun but suggested that the bullet was fired in self-defence. Nichols was in a panic triggered by the shot from Keith Harrison's gun, he argued. Harrison might very well have been nervous – he had no radio and could not get any backup – so it was not impossible that he had in fact fired first. Cairns submitted that Nichols was not the sole cause of the tragedy. He was entitled to claim a verdict of not guilty. People were not to be tried by newspapers, radio, TV, or rumours, but by a jury of their peers.

Macdonald argued on behalf of Janise that there was not enough evidence to show that she knowingly participated in a robbery, knowing that guns were to be used, and knowing that the tragic death that followed would be a probable consequence. He tried to make sure that the jury would not consider what Nichols was supposed to have said to Detective Goetjen, since it could not be used against her and they had no idea of what Nichols's motivation for having made the statements might have been. One of Macdonald's toughest hurdles was the fact that Janise had given no evidence and he had to deal with that head on.

> Bear in mind what I told you earlier: in criminal proceedings it is not up to her to prove her innocence, it is up to the Crown to prove her guilt.
>
> I would also ask you to bear in mind the decision to call or not to call evidence in a criminal case: that is my responsibility, my job. I decide that, she doesn't. She doesn't decide that. It is the thorniest question, I submit to you, that a lawyer can ever have to deal with: Is there enough there to put her on, to take this girl, who has lost a husband, who has been through an extremely trying experience, and subject her to the rigours of a court hearing? That is the decision I have to make: is there enough there? I say to you, ladies and gentlemen of the jury, two things. If there was enough evidence in the Crown case which I felt needed answering, then I could have told her to go on, and if the evidence of her defence was not already before you – you have heard it all week long – then maybe the answer would have been different and maybe you would have had her evidence, but bear in mind as I said at the outset, that is my job, that is why I am hired, I live with the decision. And when you bear in mind again where the burden lies, the girl is presumed to be innocent and I say to you that, in my opinion, the decision I make says to you, no, the Crown hasn't proven their case.

Macdonald worked through the fingerprint evidence, basically acknowledging the evidence was sound, despite a desultory challenge to the expertise of the police officer, but saying that no one could tell how it got there or when, and that Janise had been in the back of the car, where the fingerprint could easily have got there. There was no evidence as to whose handwriting was on the envelope. He challenged the evidence of Sharon Homan and said they should prefer that of Tracie Perry, who had said that it was she, not Janise, who was in front of the bank and that Janise was in the car. Similarly, the evidence of Janise driving away did not accord with what one might expect if she knew there was a robbery in progress. Surely she would not have allowed Tracie Perry to go off wandering and shopping if she had knowledge of what was going on.

At the scene of the shooting, no one had seen her with a gun. The jury knew that she did not fire a shot; they knew which gun killed Harrison; they knew that she didn't have a gun in her hand and wound up flat on her back screaming. When the car left the scene, Janise and Tracie Perry were screaming, "What is happening? What is happening?"

At this point, Macdonald said, the situation changed dramatically. You had Nichols, a man whose psychiatrist said did not respond well to pressure and might panic, and Gamble, who was at best irrational and at worst, an animal. The combination was explosive, and all Janise did was follow Gamble and Nichols. Having lived with Gamble and taken the beatings she took, would she be arguing with him in these circumstances, a situation that was out of control, certainly out of her control? She wanted to stay with Gamble, perhaps because she knew that if she were with him, she could prevent the worst from happening. When she left him, she was crying. It was not guilt: it was love.

He finished his address with the following summary:

So, look at the note: it is equivocal. Look at the identification: I say it is unreliable. Look at the driving of the car: I say it is not consistent with the way she handled Tracie Perry at the time. View it all against the overall scheme that you have heard throughout this case, that she didn't know, and I suggest to you, ladies and gentlemen, that you have not got proof beyond a reasonable doubt that she was no more different than Tracie and that when you look and look for that moral certainty, you aren't going to find that you can be morally certain that she planned and was in on that robbery and knew that guns were going to be used and knew that death was going to ensue, and I think you will agree with me, when I made the decision not to put Janise Gamble on the stand, I was right. There was not a case to meet, the Crown hasn't proven its burden of proof beyond a reasonable doubt, and that young lady is entitled and I ask from you a verdict of acquittal.

In criminal cases a high standard is demanded of the state, proof beyond a reasonable doubt. This standard is one of the reasons that many criminals go free at the end of the day and why many cases are not even brought before the courts. The philosophy has always been that it is better for many guilty persons to go free than to convict someone who is innocent. That is a bulwark of our system of criminal justice.

One slight but important advantage given to the prosecution is that it speaks last in summation. This is to make sure that the jurors are not overly influenced by emotional pleas from defence counsel to render verdicts that may be more sentimental than based on the facts in evidence before them. That was Chrumka's job: to make sure that the jury did not get led off the trail, which he did by reminding them of what was involved.

There are, of course, in the indictment, a number of elements that the Crown must prove and there are at least four that I can say there is absolutely no doubt about.

The place of the offence – it happened in Calgary.

The date of the offence – the 12th of March.

The victim – Allan Keith Harrison.

That he was acting in the course of his duties – he was a police officer on duty attempting to make a lawful arrest and that he was in fact killed while acting in the course of his duties.

Now the other elements are:

How was he killed? He was shot.

Who actually killed him? The accused William John Nichols.

Did anyone assist, aid, or was anyone else a party to the killing? I submit John Gamble was and I respectfully submit that Janise [sic] Gamble was.

On at least the first six elements that I mentioned, I submit that there is no doubt. The only elements on which you may, which you have to decide, are whether the accused knew he was a policemen, secondly – who did they think they were shooting at? Thirdly – was Janise Gamble a party to that offence?

Chrumka then focused on the elements that he considered important to establish that Janise was a party to the crime. He said it was
common sense that robbers use lookouts and that they move back and
forth. There was no question that both Janise and Tracie Perry were at
the scene. The evidence was that the men were in the credit union for
about three minutes. The witness, Mrs Homan, had seen Janise for
about forty seconds, not a fleeting glance. The elements of much of
Janise's appearance – sunglasses, leather coat, slacks – had been confirmed by Tracie Perry and Diane Perry. Janise was identified in a lineup. He even cast doubt on whether Tracie Perry did leave the car and
whether she did stop to look for change. This was evidence from his
own witness. He vigorously defended the identification made by Mrs
Homan. He provided a sinister interpretation of the fact that Janise
was driving as the car left the credit union.

> First, she drives the car from the scene. From Vancouver to Cal-
> gary she never drives. In Calgary she is the driver. Two men rob
> that Credit Union, they get in the back seat. Why? I suggest you
> can consider this: would the police, if they heard that a robbery
> was perpetrated by two men, be looking for a male driver of a car
> or would they be looking for a female? Would they be looking
> for two girls in the front seat of a car? Or, if two men did rob the
> Credit Union and they got into the back seat, on the approach
> of the police, is it easy to duck down and conceal one's self?

The envelope, he said, had been purchased by Janise and no reason
was given for its purchase. He was perhaps unduly aggressive in his
construction of the facts relating to the fingerprint on the note:

> Remember how, what position the fingerprint was placed. Maybe
> she got it when the note was thrown out the back – there is no
> evidence she threw it out. You are asked to speculate that. But
> there is this: would a distraught woman, screaming, have the pres-
> ence of mind to pick up a holdup note and throw it out the win-
> dow unless she knew what it was? Would she have the presence
> of mind to destroy evidence unless she knew what it was?

Chrumka was equally aggressive about why Janise decided to get
out on the passenger side of the car. Was this to use the car for cover,
or was it to obstruct Harrison's view of Nichols? Instead of scrambling

over the seat, why did she not get out of the same door that Nichols had used? Here, he had perhaps misunderstood the evidence, which had been that Nichols had said to stop the car, that he was going to drive, and that as he got out, Janise had not got out the driver's side but simply, as a very petite person, flipped into the back. It was not that movement that had caused Harrison to turn around; it had been her exit from the car, which Chrumka claimed was with a gun in her hand, despite the fact that there had been no evidence whatsoever that she had been seen with one. Even if she had a gun – they all seemed to think that it was in her purse or in her coat – both constructions were completely at odds with her having come out of the car with it in her hands. And the only person who had said she had a gun was Nichols, and he recanted on whatever statement he might have made. Apart from that, it was a statement completely inadmissible against Janise, as a matter of law, but one which the prosecution knew would have a significant impact on a jury dealing with the death of one of its local police officers. Chrumka, however, repeated several times that she had got out of the car with a gun. He followed this up with extensive references to the testimony of Diane Perry and the search for a gun at the hostage scene and was at pains to draw further attention to Janise's participation in the hostage elements.

Her desire to commit suicide, Chrumka said, was evidence of her guilt. It was guilt rather than love that was driving her towards suicide, and only at the last minute was she thwarted in that plan. The John Gamble who had so often beaten her and treated her so inhumanely yet she so loved forced her out of the house and no one made a request for amnesty or immunity from prosecution for her. (This was clearly wrong. It had been requested by the two men and by Jim Hogan. There was no evidence upon which Chrumka could have made that statement.) She wanted to die with the others, he said, and it was because of her implication in the offences, not for any other reason.

He finished with a reference back to the testimony of the attending physician, whose testimony and the identification of the bullet that had killed Harrison were electric moments during the trial. They had driven home the fact that there had been a murder, with real bullets and a real victim. The surgeon had broken down in the course of giving his evidence. This had sobered everyone who had just come for the atmosphere of the trial, and it was a good trial tactic for Chrumka to have seized upon for his final words:

I submit that this case was put in its proper perspective by Dr. Dubienski, who came, was overcome with emotion when recalling that after three hours of effort he was unable to save the life.

The evidence, I submit, indicates that the shooting started when Janise Gamble came out of the car, when she was ordered out. It is not necessary that she had fired the first shot but if she did anything that caused to police officer to turn and if she was armed at the time, and I submit that the evidence points to her having a gun and to her losing it.

Now, ladies and gentlemen, I want you to just consider this: this is the bullet that killed Detective Staff Sergeant Keith Harrison and this is the gun that fired it and that is the man that fired the gun and I submit, on all of this evidence, both have committed first degree murder.

With that, Chrumka sat down.

CHARGE TO THE JURY

Following argument by the defence and the Crown, Judge Shannon delivered his charge to the jury. This is an important part of the process in a jury trial, especially one for murder. The judge has the duty to explain the applicable law in terms understandable to a lay jury and to review for them the facts that have been presented. This is essential for the jury, who must reach conclusions that have enormous consequences for the accused and, to do so properly, they must know what are the legal standards that govern the facts presented to them during the course of the trial. The charge is also important to the lawyers for both the accused and the Crown, who concentrate on every word to be certain that the proper nuancing of the facts and law are conveyed by the judge, since they may have an immediate and possibly determinative impact on the outcome of the trial.

For the Crown, an acquittal is for all practical purposes the end of the road. It is almost impossible to get a reversal of a jury verdict of not guilty. For the accused, it is not quite the end of the road, since there is always the possibility of an appeal. But to the extent that the charge may affect the perceptions of the jury, everything in the evidence that favours the accused should be presented to it.

The charge is a matter of huge importance to the presiding judge as well. First, it is the duty of the judge to be sure that the jury is properly instructed; that is a fundamental element of any criminal trial. Second, however, although it is an unstated premise of the process, trial judges know that if there is a conviction, there will almost certainly be an appeal, and in that process every word that they utter will be examined with great care and presented on a platter to the appellate courts in search of a reversal of the conviction or a new trial. As a matter of personal and professional reputation, judges do not want to be told by a higher court that they have made an error, so as they work through the elements of the charge, they have an eye on the possible record that will form part of any appeal. Judges within a court often share charges that they have used on other occasions and may even have background material they have collected over the years of charges that have been approved by higher courts or, more importantly, charges that have led to new trials or reversals because they were defective in one or more particulars. The language used in the charge will be carefully selected to fit with language which has been judicially approved in other cases.

Trial judges also do not fly "blind" throughout the trial. It is too important for the judicial process for them not to be aware of what the opposing parties consider to be important in the particular case before the court. It is the duty of counsel for the prosecution and the defence to provide the presiding judge with memoranda of the theory of the case as they see it and to call the judge's attention to those points of law, evidence, and procedure of which they believe he or she should be aware as the drama unfolds. The judge will be called upon throughout the trial to make rulings that may have a decisive effect on what is presented to the jury, and the body of evidence that is before the jury is the sole basis (at least in legal theory) for the decision the jury will reach. It is generally acknowledged that it is far more stressful to be a trial judge than to sit in appeal. There is a view, which has some merit, that appellate judges should have some experience sitting as trial judges before they go to a court of appeal, in order to know how matters develop in real life, so that when they read the record of a trial, all neatly typed and bound, they can do so with a personal contextual knowledge of how it may have come about.

So, before Mr Justice Shannon delivered his charge in this case, he had the benefit of three memoranda containing the submissions of counsel for the Crown, Nichols, and Janise Gamble. These memoranda do not, however, form part of the official record of the case. Nor does the jury ever see or hear them. But they telegraph, at least to the trial judge, the areas that may be important if an appeal is to be launched.

In structure, the charge in this case was fairly standard for such matters. Mr Justice Shannon reminded the jury of the right of the accused to have their guilt or innocence decided by twelve of their fellow citizens. The jury were to be the sole judges of the facts, and he was to be the sole judge of the law. He was to instruct them in the law as it applied to the case, and they were bound to follow the law as he stated it to them. They were to approach their duties objectively, without pity for the accused, without prejudice or passion against them. They were to determine their guilt or innocence solely on the basis of the evidence introduced in the trial. Nothing said by the lawyers or by him was evidence.

When they retired, he said, they should choose a foreman to preside over the discussion, acting as chair to assist in examining the issues in an orderly fashion. As soon as they entered the jury room, their attitude, in his opinion, would be of considerable importance. It would not be a good approach to their responsibilities to make an emphatic expression of opinion at the outset and to express strong feelings for a certain verdict. Pride might become involved, and it might be difficult for them to change their minds if they were to be persuaded by the wisdom of a fellow juror. They were not partisans, they were not advocates – they were judges. In the jury room, he said, there is no triumph except the ascertainment of the truth.

The jury members were also cautioned to consider his instructions as a whole. He reminded them that, after they retired, counsel would be invited to submit any matter on which they might request that he give them further instructions. He warned them that, if they were recalled in the midst of their deliberations, they might place undue emphasis on what he said when they returned. They were not to do that; whatever he might say then should be considered part of what he was now saying and as part of his instructions as a whole. The matter of penalty or punishment should not be discussed or considered. They were not involved in the matter of sentencing.

He then turned to the matter of the burden of proof. In a criminal case, accused persons are presumed to be innocent until the Crown has proven their guilt beyond a reasonable doubt. The Crown must prove their guilt, and the onus is on the Crown throughout. It is not for accused persons to prove their innocence. If the Crown fails to prove guilt beyond a reasonable doubt, they must acquit the accused persons. "Now proof beyond a reasonable doubt does not mean proof beyond any possible or imaginary doubt, because everything relating to human affairs is open to some possible or imaginary doubt. Proof beyond a reasonable doubt is when you as jurors feel sure of the accused persons' guilt with an abiding conviction amounting to a moral certainty. It is that degree of proof which convinces the mind and satisfies the conscience, and you, as conscientious jurors, feel bound to act upon it."

He reminded them again that they were the sole judges of the facts and that questions of fact were of fundamental importance in a criminal trial. He might, however, give his opinion as to what the evidence had established in relation to different factual issues in the case or as to the testimony of witnesses. Were he to do so, he would try to do so cautiously and only if he thought it would be of help to them. However, he emphasized, any and every expression as to the facts made by him at any time during the course of the charge would be subject always to what he was about to say, and if they did not agree with any opinion of his as to what they thought were or were not the facts, it was their duty to disregard his opinion to whatever extent seemed proper to them. They, the jury, alone, after giving faithful consideration to the whole of the evidence, must make the findings of fact in the case and render a verdict according to the evidence and according to the oath sworn by each of them. In assessing the evidence, they were entitled to use the ordinary, everyday common knowledge that we all acquire as we go through life; that is, they were able to use plain ordinary common sense.

He then went on to a discussion of evidence and credibility. Credibility referred to what they believed, or did not believe, of testimony they had heard from different witnesses.

It is simply common sense that you are not bound to accept and believe every word every witness has said in the witness box. In many cases that would be impossible, because in almost every case, especially this case, there are inconsistent statements made by witnesses and sometimes conflicting and irreconcilable testimony. It is your duty to consider all of the evidence and to decide which of it you accept and believe. Having carefully weighed that acceptable and credible evidence in the light of my instruction to

you in this regard, it is for you to say whether or not the guilt
of the accused persons has been established beyond a reasonable
doubt. As to each witness, you have no doubt formed an estima-
tion of his or her truthfulness or untruthfulness, their powers of
observation, their capacity to tell accurately what he or she observed and remembered, integrity, fairness, candour, or the lack of
any of those qualities. Has the witness a motive in favouring one
side or the other? Has he or she an interest? If you do not believe
the whole of the evidence of any witness, you must make up your
mind as to what part or parts, if necessary, you believe or which
you reject as unworthy of belief. In doing so you should consider
the demeanour of the witness and the impression that he or she
made upon you while giving evidence in court. This applies to
all of the witnesses. You are entitled to accept or reject the whole
or any part of the evidence of a witness.

The next topic was the difference between direct and circumstantial evidence. Direct evidence was given by the production of things
such as exhibits that they could see for themselves, or by the testimony of someone who had seen something or had spoken of his or her
own knowledge of it as a result of his or her observations. Direct evidence might also consist of statements that had been made. Circumstantial evidence was of an entirely different nature. When certain facts
are proved, the existence of another fact or facts may be logically inferred from the proven facts. In drawing such an inference or, in other
words, finding a fact by circumstantial evidence, they must first be sure
that the facts upon which the inference was based were proven beyond
a reasonable doubt. If they were satisfied as to this, they might then
draw an inference from such facts, but such inference should be proper, reasonable, and logical and lead to an irresistible conclusion as distinct from mere speculation, conjecture, or supposition. He pointed
out as particularly important that where circumstantial evidence is relied upon, the inference drawn from it must not only be consistent
with the guilt of the accused but inconsistent with any other reasonable conclusion.

These two forms of evidence, direct and circumstantial, are equally admissible, but the superiority of direct evidence is, of course,
that it contains only one source of human error, namely, the unreliability of human testimony. Circumstantial evidence, on the

other hand, in addition to the unreliability of human testimony involves an additional difficulty of going one step further and drawing a correct conclusion or inference from established facts. That is why I have said that when circumstantial evidence is relied upon, the inference therefrom must not only be consistent with the guilt of the accused, it must also be inconsistent with any other reasonable conclusion.

This recitation of basic principles complete, his lordship then embarked on a review of the indictment and the applicable provisions of the Criminal Code. The indictment read as follows:

Janise Marie Gamble and William John Nichols stand charged that they, at Calgary, in the Judicial District of Calgary, Alberta, on or about the 12th day of March, A.D. 1976, did unlawfully kill Allan Keith Harrison, a police officer acting in the course of his duties, and did thereby commit first degree murder, contrary to the Criminal Code.

He told the jury, "We are going to have a little trip through the Criminal Code now, touching or dealing with those sections that are important to this case, so that you will understand what murder is." This portion of the charge involved explanations of homicide, culpability, murder, culpable homicide, assault, robbery, first and second degree murder, and the effect where the victim happens to be a police officer acting in the course of his duties. The Crown, he said, took the position that the victim was a police officer acting in the course of his duties and that the particular section of the Criminal Code applied. "Certainly that section is the law, and if you decide that the Crown has brought itself within it, it is your duty to give effect to it." The allegation was that Nichols actually killed the victim and that Janise was a party to that crime. He would have more to say later on about being a "party" in law.

The next portion of the charge was a review of the evidence. Most of the review concentrated on the robbery and subsequent events. Interestingly, he noted in respect to the time the robbery was occurring, "While they were doing that, Janise Gamble moved from the rear seat to the front seat behind the driver's wheel. Tracie Perry left the car and purchased some aspirins." Regarding the suggestion that Janise had acted as the "lookout," he merely observed, "The Crown claims also

that Janise Gamble went to the front of the Credit Union and was walking back and forth in front of the Credit Union." His recitation of the
evidence accorded generally with the manner in which it was presented
during the trial.

Of particular importance to the charge against Janise was the portion of the trial judge's instructions regarding the statement Nichols
was alleged to have made about her role. He was doing this, he said,
not to give the evidence special importance; all the evidence was to be
considered in context and they were to give it such weight as they
thought proper. But because of certain rules of law applicable to evidence, he must mention some items.

> The first one is the statement of the accused Nichols or the al-
> leged statement of Nichols to Detective Goetjen, depending upon
> your findings in that regard. There has been admitted in evidence
> the oral statements made by the accused William John Nichols to
> Detectives Goetjen and Snaith at the Foothills Hospital on April
> 29th, '76. You are the sole judges of fact and it is for you to de-
> cide first of all whether the accused William John Nichols made
> the statements; if you decide that he did then you will have to
> decide whether the statements are true in whole or in part.
>
> Evidence has been given showing how, when, and where the
> alleged statement was obtained. You have heard the evidence of
> Detective Goetjen on that subject, who testified to the effect that
> when he went to the hospital that day to Nursing Unit 1001,
> Nichols was to be released and they went there to escort him to
> the Calgary Remand Centre. Goetjen introduced himself and ad-
> vised Nichols that he was investigating the murder of Police Offi-
> cer Harrison and asked Nichols if he understood that. He said
> that he did – his lawyer told him. He was then told that he didn't
> have to say anything and Nichols said that he knew that and then
> proceeded to answer and make a statement and answer a number
> of questions put to him by Detective Goetjen.
>
> Now, Nichols testified about that incident. He said that when
> Detective Goetjen knew he was Bill Nichols, he told Detective
> Goetjen to "fuck off." He said that he did not want anything to
> do with the police. He denied saying that he thought they were
> followed by a policeman and he knew it was a policeman when
> he had his gun out. He also denied making remarks about Janise

Gamble that Detective Goetjen attributed to him, that is, as to her part in the shooting incident.

Detective Snaith also testified. He said that he played no part in the conversation other than to be briefly introduced by Detective Goetjen when he entered the room in the midst of the conversation.

If, after considering all the evidence, you come to the conclusion that the Crown has proved to your satisfaction beyond a reasonable doubt that the accused William John Nichols made the statements, then and in such circumstances it will be your duty to consider the statements very carefully and to decide whether you believe everything in them, or some of the things in them, or none of them. If there is anything in the statements which tends to exonerate the accused, you must give that careful consideration.

Needless to say, any statements made by the accused William John Nichols affect him only and must not be accepted by you as evidence in any way whatsoever against the other accused, Janise Marie Gamble. That applies to all statements made by him, including those to [newsman] Jim Knowler. It is only statements that he made in her presence, which she by her words or conduct adopted as her own, that can be evidence against her.

The review of the balance of the evidence against Nichols and his defence of provocation made it reasonably clear that the judge was quite satisfied with the sufficiency of that evidence and that the defence had little merit.

Then came the portion of his instructions with respect to Janise. Her defence was that she was not a party to the offence. Section 21 of the Criminal Code deals with parties, and the judge read it to the jury. No quarrel can be taken with his general explanation of the law:

Therefore, in addition to the person who actually commits the offence, a person is liable as a party if he aids or abets it. Of course, to aid is to assist. In the Oxford English Dictionary the word "abet" is defined as "to encourage", "to urge on", "to incite", "to instigate." This means that if any person does, or omits to do something, for the purpose of aiding another person to commit an offence, then such person who aids or abets is just as guilty of the offence as is the person who actually commits the offence. In other words, a person who aids or abets another person in the commission of an offence is not merely guilty of aiding or abetting, he is guilty of the offence itself.

Of course, such a person who is alleged to have aided or abetted another person to commit an offence must have done so with a guilty intent before he can be found guilty of the offence itself. If he or she aided or abetted without any guilty intent, he cannot be found guilty of the offence itself.

In addition to the person who actually commits the offence, a person is liable as a party if he has formed a common intention to carry out an unlawful purpose and if he knew or ought to have known that the commission of the offence would be a probable consequence of carrying out the common purpose.

Now, common intention is found from the conduct of the parties. What takes place at the scene of the crime is material, and the conduct of the parties leading up to it and after, is also relevant.

It is for you to decide from all the evidence if the accused Janise Marie Gamble falls within the ambit of those provisions which I have just read and explained to you.

In order to bring her under subsection (2) of Section 21, the Crown must prove to your satisfaction beyond a reasonable doubt:

> (1) that the two accused formed an intention in common to resist lawful arrest and assist each other in doing it,
> (2) that it was in fact a probable consequence of that common purpose that William John Nichols would, to facilitate the offence of resisting lawful arrest, intentionally cause bodily harm to someone,
> (3) that it was known or ought to have been known to Janise Marie Gamble that such a consequence was probable,
> (4) that in fact the death of Sergeant Allan Keith Harrison ensured from such bodily harm.

It was only when the judge began to summarize the evidence regarding Janise's possible role in the shooting that it became clear that he had little doubt as to where the jury should be headed.

Since in this case two persons are indicated, you must be careful to separate the evidence relating to each one of the accused from the evidence relating to the other accused.

Now, with respect to the accused Janise Marie Gamble and the Crown's contention that she was a party to the murder committed by William John Nichols, that is the Crown's position is that he committed the murder and that she was a party to it. With respect to her position as a party, I suggest that you consider the following items of evidence. First, there is Mrs. Homan's evidence that she saw Janise Marie Gamble in front of the Credit Union pacing back and forth and John Gamble and William John Nichols were inside robbing it. The Crown's suggestion there is that you should draw the inference that she was acting as a lookout. On that point, though, you must remember Tracie Perry's evidence to the effect that she was in front of the Credit Union when she went out to buy some aspirins and there is a possibility of mistaken identity. You have to consider that.

Secondly, there was evidence led, that you may not believe, that her fingerprints were on the holdup note. I think that, and I express this point of view to you which you can accept or reject as you see fit, but I think that fingerprint evidence in itself is not of much value unless you have evidence as to the circumstances under which the fingerprints got onto the document, the time it got on and the circumstances. This fingerprint evidence is something for you to consider and attach such weight to it as you see fit.

Thirdly, the .38 special pearl-handled loaded revolver was found at the scene of the shootout near where the evidence indicates she fell down or was knocked down. At least there is testimony to that effect.

Fourthly, there is the evidence of Diane Perry that she overheard Janise Gamble talking to her husband in the living room at the Ingram house where the hostages were held and that she could not find her .38 and searched for it in her coat and purse. Mrs. Perry went on to say that at about 4:00 A.M. on Saturday morning Janise Gamble said that she probably dropped the gun when Bill ran over her leg with the car at the scene of the shootout. Mrs. Perry said that she said, "I probably lost it when he ran over my fucking leg," and then they laughed about it.

Next, Mrs. Diane Perry said that Janise Gamble was the first person to commence looking for the gun at the house, although on cross-examination Mrs. Perry admitted that she couldn't be sure that Janise Gamble had used the words, "my gun" in the conversations.

Next, Mrs. Diane Perry also said that John Gamble at the house, John Gamble gave Janise Gamble the money to count and it came to $1,601.00.

Next there is the evidence of Mr. and Mrs. Jivraj, and they said it was Janise Gamble and Tracie Perry that took the money from the cash register at their restaurant. There is the testimony of Mrs. Diane Perry and Mrs. Jivraj that it was the two girls that tied them up, it was the two girls that held the knives to their throats, although there was testimony to the effect that they did that on the instructions of the two men.

The testimony of William Nichols, the accused William Nichols, tended to exonerate her from criminal activities. You will recall that this testimony on that subject, he said that she knew nothing of the plan to rob the Credit Union and that he never saw her carrying a gun. Indeed, he said the men took steps to conceal the weapons from her and Tracie Perry.

Now those are some of the items that you can consider in determining whether or not Janise Gamble was a party. I'm sure that there are others that I have not thought of and have not mentioned. The decision as to her role is for you to make.

Before I leave the subject of parties, I want to say one more thing. The Crown has placed a lot of evidence before you to establish that it was the accused Nichols that fired the fatal shot. I have already reviewed that evidence. If you are satisfied beyond a reasonable doubt that he did do that, then that issue of fact is settled and you will hold that he did do that. If, however, you are not totally convinced that he did fire the fatal shot and that it might have been John Gamble, or even Janise Gamble that fired it, you should bear in mind that if the three of them, that is Nichols and the two Gambles, were acting in concert so as to make each of them a party to the actions of the other as contemplated by Section 21 of the Criminal Code, it does not matter which one fired the fatal shot. In such circumstances, if one of them murdered Detective Sergeant Harrison, the others are equally guilty of murder. You will, of course, look at all of the evidence, but on that, I thought I would draw to your attention something that was in the testimony of Mr. Zimmerman. Mr. Chrumka put a question to him in direct examination and it was this.

"Now, did you see anything with respect to the vehicle just as Detective Harrison, as you have described it, turned to go back to his vehicle?"

Answer: "At the moment that John [sic] Nichols was placing his hands on the car, his head went down between his hands which would indicate to me as if there was a word given or something was said and a commotion started in the back seat, and at that very instant Detective Keith Harrison turned back to run towards his car."

You will have to decide what weight you want to give to that evidence and you should not, of course, consider it in isolation, as I am sure you will not. It was only part of the entire evidence, but I bring it to your attention because it does seem to bear on the question of concerted action on the part of the accused.

The judge's concluding remarks were that if the jury were to acquit Nichols, they must also acquit Janise. If they were to decide that he was guilty as charged or guilty of second degree murder, or guilty of manslaughter, then they would have to decide whether or not she was a party to the offence, giving her role individual consideration. If they concluded beyond a reasonable doubt that she was a party, it would be their duty to bring in a verdict of guilty for either first degree murder, second degree murder, or manslaughter against her also. It would have to be the same verdict as that found against her co-accused, Nichols. If they had a reasonable doubt, then they must give her the benefit of it and acquit her. The jury was then discharged with an expression that is was desirable, but not mandatory, that they reach a unanimous verdict.

Counsel were then invited to submit any objections they might have regarding the charge to the jury. Pope and Macdonald both raised points, including that the jury should be further instructed about not being influenced by what happened after the shootout if they were to decide that Janise had not been a party at the time of the shootout; the statements made to detective Goetjen and Jim Knowler; the ability to have different verdicts for Janise and Nichols; the reliability of eyewitness identifications; the probable consequences of guns being involved where Janise might not have been aware that the men had guns; the fact that no one had seen her with a gun; and the gun found by the side of the road being at the same spot where Gamble's glasses had been found. Justice Shannon was not persuaded by their submissions, and the charge as delivered stood.

There was obviously some concern on the part of some of the jury members regarding Janise, however, since they came back shortly after retiring to ask a question about the effects of a wife following the orders of a husband. This led to a lengthy debate between the lawyers and the judge.

THE FOREMAN: My lord —
THE COURT: Yes?
THE FOREMAN: We had one question in regard to the marital status of a woman following her husband.
THE COURT: Yes?
THE FOREMAN: Did you receive that question, my lord?
THE COURT: Mrs. Kain delivered a message to me that you had a question of some kind along those lines. Would you state what your problem is.
THE FOREMAN: It was wondered, my lord, whether or not a woman is bound through marriage to follow her husband through an illegal act.
THE COURT: I see. I think that I can gather what you are concerned about and that is the question of compulsion. My instruction to you in that regard is, and I'm sure you are thinking about the position of Janise Gamble, the accused Janise Gamble and her relationship with her husband or former husband, John Gamble: I can tell you that compulsion does not provide a defence to a charge of murder. Section 17 of the Criminal Code says this: "A person who commits an offence under compulsion by threats or immediate death or grievous bodily harm from a person who is present when the offence is committed is excused for committing the offence if he believes that the threats will be carried out and if he is not a party to a conspiracy or association whereby he is subject to compulsion, but this section does not apply where the offence that is committed is high treason or treason, murder, piracy, attempted murder, assisting in rape, forcible abduction, robbery, causing bodily harm or arson."

This being a charge of murder that you are dealing with, the defence of compulsion is not applicable. I might say that there is another section of the Criminal Code, Section 18, which says this: "No presumption arises that a married person who commits an offence does so under compulsion by reason only that she commits it in the presence of her husband."

You may now retire to consider your verdict.

This prompted an immediate response from Macdonald, and the jury was removed while the point was argued. There had been a decision of the Supreme Court of Canada less than two months earlier that had an impact on whether the defence of duress might be available. Chrumka tried to head off the argument by saying that the defence might be applicable with respect to robbery but not to murder. He was satisfied with the direction the court had given to the jury. Justice Shannon asked for a copy of the case and retired to read it. When they resumed, he announced that he had had time to read it and asked Chrumka whether he had as well, who said he had and that he had been in error, since Janise had not been a principal in the robbery but only a party to it. The charge had, therefore, been incorrect, and the jury had to be re-charged on that point.

> Ladies and gentlemen of the jury, you asked me about the matter of compulsion insofar as the accused Janise Gamble is concerned and the possibility that she would be under compulsion provided by John Gamble, the deceased. I told you that that would not provide a defence and I referred you to Sections 17 and 18 of the Criminal Code. You then went out and I heard submissions from counsel and I was provided with a recent decision of the Supreme Court of Canada which leads me to believe that I instructed you improperly and incorrectly on that subject and you should ignore what I said previously on that subject and I will now provide you with a new instruction in that regard.

The judge reviewed the major portion of his earlier charge and finished with a reference to the case drawn to his attention by counsel.

> As I have said, as a result of this decision of the Supreme Court of Canada, which I have just now had a chance to read during the adjournment, I have come to the conclusion that section 17 of the Code, which I just read to you, applies only to the person that actually commits the offence but it does not apply to a person

who is in the position of being a party or an alleged party so it is not applicable to Mrs. Gamble because the Crown says she is guilty as a party so you should ignore Section 17 in considering her position.

You can consider whether her actions were dictated by fear of death or grievous bodily harm on the part of John Gamble. You can take that into account in deciding whether or not she had the requisite guilty intention so that she could have aided, abetted or formed a common intention so as to make her a party under Section 21 of the Criminal Code. If you decide that she did not have such an intent or you have a reasonable doubt of that, you must give her the benefit of that doubt and acquit her.

Now, with respect to the evidence on that subject, I might say to you once again that there was, as I recollect the evidence, no evidence placed before you that anyone threatened her, and that includes John Gamble, in any way so as to make her do what she did on the day in question, the actual thing that occurred on Memorial Drive; however, you can look at the entire course of action and the way she was treated by her husband and you may decide that you can draw a reasonable inference from that evidence that she was acting under that kind of compulsion: That is for you to decide and I leave the question with you.

You may now retire and continue your deliberations.

In the end, and in only four hours, a jury of eleven convicted William Nichols and Janise Gamble both. Juror number eight, suffering from hypoglycemia, was excused by the judge after a couple of hours of deliberations. After polling the remaining eleven, the judge dismissed the jury.

You may now leave the jury box; you may remain in the courtroom if you wish, that is for you to decide, but you will now leave the jury box.

Janise Marie Gamble, would you stand up, please?

You have heard the verdict of the jury. Is there anything you wish to say before I pass sentence on you?

ACCUSED GAMBLE: (No response)

MR MACDONALD: She has nothing to say, my lord.

THE COURT: Pursuant to the provisions of Section 669 of the Criminal Code of Canada, I sentence you to imprisonment for life and you will not be eligible for parole until you have served twenty-five years of that sentence. You may sit down. Mr. Nichols, stand up, please? You have heard the verdict of the jury. Have you anything that you wish to say before I pass sentence upon you?

ACCUSED NICHOLS: No, I don't

THE COURT: Pursuant to the provisions of Section 669 of the Criminal Code, you will be imprisoned for life, that is the sentence of this court, and you will not be eligible for parole until you have served twenty-five years of that sentence. You may sit down.

The court is now adjourned.

A verdict had been rendered and a sentence passed on both accused. They had been found guilty as charged, and the maximum sentence permitted under the law had been imposed: life imprisonment, coupled with the injunction that the possibility of parole could not be considered for at least twenty-five years.

There could have been few indeed who did not think that Nichols's conviction was fully justified. The case against him was perfectly clear. He was an outsider and had committed his crime in Calgary against a Calgarian and a peace officer to boot. He had shot and killed Harrison, knowing at the time that he was a police officer. Many deeply regretted that the death penalty for capital murder had been taken off the books. That outcome would have been much preferred for those who favoured the Hammurabic "eye for an eye and a tooth for a tooth."

The larger question, especially with respect to Janise, was whether justice had been done. It might have been an interesting challenge for a jury, had it been faced with a decision that would have led to capital punishment for Janise (even though the jury is not meant to consider the issue of penalty), given the huge difference in the quality of the evidence against her when compared with that against Nichols. The same challenge would also have been there for the judge in the assessment of the evidence and the weight to be given to various portions of it. Imprisonment, however, was much less visceral to each member of a jury than hanging. How many of us would eat steak if we personally had to first kill and gut the animal?

As one columnist from the *Calgary Herald* observed following the trial, it would have been the height of wishful thinking to believe that the many spectators who filled the courtroom throughout the trial were there to make sure that justice was done. Judging from conversations overheard, many minds had been made up long before the trial finished and probably before it started. In addition, it seemed clear that the jurors were aware of some of the information that circulated in the media, some despite the orders of the trial judge regarding non-publication of information or statements made out of the formal presence of the jury. Public figures were clamouring for explanations as to how Nichols and Gamble were out on bail. The two men's backgrounds, which should have been completely irrelevant to the Calgary proceedings, were highly prejudicial and would have an obvious impact on people's perception of their character and statements. Anyone living in Calgary would have had to be almost wilfully blind not to have been aware of the entire sordid story long before becoming a member of the jury. That line of argument had been raised by Nichols's counsel when he addressed the jury. It is true that he did not have many arrows in his quiver by the time the evidence was in, but the swirl of it all made it far more likely that both accused would be convicted. The most dangerous jury in any criminal trial, whatever the crime and wherever the trial, is one that wants to convict.

No one from the police ever acknowledged making the statement that Janise said she heard when she left the hostage scene: "You had better hope that he [Gamble] comes out alive, or you're going to do his time."

She was about to do his time.

CHAPTER 9

APPEAL AND REJECTION

THE ALBERTA COURT OF APPEAL

It was a foregone conclusion that both Nichols and Gamble would appeal against their convictions. Appeals in criminal cases differ in many respects from normal appeals, especially where a jury has been involved. Juries are masters of the facts in a criminal case, and it is very rare for the presiding judge to say that the verdict is so clearly wrong that the court renders a judgment which does not conform to it. From time to time there may well be directed verdicts, in which the trial judge will, in effect, indicate to the jury that it should render a certain verdict. In almost every one of these cases it would be a verdict of "not guilty" usually on the basis that some element of the charge or the crime had not been established. On appeal, a Court of Appeal can reverse the verdict if the directions in law are clearly wrong and enter the verdict that ought to have been rendered at the time, had the charge been correct.

Mostly, however, a criminal appeal involves an effort to try to get a new trial, with the hope that the exclusion of sufficient evidence may make it possible to create a reasonable doubt on the next occasion. On some lesser charges than murder, the Crown may even lose

interest in prosecuting the matter a second time. Witnesses may die
or forget, documents may disappear – one never knows what may
happen the second time around. For example, counsel might, on another occasion, have allowed Janise Gamble to give evidence on her
own behalf. But the appeal itself is most often concerned with attack-
ing the rulings made by the trial judge regarding admissibility of prejudicial evidence or evidence that was excluded and that might have
been helpful to the accused.

The other principal area for attack is the charge to the jury given
by the judge at the time of the trial. Here the effort is to try to show
that the verdict reached by the jury might have been influenced by an
incorrect charge by the trial judge, either as to the law or as to the summation of the evidence. This means the charge is analyzed in excruciating detail, put under a legal microscope to see what errors may have
occurred. Charges, especially in murder trials, are minefields for the
trial judge, even more so than the minute-by-minute rulings that are
made as the trial proceeds, which can, over the course of the trial, have
a profound effect on the outcome. It is for this reason that counsel are
normally required to provide the trial judge with a memorandum of
the points that they believe should be brought forward by the judge on
behalf of the prosecution and the defence.

Other than the admission of the Nichols confession, almost all of
the challenges in the appeals by both Nichols and Gamble arose from
the charge. Most of the points were points of detail. Courts of appeal
tend to focus on the charge as a whole, which the trial judge knows
perfectly well and for this reason, if no other, the trial judges normally have a lot of generalized content in their charges that is designed to
give an appeal court a way out, especially as it relates to the findings of
fact and the responsibility of the jury to make such findings in the
course of their determination of guilty or not guilty. Judge Shannon
proved to be no exception to the general rule, and the Crown could be
expected to reinforce the overall nature of the charge.

The first factum was filed on behalf of Nichols and was received by
the Court of Appeal on 22 July 1977. Eleven of its twenty-nine pages
were taken up with a summary of the facts, one to describe the
grounds of appeal and seventeen to present the arguments in support
of the appeal.

At the trial, Nichols's main defence had been that he had acted in
self-defence when he shot at Harrison. Issue was taken with the judge's
charge, which, his counsel argued, had left the onus on the accused

and specifically that portion of the charge that indicated that if Nichols knew Harrison was a policeman, the self-defence argument must fail. The second defence was provocation, which the trial judge had instructed the jury could not apply if Nichols knew that Harrison was a policeman. It was suggested that Shannon had made a finding of fact on this matter and therefore had usurped the position of the jury. The other appeal grounds were even less compelling. Nichols's counsel argued that the theories of the defence were not put to the jury and, particularly, that the judge did not place the evidence upon which that defence rested before the jury. In the twenty-nine page charge, only six and a half pages were given to the defence, and many of the aspects of Nichols's defence had not been dealt with. The trial judge had referred to only parts of the appellant's evidence and failed to point out that there was some probative evidence that would assist the theory of the defence. In addition, he had given no instructions as to the legal effect of surrender and the abandonment of any common intention to escape.

The fourth ground was in relation to the admission of the statement made by Nichols to Detective Goetjen, who had been alone at the time. The nature of Goetjen's caution to Nichols was attacked. It was argued that there was a burden on the part of the Crown to establish that the confession was voluntary. Issue was also taken with the fact that some of the questions and answers given during the course of that conversation had not been included. The fifth ground was that the judge had allowed cross-examination in relation to an inadmissible document, namely the recording of the conversation with Jim Knowler, following which the judge had allowed the Crown to call rebuttal evidence. This was said to have been unfair, because the knowledge of the character of any such evidence was known in advance and Knowler could have been produced as a witness during the trial. Finally, objection was taken to the admission of all evidence after the events having been admitted at trial. There were other indictments that covered events before and after those included in the indictment, and they were gravely prejudicial to the accused in this case. The trial judge had failed to advise the jury as to how any such evidence regarding the indictments then before the Court could be used.

The factum on behalf of Janise Gamble was not received by the Court until 4 January 1978. It consisted of sixty-two pages, of which forty-nine were devoted to recitation of the facts and the remaining thirteen to argument. There was no section of the factum that indicated the errors that had been made. Macdonald adopted the arguments of Nichols with respect to the self-defence and provocation and said that the effect of the charge had been to remove that defence and not to permit a lower offence of manslaughter to be available. This was a piggyback position for Janise, since it would have meant that Nichols might not have been found guilty of first-degree murder and, therefore, neither could she.

Macdonald went on to say as a second ground that the court erred in its directions on common intention. Common intention was required, but the trial judge did not properly indicate how the jury was to determine whether the common intention had been formed and did exist at the time of the shooting. He argued that this constituted a non-direction on this point, which amounted to a misdirection that was fatal to the conviction. His third point was that the trial judge did not instruct the jury on matters crucial to the defence, namely the formation of common intention, and there was no reference to a series of critical facts (which he listed) on which the defence had relied to demonstrate that there had been no common intention, and the judge had an obligation to refer to evidence which supported the theory of the defence.

A fourth ground was that there was a misdirection by the trial judge on the conduct before and after the event, which was relevant only if it intended to show a common intention to resist arrest. The fifth ground was that Janise could have been a party to other offences without having formed a common intention to resist lawful arrest. The sixth ground was that there was a misdirection regarding the possible verdicts because the trial judge had left the impression that the verdict had to be the same for both accused, that he did not differentiate between the offences to which Janise Gamble could have been a party (e.g., robbery, but not resisting arrest) and if she did not know that Harrison was a police officer, then it could not be first-degree murder, but only second-degree murder. The seventh ground was that the statements made by Nichols should not be applied to Janise Gamble but only to Nichols. The final ground was that the trial judge erred in his charge regarding parties to offences, the charge being inadequate. The missing element, namely that Janise knew or ought to have known that the men had guns on their persons and would use them if needed, was the appropriate standard for a charge of this nature.

The Crown's factum was received by the court on 13 February 1978. It was a twenty-three page document, of which fifteen were taken up with a review of the facts, one page to the issue before the court and the balance to argument. This was a reasonably predictable document. Chrumka argued that there was no error regarding the self-defence, although he appeared to fudge a bit on the issue of the preponderance of evidence referred to by the trial judge. He argued that Nichols had no right to resort to force if he knew that Harrison was a policeman. The trial judge had previously directed the jury to both the facts and the law on this point. He noted that only Nichols testified that Harrison fired the first shot, whereas all the others appeared to have said that it was either Nichols or Gamble. There was exculpatory language used where the judge expressed an opinion, in which he made it clear that it was his opinion and that the jury must decide on its own on the basis of the evidence and, further, that the direction must be taken as a whole. Chrumka argued that Nichols's defence had been clearly put to the jury, although it might be open to question as to whether the jury had been directed not to consider some of that evidence. He said that only Nichols gave evidence with respect to self-defence, and no other witnesses supported his claim that Harrison had fired first. Nichols's defence had been put clearly to the jury, and no reasonable person would have been mistaken as to what defences had been advanced.

Chrumka argued, again predictably, that the statements Nichols made to the detectives were free and voluntary. Regarding the cross-examination on statements made by Nichols in the telephone conversation with Knowler, Nichols did not admit in his evidence that he made the statements. Therefore, it was open to the Crown to cross-examine him on previous oral statements. (The only question here is the admissibility of those questions based on a document that had been held to be inadmissible.) This was not analogous to cross-examination on a statement made to a person in authority that was not free and voluntary. Regarding Janise Gamble, he submitted that common intention is found on the basis of conduct of the parties, and the direction given to the jury regarding circumstantial evidence and the ability to draw inferences had been made perfectly clear. Janise's theory of defence had been fully and fairly put before the jury, and it was not necessary to review each and every aspect of straightforward evidence. Similarly, it was not an error on the part of the trial judge to have allowed evidence on the robbery prior to the shooting and hostage taking thereafter. The admissions made to the hostages were relevant to prove flight, to prove that they had knowledge that a police officer was involved, and to prove the involvement in the shooting. It could not have been introduced without some reference to the reasons for the presence of Diane Perry and the Jivravs in the house. Even though these facts showed that other crimes might have been committed, they were still relevant. Nichols had argued that there was no direction as to what use such evidence could be put and, more importantly, what use to which it could not be put. Finally, Chrumka submitted that the trial judge had made it clear that statements about Janise Gamble could not be used against her unless they were made in her presence and were adopted by her by word or conduct.

The Alberta Supreme Court, Appellant Division, gave the matter a speedy hearing, before justices Sinclair, Moir, and Haddad. A unanimous judgment was rendered on 6 April 1978, less than two months after Chrumka's factum had been filed with the court. The judgment began with a brief resumé of the facts. The court had no quarrel with the standard portion of the instructions to the jury that were essential to every charge. The court did take issue with portions of the charge. While recognizing that a trial judge, at the conclusion of a lengthy trial involving a host of witnesses and exhibits, was anxious to give the jury careful instructions as to all relevant sections of the Criminal Code, the appellant court believed that many of the portions of the law to which the trial judge referred were unnecessary.

As to Nichols, the principal submission had been that the trial judge erred in charging the jury with respect to self-defence when he had said:

> If, when considering whether the accused was or was not acting in self-defence, you come to the conclusion that the preponderance of credible evidence shows that he was acting in self defence, it will be your duty to find him not guilty of the offence of which he is charged, or, if you have reasonable doubt whether he was acting in self-defence, it will be your duty to give the accused the benefit of the doubt and find him not guilty of the offence with which he is charged.

The argument had been that the jury was misdirected because of the reference to a "preponderance of credible evidence" showing that Nichols was acting in self-defence. The court said that when the passage from the judge's speech was read in the context of the directions as a whole, no reasonable jury could have concluded that there was an onus on the accused to prove self-defence by preponderance of credible evidence. The second point on the same defence was based on the following extracts from the charge:

> Now, in this case, counsel for William John Nichols submits that you should acquit his client on the basis that he was merely defending himself when he shot Detective Sergeant Harrison. That submission based primarily on the evidence of the accused Nichols, also to some degree Tracey Perry, is that when Detective Sergeant Harrison appeared with his gun drawn, screaming at them to drop their guns and put their hands up, William John Nichols did not know that he was a policeman performing his duties. That of course has to be his state of mind if the defence of self-defence is to be accepted.

And the following passage:

> If, on the evidence as a whole, you are satisfied beyond a reasonable doubt that William John Nichols knew that Detective Sergeant Harrison was a police officer acting in the course of his duties, then the defence of self-defence must fail. In the circumstances of this case Nichols had no right to resort to force of any kind if he knew that. If he knew that, he knew that Harrison was a police officer performing his duties as a police officer, making a lawful arrest and the accused Nichols had no right to resort to force. If you find as a fact beyond a reasonable doubt that Nichols had such knowledge, then the defence of self-defence fails and you need not consider it further.

The main argument on that point was that once the jury found as a fact that the appellant knew that the victim was a police officer, the judge's direction effectively deprived the appellant of his right to full answer and defence. While the court felt that, in some circumstances, it would be a misdirection for a judge to tell a jury that the defence of self-defence is not available in respect of acts of a police officer done in the course of his duty, it was nevertheless of the opinion that, upon any view of the evidence, such circumstances did not exist in this case. What Nichols was trying to argue was that his evidence of what took place when the car stopped, coupled with that of Tracie Perry, if accepted by the jury, was such that the jury could have found that the occupants of the getaway car had in fact surrendered and that their flight was ended.

The Court of Appeal dealt with this by making three observations:

> I will make three observations with respect to Nichols' evidence on this point. First, he says he did not drop his gun and put up his hands as requested by the police officer. Instead, he put his gun on the roof of the car and placed his hands beside the car. Secondly, Nichols and Tracey Perry testified that the reason the get-away car stopped was so Nichols could take over the driving from Mrs. Gamble. Thirdly, once the shooting was over neither Nichols nor the occupants of the car stayed at the scene. Instead, they continued their flight. In my opinion, no jury could have come to a conclusion other than that the flight from the robbery continued until the four persons and their three hostages entered the house where the series of events ultimately came to an end.

The court went on to say that the direction given by the trial judge that "in circumstances of this case [those words were emphasized] Nichols had no right to resort to force of any kind if he knew ... that Harrison was a police officer" was not given in isolation. There was no evidence that the first shot fired by the detective was other than as a warning. The court also pointed out that it had to be remembered that the police officer was facing armed men who had just robbed a credit union. Guns had been used in the holdup, and the robbers were holding guns when they got out of the car. There were two other persons in the vehicle. There was movement inside it. The court concluded that there was no evidence in this case, including that of Nichols and Tracie Perry, upon which the defence of self-defence could be based. The court further pointed out that the trial judge was perfectly justified in not instructing the jury as to sections 25, 26, and 27 of the Criminal Code.

The issue of provocation had not been raised by Nichols's counsel in his address to the jury but was mentioned by the judge in his charge. The argument as to provocation is essentially the same as that made with respect to self-defence, and it was not necessary to deal with it further, as the court saw no merit in it.

The court then moved swiftly through the remaining grounds. Such evidence as might tend to support the proposition that Nichols did not know the person who came out of the car behind him with a gun, screaming at the occupants of the getaway car to drop their guns and put their hands up, was a policeman had been fairly put to the jury in the charge. Regarding the theories of the defence, the trial judge had reviewed the substantial parts of the evidence and given the jury the theory of the defence so that they might appreciate the value and effect of the evidence and how the law was to be applied to the facts as they found them. The charge was fair to the appellant, and all that could have been said on his behalf was said.

Counsel had abandoned the argument contained in the factum that the trial judge had improperly admitted a statement made by Nichols to the police on 29 April 1976. As to the cross-examination of Nichols on a private communication previously ruled inadmissible and thereafter allowing the Crown to call evidence of the communication in rebuttal, the court reviewed the admissibility of the wiretap evidence with respect to the statement made to Knowler. Nichols had testified that he either did not recall making the statement or that he did not know whether or not he had made it. In the circumstances of the case, the court decided it was unnecessary to decide whether the evidence of Knowler was properly admitted in rebuttal because, even if it were convinced that the evidence was improperly admitted, it was firmly of the opinion that no substantial wrong or miscarriage of justice had occurred.

The court went on to indicate that it was its view that the wiretap evidence of the telephone conversations were private communications within the meaning of the Criminal Code. The court found it hard to conceive that the bandits, holed up inside a house for nearly two days with hostages and surrounded by police, as they well knew, were using the telephone under circumstances in which it was reasonable for them to expect that their calls would not be intercepted. In addition, the court could not see how the provisions of the Code could be interpreted as inhibiting the recipient of a private communication from testifying as to the contents of that communication. No question of interception arises. Finally, regarding the admission of evidence subsequent to those alleged in the indictment, the court did not accept the argument made on behalf of Nichols. He had made statements to the hostages and others which were relevant not only to flight but also to establish that the accused knew Keith Harrison was a police officer. There was evidence touching upon the involvement of the two appellants in the shooting that was clearly relevant to the murder charge. The court could not see how evidence of the kind mentioned could have been put to the jury without telling the whole story.

Beyond that, even had there been imperfections in the charge or improperly submitted evidence, the court was convinced that the verdict of the jury would necessarily have been the same if the charge had been correct and evidence properly submitted. It could not see how any jury could come to another conclusion once the evidence was related to section 213 (d) of the Code (which says that culpable homicide is murder where a person causes the death of a human being while committing … [robbery] … whether or not the person means to cause death and whether or not he knows that death is likely to be caused to any human being, if he uses a weapon during or at the time of his flight and the death ensues as a consequence). In any event, the court was of the opinion that no substantial wrong or miscarriage of justice had occurred.

Turning to consider the appeal of Janise Gamble, the court thought that the charge relating to aiding and abetting ought to have been differently framed, as Macdonald had contended, and in that respect did agree that the charge derived from the cases Macdonald had cited would have been more appropriate. The evidence referred to in the charge given to the jury by the judge had included eight elements of the evidence which the court felt the judge had summarized in a manner that was favourable to the accused. Counsel had argued that nowhere in this critical portion of the charge did the trial judge instruct the jury that, if they believed that evidence, they might draw the inference that there was a common intention to resist arrest. It was argued that the judge did not make it clear that it was for the jury to draw any inferences and that the matters to which the judge referred did not of themselves constitute proof of the formation of an intent to resist arrest. Such a distinction, it was urged, was fatal.

The court said that the charge, read as a whole, did not support the contention that the jury would be under the impression that these matters would constitute proof of an intention to resist arrest rather than merely being evidence from which it could make such an inference if it chose to do so. Again, the court referred to the standard part of the charge in which the jury members were instructed that they were to be the sole judges of the facts. They were, moreover, told how they could draw inferences from the proven facts. Just before the section of the charge to which complaint was made, the trial judge explained to the jury that common intention is found from the conduct of the parties. In the very important part of the review of the evidence dealing with the Crown's contention that Janise Gamble was a lookout, he had said: "The Crown's suggestion there is that you should draw the inference that she was acting as a lookout." There was, in the court's view, no misdirection.

Nor was the court particularly impressed with the argument that the judge had failed to refer to evidence that the defence had relied on to show that there had been no common intent. These points had included: no eyewitness to the shooting seeing Janise do anything that could be considered as resisting arrest; no one seeing a gun in her possession at any time; Janise falling to the ground and screaming during the incident; the shooting starting as she and Tracie Perry were in the process of getting out of the car; Janise screaming and saying, "What is going on?"; her conduct in the car behind the credit union before and after the robbery; the evidence that the loaded pearl-handled gun was placed on the passenger side by John Gamble and was found near his glasses on the road; the evidence as to how she treated the hostages in consoling them and untying them; and the situation in general at the house where the hostages were taken. It merely observed that a trial judge is not obliged to refer to every piece of evidence in favour of an accused. Moreover, it noted that he could have, but had not, referred to other evidence which, if accepted by the jury, was damaging to her, including her purchasing on the morning of the robbery the large envelope on which the holdup note was written; the evidence of Diane Perry that Janise had said a spent bullet shell fell out when she took off her coat at the restaurant; and the fact that the only time she drove the car was just after the robbery of the credit union. There had, in the court's opinion, been no miscarriage of justice arising out of the charge to the jury.

It was only when the court heard argument on the appeal that a matter essential to the sentencing of Janise Gamble arose. None of the parties had referred to the issue in the factums that had been filed, and the question arose during the course of argument. By way of review, the events that occurred were as follows:

12 March 1976 Offences committed.

29 April 1976 Information sworn.

14 June 1976 Preliminary hearing commences.

25 June 1976 William Nichols committed for trial.

30 June 1976 Janise Gamble committed for trial.

26 July 1976 Provisions of Criminal Law Amendment Act
   (No. 2) 1976 proclaimed in force.

30 August 30, 1976 Indictment preferred.

The jury was charged on the basis of section 214 of the Criminal Code, as enacted by the Criminal Law Amendment Act (No. 2), which came into effect on 26 July 1976. There were transitional provisions applied, the most important of which was section 27(1) which read as follows: "Where proceedings in respect of any offence of treason, piracy or murder, whether punishable by death or not, that was committed before the coming into force of this Act are commenced after the coming into force of this Act, the offence shall be dealt with, inquired into, tried and determined and any punishment in respect of the offence shall be imposed as if the offence had been committed after the coming into force of this Act irrespective of when it was actually committed."

The problem that arose came from the operation of this provision. Clearly the offence of murder had been committed before the coming into force of the amended act and therefore before the coming into force of the new Section 214. However, the subsection said that where the proceedings were commenced after the coming into force of the amendment act, the offence was to be dealt with, inquired into, tried and determined, and any punishment imposed as if the murder had been committed after the coming into force of the amendment act. The court concluded that the proceedings in the present case had commenced before 26 July 1976. There was no specific provision in the Criminal Code to indicate when proceedings involving indictable offences are considered to have commenced, but at least in respect of summary conviction offences, proceedings are considered to commence upon the laying of the information. The court concluded that the offence had clearly been dealt with and inquired into before the coming into force of the amendment act and therefore was of the opinion that the proceedings in the present case were commenced before 26 July.

The court then attempted to consider the effect of deciding that the trial ought to have been conducted as if the offence had been committed before the coming into effect of the Amendment. The first thing to do was compare section 214 as it read before the amendment with the section as presently worded. The former section 214 read:

> 214(1) Murder is punishable by death or is punishable by imprisonment for life.
>
> (2) Murder is punishable by death, in respect of any person, where such person by his own act caused or assisted in causing the death of:
>
> (a) a police officer, police constable, constable, sheriff deputy sheriff, sheriff's officer or other person employed for the preservation and maintenance of the public peace, acting in the course of his duties, or
>
> (b) a warden, deputy warden, instructor, keeper, gaoler, guard or other person or permanent employee of a prison, acting in the course of his duties, or counselled or procured another person to do any act causing or assisting in causing the death
>
> (3) All murder other than murder punishable by death is punishable by imprisonment for life.

Subsection 2 was the important provision in this case. So far as it was germane to the proceedings involving Gamble, it said that murder is punishable by death, in respect of any person, "where such person *by his own act* caused or assisted in causing" the death of a police officer acting in the course of his duties. On the other hand, subsection 214(4) of the present Criminal Code said that, irrespective of whether a murder is planned and deliberate on the part of any person, murder is first degree murder when the victim is a police officer acting in the course of his duties. The court noted that there was clearly a difference between the old and the new subsections as regards the test to be applied in determining culpability for the murder of a police officer acting in the course of his duties. As regards Nichols, there was no practical difference between the two wordings since it was clearly an act of Nichols, the firing of his gun, that caused the death of Harrison. However, as far as Janise Gamble was concerned, her position under the old section might have been different, for the Crown would have had to prove beyond a reasonable doubt that she, by her own act, caused or assisted in causing the death of the police officer, rather than simply establishing as required by the new section that the victim was a police officer.

The court noted that in such circumstances an appellate court would ordinarily direct that there should be a new trial so that it could be conducted in accordance with the law that was properly applicable. So far as concerned the appeal before it, however, subsection 27(2) of the Amendment Act provided that such a new trial would be conducted, and punishment imposed, as if the offence had been committed after the coming into force of the Amendment Act. The practical effect of that subsection, said the court, is that the law applicable to the new trial would be the same as that which was in fact applied at the trial already held and with respect to which the appeal was concerned. The result of all of this, it concluded, was that no substantial wrong or miscarriage of justice had occurred. It followed, in the view of the court, that the appeals of both Nichols and Gamble should be dismissed.

What the court appears to have overlooked, however, is that the principal purpose of the amendment was to remove the death penalty in respect of offences that had previously been punishable by death. It was, therefore, a mitigating provision, not one that was intended to impose a harsher punishment than had existed under the old law. But that, of course, is exactly what happened to Janise Gamble. Even on a worst-case analysis, since it was clear that she had not by her own act caused or assisted in causing the death of Sergeant Harrison, the harshest punishment that could have been applied to her under the old provision was life imprisonment. If such a sentence had been imposed, she would have been eligible for parole in ten years. Under the sentence handed down under the new provision, she was sentenced to life imprisonment with no possibility of parole for twenty-five years, an effective punishment two and a half times greater than that to which she would have been liable under the provisions of the law in force as at the time of the offence.

This sentencing impact does not appear to have been considered by the court or by the lawyers for Gamble or the Crown, an oversight that is remarkable in the circumstances. While the matter had clearly not been considered by anyone prior to the hearing in the Court of Appeal, once the line of inquiry had been raised, one should have thought that by the time an application for leave to appeal was filed with the Supreme Court of Canada, the issue ought to have been identified as a glaring miscarriage of justice in all circumstances of the case. At the stage of deciding what to do with the indictment, the Crown knew it would never get the death penalty, because everyone knew the new legislation was on its way, so it simply waited until the new provisions were in place and charged the accused accordingly.

LAST CHANCE: THE SUPREME COURT OF CANADA

The application for leave to appeal to the Supreme Court of Canada, case number 15183, was heard on 3 October 1978 by Justices Martland, Ritchie, and Dickson. Webster Macdonald, Jr. appeared for Janise, and Paul Chrumka represented the Crown. In those days applications for leave to appeal were still heard by a panel of three judges; now they are presented only in writing. The hearing began at 3:22 P.M. and finished at 3:49 P.M. Chrumka said that the judges did not show particular interest in the matter and, when one of them asked whether the accused had given evidence at the trial and was advised that she had not, showed even less. This suggests very strongly that the judges had not read the transcripts of the trial in advance, as they would undoubtedly have done if the appeal were to have been fully argued. Chrumka was not even called upon to speak on behalf of the Crown, and the application was summarily dismissed. In accordance with the court's usual practice, no reasons were given.

That was the end of the line for Janise Gamble. The gates of the Kingston Prison for Women were actually and metaphorically closed around her until December 2001, twenty-five years after she was sentenced or, if she were lucky, March 2001, twenty-five years after she had first been incarcerated.

CHAPTER 10

SECOND THOUGHTS

There was always some lingering doubt as to whether Janise had been properly convicted and whether the sentence she received was too harsh. The Elizabeth Fry Society, which operates a halfway house in Kingston, Ontario, was concerned that her conviction might have been tainted and was vociferously of the view that something needed to be done to provide some relief. Even the Calgary branch of the society felt the same way. It seemed, however, that nothing could be done, especially since, until the Supreme Court of Canada had rejected the application for leave to appeal against the conviction, the matter was technically still before the courts.

Fortunately for some of the prisoners in Kingston, Queen's University has a faculty of law, established in 1957 (it is slyly rumoured among some other law schools, for the express purpose of keeping star football player Ronnie Stewart at Queen's for a few more seasons. If that were the case, it was a huge investment, since he left after only a year). Because of its location in Kingston, it seemed only natural that the Queen's law faculty would develop a concern about the legal rights of prisoners, and in the early days this interest was headed up by professor H.R.S. Ryan.

In the late 1970s the faculty included Allan Manson, an Ontario lawyer who had done graduate work before articling with the Toronto firm of Benson, McMurtry. When he was called to the bar, Manson had decided that he wanted to practise criminal law. The best known of the partners in the firm was R. Roy McMurtry (later chief justice of Ontario), prior to his earlier appointment as attorney general of Ontario. McMurtry had been working on a large file, a commission of inquiry, with Barry Percival, and Manson had gone to the firm to help work on that file. He was also given some other criminal files, one of them the case of Ernest Luffman, who arrived at the firm in 1975 with a shopping bag full of letters, including ones he had sent to the queen, Pierre Elliott Trudeau, and Chief Justice of Canada Bora Laskin, complaining about the length of the prison sentence he had just served. In the pile of letters was an open letter from Professor Ron Price, director of the Queen's University Faculty of Law's Correctional Law Project. The bag also included a letter from the director of the Correctional Law Service, explaining why he was wrong. The oddest part of Luffman's situation was that he could no longer survive outside prison, and he attempted a break and entry as soon as he got out.

The letter, and the effort to fashion an argument on behalf of Luffman, led Manson into a new array of statutes and cases which he now recognizes as prison law. After some research that built on this background, he connected with the two Toronto lawyers he knew who did prison work, Paul Copeland and David (now Mr Justice) Cole. In December 1975 the entire Special Handling Unit at the Millhaven Institution west of Kingston was tear-gassed. An inquiry was set up, and the twenty-seven prisoners hired Copeland and Cole. Manson had just moved in to share premises with them on Madison Avenue. They had busy practices and were worried about how they could adequately represent their clients at the inquiry. Remembering Manson's questions about Luffman, they seemed to conclude that he knew some prison law. In fact, when Manson went to Millhaven before the inquiry began to meet with the clients one by one, it was his first visit to a Canadian penitentiary. He spent much of the next three months in Kingston and met with Professor Price. In 1977 he left the practice of law in Toronto to join the Correctional Law Project, co-sponsored by the Queen's University Faculty of Law and Ontario Legal Aid. He has been at Queen's ever since. He brought to the project a distinct service orientation, with test cases and other minor procedures that would help students learn. Within the Law Society of Upper Canada, the governing body for the practice of law in Ontario, he became aggressive about providing services to and on behalf of prisoners.

One of his students had met Janise in the course of a visit to the Prison for Women and described her situation to him – the conviction under the wrong law and the refusal of the courts to do anything about it. He told the student he would see Janise, having remembered watching the hostage scene unfolding on television in March 1976. He went to see her in 1978, just after her application for leave to appeal to the Supreme Court of Canada had been turned down. She told him her story.

As someone often consulted by inmates, each of whom was convinced that his or her conviction was unwarranted or the sentence extreme, Manson knew he had to be careful about not being too gullible. He told her he would have to get the judgments and the record of the trial and study them. He got Janise's permission to call Webster Macdonald and tried to contact him but got no reply. Nichols's lawyer was much more helpful and Manson eventually got a set of the transcripts. He determined to try to help her.

His initial effort in February 1982 was multifaceted. He first asked that the minister of justice order a new trial in Alberta; or that the Cabinet direct a question of law to be decided by the Supreme Court of Canada; or that Janise be considered for the exercise of the Royal Prerogative of Mercy to effect her immediate release in light of her personal circumstances, the circumstances of the offence, and the years of incarceration that she had already undergone. This involved some degree of risk, because there was not much on the official record that might suggest that any of the suggested recourses would be appropriate. Manson's strategy also involved generating some public interest in her case. He was aware that a program eventually produced by CBC's *the fifth estate* was in preparation. Opinion polls were conducted and questions were raised in the House of Commons. Manson knew that, generally, ministers only act when there is a certain level of awareness created amongst the public, especially where prisoners are involved.

Under section 617 of the Criminal Code at the time, the minister of justice had the power to order a new trial, whenever there existed a reasonable apprehension that a miscarriage of justice had occurred. The jury that determined Janise's guilt, said Manson, did not have the opportunity of hearing her account of her involvement in the events to which she was a party, and the critical questions relating to common intent and knowledge of the circumstances, by her own account, were not placed before the jury. The big problem here for Manson was that Janise could have testified at the trial, but on the advice of her counsel, chose not to. Her affidavit supporting the petition stated that the reason why her counsel advised her not to testify was due to concerns about her mental state. A lawyer arguing for the Crown would certainly have taken the position that counsel advised her not to testify because good cross-examination might well have shown that she was very much involved in the robbery and that she did have a gun. Manson put forward the only two arguments at his disposition: her impaired mental state should be considered in relation to the decision not to testify at the time, and that neither she nor her lawyer could have been expected to know that the trial judge would misdirect the jury to the effect that the verdict for Janise must necessarily be the same as that for Nichols.

Manson also sought to bring forward far more evidence than had been made available to the jury regarding Janise's physical abuse by Gamble and the manner in which that abusive and dominating relationship affected her behaviour and mental state between 11 and 13 March 1976 and may have created a situation of duress, which might have constituted a defence.[1] Here again his case was hampered by the decision made by her trial counsel not to have any such evidence put before the jury, even though it would have been available at the time. In fact the jury on its own accord, faced with the bits of evidence of the relationship that were before them, made a special request of the trial judge for directions. Whether or not Janise was going to testify in the end, such evidence could only have been helpful to her, but it was not led. The trial judge made that all too clear when he re-instructed the jury, by pointing out that there was no evidence that anyone, including Gamble, had threatened her in any way so as to make her do what she did on the day in question.

There was also the interesting matter of the discharge of Ruth Browning, juror number 8, very late in the proceedings, after all the evidence had been heard, arguments had been given, and the judge had given the charge to the jury. The juror apparently suffered from hypoglycemia, and she fainted as she came out into the corridor. She was assisted by a paramedic and did not return to the courtroom be-

---

1 See, for example, *Director of Public Prosecutions for Northern Ireland v. Lynch*, [1975] A.C. 653 at 670 and 675.

cause she did not feel well enough. The trial judge had asked Irene Kain, the deputy sheriff, for an opinion, and she said she did not feel that the juror was capable or well enough to resume her duties as a juror. Manson made the point that the trial judge should have heard some medical evidence on the point before discharging the juror, who might well have been perfectly capable of continuing the following day or even sooner, had she been given some food. This decision deprived Janise of her right to be tried by a jury of twelve.[2] Who knows what the juror's opinion might have been, and what influence she might have had on the other members of the jury? Whether or not counsel may have consented to the withdrawal, he argued, a wrongly constituted tribunal cannot be given jurisdiction by consent.[3]

The trial judge had made it clear that, to convict Nichols, the jury must be satisfied that he knew that the victim was a police officer, but he had not charged the jury that there was any need to consider Janise's knowledge as to the identity of a likely victim. The jury thus had no instruction of what was the requisite quality of guilty intent for first degree murder for someone alleged to have been a party to that offence. The Alberta Court of Appeal had recognized the inadequacy of the charge, and Manson went further, saying that not only was it inadequate but that it was wrong, especially as it related to the fact that Harrison was a police officer and that the death of a police officer would be a probable consequence of the conduct. Subsequent cases in Ontario had specifically rejected the Alberta decision.[4]

His final branch of argument for a new trial was that Janise should not have been tried under the new provisions of the Criminal Code. Under the provisions of the law that existed at the time the offence was committed and the proceedings were commenced, Janise could only have been convicted of non-capital murder, unless it was shown that she by her own act caused or assisted in causing the death of the police officer. Even the Alberta Court of Appeal had recognized that, and that a different result might have been obtained. It could never have been the intention of Parliament that a person could be tried in an entirely wrong legal context and then be precluded from a re-trial. Any ambiguity in the transitional provisions should be resolved in

---

2 *Basarabas and Spek v. The Queen* (1980), S.C.R. 730.

3 *Letourneau v. Ottawa Bronson Construction* (1970), 1 O.R. 24 (Ont. C.A.).

4 The clearest rejection of the Alberta Court of Appeal's decision can be found in the decision of the Ontario Court of Appeal in *R. v. Collins* (1989), 48 C.C.C. (3d) 343.

Janise's favour. If properly tried, she would have been sentenced for non-capital murder to life imprisonment, with a parole ineligibility of only ten years or less instead of twenty-five. She ended up with harsher treatment under the new law than under the law that applied when the act occurred.

Manson also asked for a reference case to the Supreme Court of Canada, but that was an exceptional recourse that has been granted only in such high-profile cases as Steven Truscott and David Millgaard. It had to be considered as a very long shot.

He then turned to the mercy aspect. Because Janise had been counselled by her lawyer not to give evidence at the trial, many of the factual elements that might have been persuasive simply were not in existence. She was advised by Macdonald that she should not testify because with all the medication she had been given, she would probably break down. That might not have been such a bad thing, and at least the jury – which always wants to hear the story from the accused, not a string of hypotheses or legal objections by lawyers – would have had a chance to hear her version of the facts, including whether she was the so-called lookout, whether she had a gun, why she got out of the car, whether she knew the men had planned a robbery, and whatever she might have said to the hostage about a gun. Manson had, and disclosed them to the Crown, the records of the medication that had been given to her during the trial. Janise would have to be prepared to waive any solicitor-client privilege, so that all the facts could be disclosed. The Crown asked if she were ready to waive this privilege so that they could speak with her lawyer, and she agreed. She would have to expect that extensive and comprehensive inquiries would be made. She was willing for that to happen.

Manson raised in the petition such factors as her previous good character, the period of incarceration she had already served (a continuous term of imprisonment since 13 March 1976, much of it in a maximum security institution), and a good institutional record. He referred to the nature of her complicity in the offence (which, putting the Crown's case at its highest – specifically denied by Janise – made her only a marginal participant in an underlying offence, that being the robbery), and to the numerous errors in the trial process. He also pointed out that the almost seven years she had spent in custody were under the spectre of a minimum term of imprisonment of twenty-five years – a more difficult experience than someone who had spent exactly the same time in custody looking forward to release in the realistic future. Janise had been denied even escorted passes into the community notwithstanding the existence of humanitarian reasons and the support of the institutional staff for such purposes.

The latter two factors were in her case particularly compelling. Kingston's Prison for Woman was a tough institution. Many, though not all, of the inmates were hardened criminals who needed to be kept there for the protection of society and who had few redeeming features. It was clear to anyone that Janise was not of the same character. Indeed, she needed protection from some of them and was befriended by other inmates. An incident in 1994, the strip-searching of eight women in the middle of the night in segregation on the pretext of looking for drugs and weapons, and the response of the authorities to those actions, demonstrated the general brutality of the conditions. A Royal Commission headed by Justice Louise Arbour, then a member of the Ontario Court of Appeal and later a judge of the Supreme Court of Canada, made this all too clear to the public at large.

The other aspect that made the conditions so unbearable was that there were virtually no programs of education available to Janise to make her eventual re-entry into society as smooth as possible. The Prison for Women was the only federal penitentiary for women prisoners in Canada. Because the sentences were generally long, there was apparently no useful purpose seen in preparing the inmates for their release by equipping them to assume normal jobs, and so no training was provided to help them do so. The most common vocational training at the institution was hairdressing. Although Janise had access to whatever jobs and programs were available within the institution, she could not work towards participation in any vocational or re-integrative programs that would involve leaving the confines of the institution. There were no educational facilities at the Prison for Women, and anything that had to be done was done at the men's prison. The central element of her confinement, and the primary obstacle even to contemplating any plans for the future, was the lengthy period she faced of ineligibility for conditional release. She had applied to participate in a microfilming course conducted at Bath Institution, a penitentiary operated by Corrections in the village of Bath to the west of Kingston. A number of prisoners from the Prison for Women were transported there daily. But Janise's request was denied by the warden because of the number of years she still had to serve before she would have the opportunity to seek authority from the National Parole Board to re-enter the community even on a limited and conditional basis. The prison time being served, therefore, had no purpose but to confine many of the inmates, who were given nothing to look forward to at the expiration of their terms.

The section 617 application had begun in the summer of 1982. Mark MacGuigan, a former law professor at the University of Windsor before entering politics, was then minister of Justice. It would be he who, if convinced of the equities of Janise's case, would make the recommendation to Cabinet that the Royal Prerogative of mercy be exercised, or agree to any of the other suggested recourses. It would be an uphill struggle. The Justice lawyer charged with management of the file was S. Ronald Fainstein at the Criminal Prosecutions section of the Department of Justice in Ottawa. Manson himself was hampered to some degree by the fact that his familiarity with the case was derived almost entirely from trial transcripts and the factums filed by the various parties and that he had not acted on Janise's behalf during any of those proceedings. He made this clear and stated that, were there any additional facts to be required in order to reach a decision, he would be willing to obtain them. This was prior to the days of mandatory disclosure of evidence; the Crown did not have to disclose everything it had, just everything it intended to use. Manson wanted to be sure that if the minister were going to rely on any material beyond that which Manson had in his possession, it would set up an "unfairness" argument for subsequent legal proceedings. Therefore, he spelled out what he had and asked the Crown to tell him if there was any other relevant material. The real point was not his own willingness to obtain more material but to make sure that the Crown could not rely on any information now without disclosing it to him.

Fainstein was a career lawyer in the federal Department of Justice, with a great deal of experience in criminal law. My impression, when I interviewed him, was that he was a very careful, dedicated civil servant, concerned that the right thing be done, especially in a matter of such importance. He was thorough and as impartial as possible, taking into account that he, in effect, represented one of the parties to the proceedings. He did everything he could to make sure that the advice he would provide to the minister would be complete and reflect the sum of the information available as well as the arguments and submissions that were received. Once the minister reached a decision, Fainstein would be responsible for writing the letter conveying that decision to Manson. There was no real basis for ordering a new trial, and the reference case option was not considered appropriate, so the main crux of the matter would be reduced to the matter of clemency. Mercy was a matter for the minister of Justice and clemency (if the penalty were too harsh) a matter for the solicitor general.

The appreciation of the facts was crucial. Fainstein's report to the minister described the background summarily, although reasonably fairly (perhaps with a bit of a Crown "spin") including some of Janise's beatings by Gamble. On the day before the robbery she had got out of the car after one of them, and Gamble had told her to "go home," but she would not. In Calgary they had gone to Eaton's to buy suitcases for the trip back east – they had planned to catch the 3:50 P.M. train from Calgary to Toronto – and the men had packed the cases so the girls would not see the guns. Janise also purchased a large envelope that was used as both the note in the holdup and the container for the stolen bills, and the police had found one of her fingerprints on it, along with several other prints. The handwriting evidence as to the note was inconclusive, but Fainstein noted that the purchase of the envelope was never explained. The evidence of Mrs Homan, who had identified Janise as the person pacing about in front of the bank, was noted. Janise had changed her hairstyle from long and blond to short and brown, but the witness had no trouble identifying her at trial, nor at the preliminary hearing. Tracie Perry, summoned as a Crown witness, had said that she was the one who got out of the car, but she had been in the same police lineup as Janise and had not been identified. The argument was that Janise would never have let Tracie go to the drug store if she had known there was a robbery in progress.

Following the robbery, there had been only thirty-five minutes to get to the train station. Less than a mile from the credit union Nichols told Janise to stop driving and said he would drive. This had been apparently the only time she had driven during the trip. Regarding the shooting, the evidence of Hunter, Cox, and Zimmerman all supported the view that the first shot came from the lead car. Nichols's head went down and words were exchanged. Janise had been the only person still in the back seat, so the commotion could only have been caused by her. Even though she had been on the driver's side of the car, she got out on the passenger side. Nichols had also run around to the passenger side, so that both he and Gamble were then on the same side of the car. Nichols's testimony at trial regarding Janise and whether or not she had had a gun was extremely prejudicial for her, but the statement had been ruled admissible against her. Nichols did not recall saying what he was reported to have said and did not believe that he had said it. The Greenwood evidence, that he had seen a female lying on the ground right where the gun had been found, was relevant, although Gamble's glasses had been found close to that spot as well.

Manson reviewed the evidence of Diane Perry and her cross-examination.[5] Janise seemed to have admitted that the conversation about a gun was about another gun, not the one found at the scene. There had been some concern on the part of the captors that the police would be able to tell who they were from the gun found at the scene of the shooting. It is not clear how this would relate to Janise, since she had never been fingerprinted, whereas of course both Gamble and Nichols had been fingerprinted in Vancouver. There was some wiretap evidence that Gamble had told Jim Hogan that Janise's prints were all over one of the guns, although that evidence was not admitted at the trial. The evidence of Diane Perry was regarded as significant, notwithstanding comments she made on *the fifth estate*. She said she had been interviewed for an hour by the producers of the program and had said many disparaging things about Janise, but the program included only the portion about Janise comforting her during the hostage scene. Fainstein said that Hogan had said something quite different about the gun and the fingerprints from what had been said to him by Nichols. Before he knew that Harrison had died, Nichols told a Canadian Press reporter that there were three persons involved in the robbery scheme. This statement had not been in evidence before the trial. This was a matter that troubled Manson. The statements were made between Nichols and a newsman named Short and Nichols and Doug Green. Manson attempted to restrict the effect of the inculpatory statements to the maker (i.e., Nichols) and emphasized that it should be given no weight by the minister because it related to Janise. The statements were also made at a time when Nichols was clearly providing erroneous information about the number of people in the house, the number of participants, and the identification of the participants.

Janise provided a further affidavit, dated 23 December 1983 and prepared by Manson, in connection with the various proceedings for relief. It addressed the matter of the statements made by Nichols to the reporters. She affirmed that any statements by Nichols or Gamble that appeared to incriminate her by raising questions as to whether she knew a robbery was to take place, whether she was a participant in the robbery, or whether she was a participant in the killing of Harrison,

---

5 At page 455 (evidence-in-chief) and page 468 (cross-examination).

were entirely false. She went on to affirm that it was not until early in the morning of 12 March that they learned that Harrison had died. Up to that point, to the best of her recollection, there had been no real discussion among Nichols, Gamble, Tracie, and her of any negotiations. It was only after they had learned of the death of Harrison that they began serious discussion about how best to extricate themselves from the situation. At that time, both the possibility of amnesty and the issue of suicide were raised.

The original proposal Nichols and Gamble made to Tracie and Janise was that they would seek amnesty for them and then take their own lives by overdosing with heroin. At that time, Janise continued, she believed she could not live without Gamble. With the knowledge of Harrison's death came a real sense of the events that had already taken place and their probable consequences. She was terrified and frightened. One idea that penetrated the fog in her mind was that the man she had loved was about to take his own life and leave her alone. She absolutely refused to leave Gamble, telling him she could not live without him and that she would rather die than leave him. Gamble ignored her plea to remain and began discussing ways of obtaining amnesty for both her and Tracie and also for obtaining heroin. She continued to badger him and eventually became hysterical. Gamble relented and agreed she could stay with him.

At that stage, her affidavit continued, Gamble realized that it was necessary to devise a scheme for the negotiations with the police in order that the planned suicides would not be revealed. He and Nichols discussed this matter privately. They approached Janise and advised her that it would be necessary to say something to the police that could implicate her in the preceding criminal events in order to make the negotiations plausible. Their view was that she had to be distinguished from Tracie Perry during the discussions with the police in order that the police not suspect that the reason for her staying behind was a mutual suicide pact. She was not advised of any details of what Gamble or Nichols planned to say to the police. She was committed in her mind to staying behind and killing herself along with them. The question of going to trial and attempting to prove her innocence was not an issue that occurred to her. Her only concern was to stay behind and die with Gamble. After he agreed to allow her to stay, she made a phone call to her mother in Peterborough. That was the only time she spoke on the telephone to anyone on 12 or 13 March. She believed that she made vague references to suicide in speaking with her mother.

However, Gamble was monitoring the conversation. An excerpt from the telephone conversation appeared on *the fifth state* program aired on 7 December 1982. She was not aware of how the CBC came into possession of that tape. However, the excerpt on the program included her statement "I can't live without him" and indicated her mother's plea that she wanted her "alive."

After the negotiations with the police commenced, the atmosphere in the house relaxed substantially, albeit with occasional flare-ups of extreme tension while everyone waited. Many of the conversations in which Gamble, Nichols, and she referred to suicide went on in the presence and within hearing of the hostages. In particular she recalled a conversation with Diane Perry, who vigorously attempted to dissuade her from taking her own life. Later, Vancouver lawyer James Hogan was permitted to enter the house. He talked privately with Gamble. After that discussion Gamble advised her that she was to leave the house along with Hogan, the hostages, and Tracie. She refused to go and began to cry hysterically, pleading with Gamble to let her stay. He and Hogan physically forced her from the house, and Hogan assisted her to a police car. After leaving the house, she had no real appreciation of what was going on around her other than that she had deserted her husband, the man she believed she loved, and the man who was about to take his own life.

She concluded by swearing on oath that the truthful account of her involvement in the events of 12 and 13 March 1976 was set out in her affidavit sworn on 18 February 1983. Any remarks that might have been made by Gamble or Nichols that gave the impression that she knew about or participated with knowledge in the criminal events that led to the tragic death of Harrison were entirely false. She had related the events to the best of her recollection and was prepared to recount this material orally and to be cross-examined upon it in any context that might seem appropriate in order to satisfy the minister of Justice as to her truthfulness.

Manson gave attention to the words "by his own act" and the position was taken by the Crown that this was not limited to a direct act in the killing itself. The words were in the Criminal Code to distinguish between a principal and a party for the purpose of delineating the scope of capital murder. One way to look at it was that Janise did participate in the killing: there had been a stable situation in which both men were out of the car and had assumed "the position" with their hands on the roof of the car (albeit that Nichols had a gun between his hands and Gamble had a gun that had not been shown or surrendered). Janise created the diversion that led directly to the killing. The jury had been instructed regarding a common intention to resist arrest, etc., which was the strongest case against her for capital murder. The same was true regarding the words "having counselled or procured," based on *R. v. Prince*.[6] The Manitoba Court of Queen's Bench had refused to quash a committal, a decision affirmed by the Manitoba Court of Appeal. Being a party to a crime, having guns and so forth, there being a killing, was capital murder. It was not a tough test.

By the time the federal government was ready to respond to the submission, the government had changed and John Crosbie had become minister of Justice. His decision was conveyed to Manson in a letter dated 28 August 1985. The letter was almost certainly written by Fainstein, who had undertaken the review of the matter within the Department of Justice. It was short and to the point. Crosbie was not willing to intercede. His view was that the evidence at trial amply supported the jury's conclusion that Janise had played an active and willing role in the events in which Harrison was slain and that she was culpable of murder. He also pointed out that there was evidence which was not before the jury but that was consistent with the jury's verdict and the opinion of the Alberta Court of Appeal. He mentioned that, he said, notwithstanding that the case was amply made without it. He was not unmoved by the treatment suffered by Janise at the hands of Gamble, but the defence of duress was raised and canvassed at her trial and her story was told "in considerable detail" by Tracie Perry and Nichols without her having had to take the witness stand and testify herself. He continued, saying:

> On this point one can't help but think of the rather poignant conversation Mrs. Gamble had with her mother from the hostage scene in which she makes it clear that she was with her husband not out of fear, but because she loved him. Her love for John Gamble cannot justify her role in the murder of Det. Sgt. Harrison. That conversation was not introduced at trial but, on the basis of the Court of Appeal judgment, would have been admissible. The case is, as I have already stated, supportable without reference to this evidence but I again note how consistent this extraneous evidence is with the jury verdict.

6 (1970) 10 C.R. (NS) 260.

Crosbie was unmoved by the argument that Janise should have been tried under the old law. His view was that the ultimate aim of the new legislation was to bring into tandem the new test of culpability and the new penalty. The rationale, he said, was that if one no longer faces the penalty of death on a charge arising from the killing of a policeman, then the test of culpability should be that laid down for first degree murder, and the penalty on conviction should be life with a minimum of twenty-five years of incarceration. Janise, he said, was tried in accordance with that rationale. Even if this trial was governed by the old provisions, the evidence manifested Janise's guilt of capital murder. By her own act she caused or assisted in causing the death of Harrison, or she counselled or procured another person to do an act causing or assisting in causing the death.[7]

The minister left Manson with the suggestion that he make an application for judicial review of the sentence under section 672 of the Criminal Code after fifteen years had been served. His department had advised the solicitor general (to whom Manson had also made an application) accordingly. He finished with a brief note of commendation to Manson for his thorough and conscientious efforts on behalf of his client.

That Manson was unimpressed with such a response is an extreme understatement. Few of his arguments appeared to have been given serious consideration, and many of the facts raised in support of his application seemed to have been completely ignored. He was in the process of considering an appeal to the Federal Court of Canada against Crosbie's decision when help from a completely unexpected quarter landed on his doorstep.

---

7 Crosbie referred to the case of *R. v. Prince, Hewitt and Craib*, referred to above, in which the Manitoba Court of Appeal held that the words "by his own act caused or assisted in causing the death of a police officer" were not limited to direct participation in the act of killing. The same case had also affirmed that the words "counselled or procured another person to do any act causing or assisting in causing death" include being a party to an illegal venture which involves the use of firearms for its perpetration and the escape of the participants. An appeal against that decision had been dismissed without written reasons by the Supreme Court of Canada. [1970] S.C.R. vi. It appears to have been a particularly factually driven case that should not have been considered as an authoritative interpretation of the provision.

CHAPTER 11

PLAN B

Had it not been for a program entitled "Janise" on CBC's *the fifth estate*, broadcast on 7 December 1982, the matter would probably have rested there. Janise would have stayed in prison until 2001. The program was one that had been inspired, at least in part, by a documentary entitled "P for W," produced by Holly Dale and Janice Cole, which aired in 1981. It was a look at the penitentiary experience through the eyes of six or seven prisoners, one of whom was Janise Gamble. Dale and Cole became good friends with Janise and visited her regularly. When *the fifth estate* showed interest in telling Janise's story, the only basis upon which she would agree to cooperate was if they agreed to hire Holly Dale as a consultant.

Like all programs assembled in formats like that of *the fifth estate*, one has to be cautious about the content and whatever the agenda may be that underlies it. Such programs involve almost limitless scope for editorial licence. The manner in which excerpts are assembled from many questions, asked in different ways in several "takes" that are on occasion influenced by the interviewers, can produce wildly biased impressions on the eventual audience. I have had several personal experiences with programs of this nature, some of which deliberately misrepresented the underlying facts in the guise of so-called investigative journalism. With some television networks I now adopt the position that I am willing to appear "live" at any time and to answer any questions, but under no circumstances do I trust them to prepare a pre-recorded program using any interview material from me. I raise the point here simply to say that quoted material in the program from those involved might well not be a full and complete representation of what they might have said or thought about the full circumstances of the matter. In any event, however, the program was deemed fit for release and was broadcast.

On the evening of 7 December 1982, staying at the Newfoundlander Hotel in St John's, while on a case, Montreal lawyer Colin Irving was sufficiently bored that he watched *the fifth estate*, not by any means his favourite television program. He was affected enough by it that he mentioned it some time later at dinner with his family. One of his daughters, with the subtlety characteristic of a teenage girl, said, "Well, why don't you do something about it then, instead of just representing large companies?" The challenge stuck with him, even though he knew precious little about criminal law and though it was probable that Janise had her own lawyers. He was, however, an experienced courtroom lawyer and one of the best constitutional litigators in the country, and had acted before the courts of all levels in Canada on major cases. Eventually, after reviewing a transcript of the program obtained from the CBC in June 1984, and after studying the decision of the Alberta Court of Appeal in the case, he wrote to Janise on 16 September 1985, offering to see what might be done.

Dear Ms. Gamble:

I read last week a transcript of the program televised by the Fifth Estate on your case and I have since then read the published decision of the Alberta Court of Appeal. I was left with the feeling that the sentence is out of all proportion to the events which occurred insofar as you are concerned and if anything can be done about it at this late date, I would be willing to give any help I can.

By sheer coincidence, I became associated with the firm of Burnet, Duckworth & Palmer in Calgary a year and a half ago when I set up an office in Ottawa, although my practise in Ontario and Quebec is almost entirely independent. I called Web MacDonald last week having discovered that he was the lawyer who defended you. He told me that he thought you had lawyers representing you in Kingston and that they may have taken some steps to have your case reviewed.

While I have little experience in criminal law, I have been much involved in constitutional matters in recent years and have dealt with a number of cases involving the Canadian Charter of Rights and Freedoms. While I would not wish to hold out any false hopes, I do think there are some issues under the Charter which at least merit serious consideration.

If you would write to me at my Ottawa office and let me know the name of your lawyers in Kingston, I would be pleased to get in touch with them and pass on the points which occur to me.

Janise replied shortly thereafter on 3 October.

Dear Mr. Irving:

I must admit to some surprise when I received your letter, dated Sept. 16, 1985. After reading it, the surprise became gratitude and appreciation.

Your timing was also incredible, as I had only received a decision from the Minister of Justice not long ago. I am enclosing a copy of the reasons for the denial for your perusal and opinions. [This was Crosbie's rejection of her application.]

I do indeed have a lawyer in Kingston, by the name of Professor ALLAN S. MANSON, and he has been acting on my behalf for the past few years. I have forwarded him a copy of your letter and asked him to get in touch with you; or if you have not heard from him by the time you receive this, you could contact him.

I, personally, would like to thank you for any help you could offer me, and certainly believe that any of your opinions and "issues" would be appreciated by Allan also.

In closing, Mr. Irving, I would again like to thank you for your kindness and consideration of my situation and express my sincere gratitude for any offer of assistance forthcoming.

Her letter reached Irving on 9 October, and he replied to her the same day, after establishing contact with Manson.

Dear Ms. Gamble:

Thank you for your letter of October 3rd which arrived here
today.

I had a long conversation with Professor Manson this morning
and it has been agreed that we will get together when I am next
in Toronto which I expect will be on October 21st or 22nd. I have
already prepared a very rough draft memorandum which I will
revise in the meantime and review with him when we meet.

I think it would be preferable to discuss any conclusions we
reach with you at a meeting between yourself and Professor
Manson, or perhaps all three of us if that is possible, as soon as
possible after he and I have met.

Manson had initially decided that the best course of action following the rejection of his petition by the minister of Justice was to apply
to the Federal Court of Appeal for judicial review of Crosbie's decision
regarding mercy. He had not taken any concrete steps before Irving
called him. They agreed to meet in Toronto the following week. Irving
explained that he had no experience in criminal matters, but when
Manson told him what he planned to do, Irving was convinced it was
the wrong approach, on the practical basis that you cannot tell the
Queen what to do with the royal prerogative of mercy. What, in any
event, would it get him? At best, another chance to appeal to the same
minister, who would be acutely aware of the political unpopularity in
Alberta of reopening the case. Their first meeting, which Irving had
wanted to have before meeting Janise personally in Kingston, was at
the Courtyard Inn in the Windsor Arms Hotel in Toronto.

He told Manson that he thought the Charter provided the answer,
with the wrong charge and a sentence that did not exist at the time of
the offence. Manson, said Irving, was very generous; he was only interested in getting Janise out of prison and did not stand on any no-
tion of affronted dignity when some other lawyer arrived on the scene
with a completely different approach to what he had been contemplating. They began the initial consideration of a recourse that would include *habeas corpus*. Manson, who had far more experience with this
recourse than Irving and knew its limitations, marshalled all the reasons he could think of why it would not work. Irving persisted, however, and said that the new Charter had led to new remedies. This led

to the approach upon which they settled. In the meantime Irving
sought a meeting with Crosbie through James Greene, a well-known
lawyer in St John's with whom he had worked in the past. However, he
never managed to get one, other than a chance encounter on an airplane when they discussed the matter generally but without substantive content.

After Irving's meeting and initial discussions with Manson, the two
lawyers later met with Janise in a workroom at the Kingston penitentiary. Once he was fully engaged, Irving, who came to like the chain-
smoking young woman and to admire her guts, saw her alone, usually
in the visiting room. He found the prison a very tough place with some
very tough characters. He wrote to her shortly thereafter on 12 December 1985 to report on progress.

Dear Janise:

I am very glad we had the chance to meet even though only
briefly.

Allan and I had a long meeting here in Ottawa last week and
we are now studying some of the legal issues which we will have
to be sure of before the Application is served.

The first question, of course, is what Court has jurisdiction
and I think we are both pretty well satisfied now that it is the
Supreme Court of Ontario. This being so, the Application could
be presented to that Court in Kingston but we don't yet know
what judges will be sitting in Kingston in the new year and what
their availability might be. Since the hearing of the Application
will take at least a full day, it may be that we will have to arrange
with the Chief Justice to have a special judge named to hear the
case. In that event the hearing would probably be in Toronto
where the Court has its headquarters.

Our present plan is to meet again next week if we are both far
enough along and then to meet again with you to let you know
where we stand. Since I am only a two hour drive from Kingston,
I will arrange to come down during regular hours so that we can
meet in a proper room. I certainly hope that we will be able to
arrange that meeting between now and Christmas.

Both Allan and I would like to aim for a hearing date as close
as possible to early March which would probably mean getting

the Application completed and served by mid-January. I hope that we can meet that target but our chances of success will be better if we make sure that all preparation and research which can be done is done before service. What we want at the hearing is something like the ads for Holiday Inns – "no surprises"!

I look forward to meeting you again shortly.

With best wishes.

Irving and Manson had agreed that since Janise was incarcerated in Ontario, the best way to take the matter forward was to bring an application for *habeas corpus* in the Ontario courts, and to combine that recourse with an application under the Charter to the effect that her continuing imprisonment under the circumstances constituted cruel and unusual punishment under section 7 of the Charter. The federal Crown had already argued before the Supreme Court of Canada that prisoners had no section 7 rights, so it would certainly be new ground. It was fundamentally important that the application not be positioned as an appeal against either the legality of the conviction or the sentence of life imprisonment. That route would have been doomed to failure, since all available recourses along those lines had already been definitively settled by the Alberta courts and by the refusal of the Supreme Court of Canada to grant leave to appeal in 1978. The only issue to be raised in the application related to the continued legality of the condition of the sentence that Janise not be eligible for parole for twenty-five years. The distinction may appear subtle, but it proved to be decisive in the end, despite continued attempts by the federal, Ontario, and Alberta governments to suggest that the proceeding was an indirect attack on the original proceedings and should be dismissed out of hand on that ground.

They considered the timing of the presentation of the application and concluded that it would be prudent to wait until a date that was at least ten years from the time that Janise was incarcerated, since their argument would be based on the availability of a life sentence under the old law, which would have made Janise eligible in not less than ten years and not more than twenty. They did not want the application to be met by a procedural claim that, because Janise had not served the minimum possible sentence, the application should be dismissed because it was premature. They therefore had to wait until at least 13 March 1986, the tenth anniversary of her period of custody. The date they filed the application was 20 March 1986, and the court officially acknowledged receipt of the application on 26 March.

Irving tried to get agreement from the lawyers representing the federal government that Janise could be present when her case was argued, but the federal government lawyer, Ivan Whitehall, said he would oppose any motion that Irving might make for such purpose. He said that all Irving wanted was to have a pretty face in court to attract the sympathy of the judge. Irving had to admit to Janise that this was true, although he did not, of course, acknowledge this to Whitehall, to whom he urged that every person should have the right to be present in court when his or her case was being argued. The federal Crown routinely opposed all such applications to be present, having determined that many prisoners were bringing frivolous motions and applications just to get some time outside of prison. Irving did not want to delay the hearing on the substantive arguments as a result of procedural wrangles, so he did not pursue it any further, other than to advise Janise that he had made the effort and that the Crown had correctly divined his real purpose.

The originally scheduled date to be heard in the Ontario Supreme Court on the application was 22 April 1986. That date had to be abandoned because of Manson's involvement in another murder case, and it was instead heard on 12 and 13 May in Toronto, before Mr Justice David Watt, a newly appointed judge with a considerable background as a tough but fair and technically expert Crown appeal court lawyer. Watt was new enough to the bench at that time that he had not yet got his judicial robes, and this, if not his first case, was among his early ones. From Irving's perspective the hearing did not go at all well. Justice Watt, although impassive and asking the odd question, seemed to be generally unimpressed with the merits of the application and considered that the Ontario courts did not have the jurisdiction to act in respect of a conviction and sentence arising in the courts of another province. There were two days of argument, in which the Alberta Crown, as well as the Ontario and federal governments, participated. Irving reported on the hearing to Janise on 21 May.

Dear Janise:

I am sorry not to have written to you before now but I just got back to my office. Allan was going to phone you last week and I assume that he has brought you up to date on the hearings.

As he will have told you we had the feeling through the first day that the Judge was not convinced that our case was serious but things went much better on the second day when Allan and I replied to the Crown's argument. As a result I am reasonably optimistic that there will be a thorough and carefully written judgment to bring before the Court of Appeal. Whatever happens please remember that it is in the higher courts that the case will finally be decided and try not to be too disappointed if things go against us in the first court.

The Ontario Court of Appeal rendered a decision just a week or so prior to the hearing which should be helpful to us in the long run but may pose a procedural problem in the short term.

The case involved two individuals named Dunbar and Logan who killed three people including a young girl in January 1976. They were not caught until 1979 and their conviction on their first trial was overturned by the Court of Appeal for technical reasons with the result that they were tried again after the Charter had come into force. They were convicted a second time and appealed a second time to the Ontario Court of Appeal. They had been charged with first degree murder as you were and were sentenced to twenty-five years without parole. On the second appeal the Court of Appeal decided that their twenty-five year sentences violated the Charter since no such sentence was provided by law at the time of the murders. As a result their sentences were reduced to twenty years without parole.

Although ten years was the ineligibility provided by law at the time of the offence the trial judge could increase it to a maximum of twenty and in the case of Dunbar and Logan killings were so horrifying that nothing except the maximum possible sentence would be appropriate. Whatever else may be in doubt no one could consider that any such consideration could apply to you. Except, therefore, for the fact that Dunbar and Logan were tried a second time after the Charter had been proclaimed, their case is very similar to yours insofar as the purely legal issues are concerned and it is for that reason that it should be very helpful in the long run.

The bad news is that their sentences were reduced on appeal from their conviction to the Ontario Court of Appeal. The lawyer for Ontario in particular seized on this to argue that your case should be brought now to the Alberta Court of Appeal and that the Ontario courts should not be involved. If our Judge agrees with this we will have to consider whether we should make an immediate application to the Alberta Court of Appeal or whether it would be better to take our present application up to the Ontario Court of Appeal first. If necessary, of course, we will do both.

I expect to be in Kingston to see Caroline [one of Irving's children, then a student at Queen's University] either this coming weekend or the weekend after and as soon as I know I will try to arrange to come and see you on the Saturday morning. Either Allan or I will call you if the judgment is rendered in the meantime.

It was not until 8 September 1986 that Justice Watt rendered his decision. He dismissed the application in a lengthy and obviously carefully considered judgment.[1] He concluded that the right remedy was to appeal against the sentence in the Alberta courts and pointed out that, although an appeal had been launched against the conviction, there had been no similar appeal in those same courts against the sentence. He was far from convinced that the minimum period prior to eligibility for parole would have been the sentence imposed under the former law. In addition, he thought that *habeas corpus* was not appropriate because it would not result in the complete release of Janise. The traditional role of the writ of *habeas corpus* was to secure the immediate release of a person in custody, whereas what was sought in Janise's application was not immediate release but simply a variation of the conditions under which she remained in custody, namely as not eligible for parole for a period of twenty-five years. He was clearly uncomfortable with the idea of the Ontario courts appearing to exercise supervisory control over other provincial superior courts, simply on the basis of the fact that the applicant happened to be confined in Ontario. To vary a sentence validly imposed by the Alberta courts might be perceived as a collateral attack on the decisions of those courts. Dealing with the Charter, he thought the application involved a retrospective application of the Charter, which the courts had been steadfast in refusing. This was, Irving and Manson knew, their toughest hurdle.

Irving wrote to Janise on 12 September:

1 (1986) 17 W.C.B. 188.

Dear Janise:

I cannot tell you how frustrated and disappointed I am in the judgment Watt J. finally delivered. After all those months of waiting he has barely dealt with the merits of the case at all. As Allan will have told you he bases himself almost exclusively on the question of jurisdiction and only rarely even mentions the Canadian Charter on which the application was based. If I am disappointed I know how you must feel but please try not to be too discouraged; this is only the first round.

Allan and I will be meeting very shortly to plan the appeal and to discuss at the same time the possibility of an application to the Alberta Court of Appeal. I am not sure yet whether these two should be pursued at the same time but this is something which Allan and I will discuss together and with you very shortly.

In the meantime remember that we have lost a battle, and not a battle on the real issue at that, but not the war.

With best personal regards.

It was then on to the Ontario Court of Appeal, after determined efforts by Irving to get a hearing as soon as possible. There were very few open dates, and several conference calls were organized to discuss them. Manson remembers a hilarious moment during one call when Irving advised all counsel that the court had a few dates during a particular week. Ivan Whitehall, representing the federal Crown, responded that he would be out of the country that week. Irving suggested, "You have a large office. Can't someone else argue this case?" to which Whitehall replied, "The people of Canada are entitled to the counsel of their choice."

In order to get an early appeal, they agreed to take a civil panel, namely one not assigned to criminal cases and one that might not include any criminal law experts. The appeal was eventually heard on 22 April 1987, before Justices Houlden, Grange, and Tarnopolsky, who gave even shorter shrift to the application and rendered a brief oral judgment on the spot, simply holding that the courts of Alberta were the proper courts to deal with the issues that were raised by the case.[2] It was obvious after the first four minutes of argument, said Manson,

2 (1987) 3 W.C.B. (2d) 88.

that the court had no interest in the merits of the case. Irving was on his feet for perhaps twenty-five minutes (from the back table, not being a Queen's Counsel, while all the lawyers for the governments, with their QCs, were in the front rows. The Ontario courts followed the British tradition that only QCs – so-called "silks," from the nature of their robes – were permitted to sit in and argue from the front rows of counsel tables). He made no progress beyond the court's suggestion that, if they wanted relief, they should apply for late leave to appeal against the sentence in Alberta.

Irving turned to Manson and said, "See if you can do anything," but after a few minutes it was clear that the court had tuned out and that was it. The court did not even bother to hear argument from the respondents. Justice Houlden announced that the court would adjourn for a few minutes and, when they returned, said to the respondents that the court did not have to hear from them, and dismissed the appeal. A discouraged Irving and Manson walked from Osgoode Hall across Queen Street to a bar and ordered a drink. They found themselves the first customers of the day. Having started their case at 10:30, they'd made it to the bar well before noon.

Eight days later, the following endorsement was signed by the three judges:

> The Appellant is not challenging the validity of her conviction or of the sentence of life imprisonment imposed upon her. She alleges that by reason of the *Charter* the sentence of the Alberta court fixing her period of parole ineligibility at twenty-five years is no longer valid. She contends that she should receive the benefit of the lesser punishment to which she would have been subject if properly charged under the *Criminal Law Amendment (Capital Punishment) Act 1973*, s.c. 1973-74, c.38 and convicted only of "murder punishable by imprisonment for life."
>
> Whether or not in a different factual situation *habeas corpus* or a declaration might be an appropriate remedy for a person imprisoned in Ontario pursuant to a valid warrant of committal issued by the court of some other province, we are all agreed that they are not appropriate remedies for an Ontario court to grant in the factual situation that exists in this case. In our judgment, the proper forum for the determination of the issues that arise in this case is Alberta: that province is where the crime was committed,

where the full record of the proceedings is located and where the order and warrant for committal were issued. The courts of that province are, in our opinion, best able to determine whether the appellant should have properly been found guilty of murder punishable by imprisonment for life, and if so, what the proper period of parole ineligibility should be.

The appeal from Watt J. will, therefore, be dismissed. We wish to make it clear, however, that we are not to be taken as approving in any way his views whether, in the circumstances here present, the application of the *Charter* would be giving it a retrospective effect.

Even before he had seen the written endorsement, Irving wrote to Janise on 24 April to give her the bad news.

Dear Janise:

As Allan will have told you the Court of Appeal dismissed our Appeal at the hearing on Wednesday.

They did so solely on the ground that in their view the issues raised could be dealt with better in the Alberta courts. It was apparent that they were troubled particularly by the question of what sentence would or should have been imposed under the old law and what the verdict of the jury might have been under the old law. My impression, however, is that the decision was really based more on policy than anything else in that with so many Federal prisons located in Ontario the court fears that it may be inundated with Charter cases arising from sentences imposed by courts outside the Province.

On the brighter side, they appeared to agree with our argument that you were tried under the wrong law and that the Charter applies even though the sentence was passed before it was proclaimed. In the brief oral judgment rendered the Court took pains to say that although the appeal was dismissed on jurisdictional grounds they were not to be taken as having agreed with Watt's finding that the Charter could not apply.

I am increasingly convinced that we are right on the main issue and I cannot tell you how frustrating and angry I am at our inability to persuade the Ontario Courts to consider the real issues. Wednesday's result on the question of jurisdiction seems to me wrong and unjust but leaves me even more determined to keep on going until we succeed in having the merits of the case determined. I know what a terrible strain this must be for you but I also know you have the strength to hang in until that day arrives.

While I haven't had the chance to think the matter through completely, my preliminary view is that the next step should be an application to the Alberta Court of Appeal for leave to appeal your sentence basing ourselves on the judgment of the Ontario Court of Appeal in Dunbar and Logan. I will be in Calgary next week on other business (would you believe I am representing the Attorney General of Alberta in a constitutional case in the Supreme Court of Canada!) and I have arranged to meet Bruce Fraser who is the Alberta lawyer in this case to arrange a date for making the application.

If leave is not granted, we would then have to appeal the decision of the Ontario Court of Appeal to the Supreme Court of Canada. Such an appeal would require leave of the Supreme Court but I am confident we would obtain such leave if the Alberta courts will not hear the case. In the ordinary course an Application for Leave to Appeal must be made within 90 days of the decision appealed from and it may be that we will not be able to make our application in Alberta within that time. If not we will make the application for leave to appeal within the delays and ask the Supreme Court to hold it in abeyance until the Alberta Court has made its ruling.

I will be in touch with you again as soon as I come back from Calgary towards the end of next week and I know that Allan will be coming to see you in the meantime.

In the end they decided that an appeal against the sentence before the Alberta courts, particularly in Calgary, where the feelings about Harrison's murder were still very strong, was not likely to be of much help. It would, in any event, have required leave from the Alberta courts even to get the matter to be heard. So Irving and Manson decided on trying to get the Supreme Court of Canada to hear Janise's appeal. They would file an expedited application for leave to appeal to that court.

Manson told Irving that courts were not generally responsive to prisoners' cases. The standard operating procedure of the Department of Justice in prison cases, he said, was to do everything possible to keep the merits of the case from adjudication and to use motions or arguments as to jurisdiction, try to demonstrate that there was no cause of action, and use interlocutory appeals until the matter got to the Supreme Court of Canada, which was where any remedy that might exist would be determined. However, it was difficult to get the Supreme Court to hear many cases, so the delay strategy usually worked. In Janise's case, since they had disclosed the full merits of the case from the beginning, and it was the government that had invoked all the procedural and jurisdictional impediments, Irving was confident that they would get a good hearing if they could manage to get the Supreme Court to hear the case. Manson was not as sure, even though the Supreme Court of Canada had opened the scope of *habeas corpus* in a series of 1985 cases. Irving, however, would eventually be proven right.

SUPREME COURT OF CANADA

Almost all cases that are heard by the Supreme Court of Canada require the agreement of the court, or special leave from the court whose decision is being appealed, before they are allowed to proceed. There are too many possible appeals from the many courts across Canada for the Supreme Court of Canada to deal with, and the court agrees to hear only a very small percentage of those presented for its consideration. With so many applications for leave to appeal, panels of three judges decide whether cases are worth hearing, although any judge who considers that a case may be worth hearing, whether on a particular panel or not, can raise the matter for discussion. In recent years the court no longer actually hears counsel for the parties seeking or opposing leave to appeal and proceeds on the basis of written submissions. Fortunately for Janise, the court was still hearing leave applications when her case came up.

The court does not regard its role as necessarily one of correcting errors in the lower courts, so the mere fact that a judgment may be wrong in law is no guarantee that the court will agree to intervene. It is instead mainly concerned with cases involving broader questions of legal policy and the possible ramifications for society generally. Thus it normally eschews the highly technical cases that may have a limited impact, as well as cases involving provisions of law that have already changed or that may have become moot with the passage of time.

Janise's application for leave to appeal to the Supreme Court of Canada was filed on 1 June 1987, along with the filing fee of $30. On 11 June the attorney general of Alberta filed a motion for leave to intervene, which was heard the following day by Justice Bertha Wilson, the first woman appointed to the Supreme Court of Canada. Justice Wilson granted the application. When the application for leave to appeal to the Supreme Court of Canada was heard on its merits, the time allotted for each party was very short, ten or fifteen minutes. It was heard before Justices Estey, Wilson, and LeDain.

On such occasions it is absolutely critical to get the court engaged in the issue and to present it as one that the court should consider important enough to hear. As the old adage goes, you never have a second chance to make a first impression. Irving's opening began: "This is a case about a young woman who has been in prison for eleven years serving a sentence that was unknown to the law at the time the crime was committed, for a crime which itself did not exist." Bertha Wilson practically rose out of her chair and said, "I beg your pardon!"

The generally sympathetic hearing that followed might have led to an expectation that the application would be dealt with quickly, but the months dragged on without a ruling. The reason for the delay became clear when Irving received a letter, almost six months later, from the registrar of the Supreme Court of Canada, Guy Goulard, dated 10 December 1987. The registrar stated that the panel of judges that heard the application for leave to appeal on 23 June had been waiting for the decision of the Court in *Milne v. Her Majesty the Queen*, which was eventually delivered on 18 November. He went on to say that he had been instructed by the chief justice to communicate with counsel in the Gamble case and to ask "whether they wish to pursue their application for leave to appeal in light of the decision in *Milne*." He asked for comments as soon as possible.

On 22 December Ronald Fainstein, representing the federal Crown, sent a letter to the court, which was received on 29 December. Irving answered it the following day and it was received by the court on 4 January 1988. Irving was certainly aware of the *Milne* decision, having been sent a copy on 18 November by Gowling and Henderson, the Ottawa agents they were using for the case. He had written to Janise the day before the judgment was issued, saying that he had learned that the *Milne* judgment was to be rendered on 17 November and that he had asked the Ottawa correspondents to get him a copy as soon as it was released. Goulard's letter had not reached him until 28 December, and he replied on 30 December that he would have to consider the matter carefully and discuss it with his client before making any final decision. To keep the ball in the air, however, he noted:

> I should say immediately however that my reaction upon re-reading *Milne* is that the two major issues requiring determination here are precisely those which the majority found it unnecessary to decide. I refer particularly in this connection to the first full paragraph on page 15 of the reasons of the majority. It was held in both *Mitchell* and *Konechny* which are referred to in that paragraph that relief under the Canadian Charter is available, if the facts warrant it, in respect of post-Charter execution of a pre-Charter sentence. That principle is the foundation of this application. It appears to me that the majority did not express an opinion one way or the other on its validity but simply left the question open. The jurisdictional issue in *Milne*, likewise left open, is identical to that raised by the Respondents and the Intervener in this case.
>
>   In all the circumstances I would respectfully request an opportunity for counsel to meet with the Chief Justice to discuss the matter before further steps are taken.

The federal Crown added fuel to the fire on 19 January. Fainstein wrote to Goulard, agreeing with Irving that the Charter issue in Gamble was not dealt with in the majority judgment in *Milne*, but that the judgment nevertheless disposed of the Gamble matter because it had accepted the Crown's argument that a collateral attack upon a sentence is impermissible. Fainstein argued that the binding legal effect of a sentence continues and is not susceptible to attack, except within the context of a sentence appeal. The resort to *habeas corpus* here was, he said, misconceived. The issue of whether section 11(i) of the Charter had any application to Gamble's case could, he said, be dealt with by the Alberta Court of Appeal on a sentence appeal, if one ensued, and could only be raised legitimately in that forum. He concluded that the application for leave to appeal should be refused.

Irving replied the next day. Fainstein's conclusion as to what the *Milne* decision stood for was, he said, directly contrary to the decision of the same court in *Mitchell*. In that case, as in this, the application was for *habeas corpus* or a declaration and was made in Ontario, where the applicant was imprisoned, in respect of the continued execution of a sentence imposed in another province. The validity of the decision in *Mitchell* had been expressly left open in *Milne*. Furthermore, in light of Fainstein's comments, he drew Goulard's attention to the fact that the case for Gamble, unlike that in respect of Milne, was that she was not "properly convicted and sentenced" under the law that existed at the time of the offence. Finally, he pointed out that Fainstein had raised a number of other issues not arising from the decision in *Milne*, all of which were canvassed in the argument portion of the leave application. If the court wished further argument on any of these issues, which he said he did not understand to be the case from Goulard's letter of 10 December, he would be pleased to make such arguments either orally or in writing.

Goulard replied on 12 January that he would wait for comments from Fainstein before bringing the matter to the attention of the chief justice. On 11 February, Irving reported to Manson that he had spoken with Goulard, who said that the matter was now in the hands of Justice Estey, who did not "for the moment" see any need to meet with counsel. It was not until 24 March 1988 that the court granted leave for Janise to appeal. The Order was issued on 30 March without the need for further argument. It turned out that Justice Estey was strongly in favour of the leave being granted.

Losing no time, Irving filed a motion for directions pertaining to the hearing, dealing with the delays to provide factums from each party. He wrote to Janise on 4 April:

Dear Janise:

Finally a piece of good news! The prospect of the Alberta courts was very unappealing and I am much relieved.

I have made an appointment with Mr. Justice Estey, who presided over the panel which heard the application, for Friday April 8th to hear an application to fix an early hearing date and to give directions on a number of technical issues having to do with the material to be filed with the Court.

I think the Court will be sympathetic to a request for an early hearing partly because of the nature of the case and partly because there was such a long delay between the application for leave to appeal and the judgment allowing leave. I will ask for a June date but at the moment I have no way of knowing if the Court will have time available before the autumn term which begins at the end of September.

I will be in touch again after April 8th to let you know what happened and will arrange then to come and see you.

All the best in the meantime

A hearing date of 17 June 1988 was fixed. Justice Estey signed the order for the expedited hearing about two days before he resigned from the court. He had made it clear to Ivan Whitehall that he, Estey, would have had no hesitation in applying the Charter in the circumstances. Unfortunately, when Estey resigned, he did so rather publicly and alienated virtually every member of the court. The attorney general of Alberta later filed an application for leave to intervene, which was granted on 3 June; he was to be limited to fifteen minutes of argument.

LAST CHANCE: ARGUMENT BEFORE THE SUPREME COURT OF CANADA

The hearing took place as scheduled on 17 June before Chief Justice Brian Dickson and Justices Jean Beetz, Antonio Lamer, Bertha Wilson, and Claire L'Heureux-Dubé. Irving argued the entire appeal on behalf of Janise, even though Manson and Franklin Gertler were shown in the court records as appearing on her behalf. Manson declared, not without some interest in the matter, that the factum in the Supreme Court of Canada filed on Janise's behalf was a masterpiece. Irving, he said, was superb at breaking a series of complex issues into pieces and making them comprehensible, while advancing the points in Janise's favour in a persuasive manner. Whitehall acknowledged that the hearing was not entirely warm for the Crown and decidedly not hostile towards Janise. L'Heureux-Dubé said nothing, while Bertha Wilson was vociferous.

The position of the federal Crown was that the case amounted to a collateral attack on the judgment of the Alberta Court of Appeal in 1978 and that all of the issues had already been canvassed by that court at the time and the Supreme Court of Canada had refused to grant leave when it had been applied for following the decision. Jeff Casey, who had appeared throughout the proceedings on behalf of the Ontario government, reiterated his legalistic argument against the remedy and the retrospective application of the Charter. Manfred DeLong, counsel for the attorney general of Alberta, spent much of his limited time pointing out that the crime had been committed in Alberta. If there was to be a remedy, it had to be in Alberta. He got an even less sympathetic response when, in the course of his argument that the Alberta courts should have jurisdiction in case of a retrial because the offence occurred there, the evidence was there, and the community interest relating to the dead police officer was there, Justice Beetz noted, sarcastically, "Maybe this time, you can hang her." It was also during argument for the Alberta Crown that Lamer said, "Isn't this the sort of case where we should put all the law books aside and sit under the old oak tree to try to decide what is right?" Delong had started to respond to this by saying that he believed there was a lot of value in those law books, when Chief Justice Dickson interrupted. He told DeLong to get on with his argument, which had included a complaint that he had had such a restrictive time constraint – fifteen minutes of argument, the same as for any intervenant in the court – placed on him.

It is one thing to believe that your hearing before the court has gone well and quite another to get the judgment for which you are looking. Many counsel have left the courtroom thinking they had won, only to get a judgment later demolishing their arguments. Of course, the reverse often happens as well, when counsel have left the courtroom in apparent tatters after argumentative questioning by the court. It is always important not to read too much into what happens in the courtroom, as the judges may be testing preliminary views that they formed prior to hearing the argument and are looking for confirmation, or otherwise, from whatever counsel may have to say. What really matters is what the judges do once they have begun to work their way towards a final judgment. Quite often divergences of opinion develop, and considerable effort is devoted to seeing whether a consensus can be reached. Only if that is not possible will the respective factions prepare their own judgments and try to persuade their colleagues to support one view or the other.

As the months went by after the hearing, it became clear that the court was having difficulty with the appeal. The members were experienced, smart, and open-minded judges, but, with the exception of the chief justice, who had some background in the area, it was not clear how many of them fully understood the conditions under which Janise was living in the Prison for Women. Had they been unanimous, it would have been relatively easy, even with the intervention of the summer vacation, to have produced a judgment fairly quickly. But in each session of the court at which its judgments were released, time after time there was no mention of Janise's appeal. Appellants' counsel often develop their own defence mechanisms in such cases, convincing themselves that a negative decision is easier to reach than a positive one, so that they should take hope from the delay. It is pretty thin gruel, however, and not easy on the nerves. On 4 October Irving wrote to Janise:

Dear Janise:

I am as tired of writing to tell you that there is no news as I am sure you are of receiving such letters.

I had hoped that the judgment might come out when the Court reopened for business on September 29th but of the 60 or 70 cases awaiting judgment only one was disposed of on that day.

I wish I could tell you when something will happen but I don't know and there is no way to find out. One of our judges (Beetz) is in hospital and I gather is not expected to return to the court until November. It is very unlikely that he would write this judgment anyway since he never deals with matters of criminal law but his absence could hold things back if his opinion has not already been recorded.

I will be in Kingston either in the weekend of October 22nd or October 29th and will arrange to come and see you. Of course if anything happens in the meantime, I will let you know.

And so they did the only thing they could: they waited for the court to decide.

JUDGMENT DAY: 8 DECEMBER 1988

Irving got word from the court that it would be rendering its judgment on the appeal in Ottawa on 8 December. He and Manson discussed what they should do to advise Janise of the outcome, since she was very depressed. The prison psychologist was worried about suicide if the appeal did not succeed. As the judgment loomed before him, Irving remembered being in Kingston visiting his daughter, Caroline at Queen's

University, and being angrily accosted by a woman from the Elizabeth Fry Society, saying, "I hope you know what you're doing, giving her hope when there may be no chance."

They agreed that Irving would attend at court to receive the judgment and that Manson would stay in Kingston to bring the news to Janise. Getting a judgment from the Supreme Court of Canada is an unnerving experience at best. Irving had been there many times before, but never on an occasion so emotionally charged as this. The pressure was excruciating, and he had practically to hold onto the railing at the end of the counsel table to keep from falling.

The decision in the case was announced by Chief Justice Dickson. "The appeal of Janise Marie Gamble is allowed, the Chief Justice and Mr. Justice Beetz dissenting." Irving almost fainted with relief – and at the narrowness of the victory – in which the two most senior judges had dissented. He left the courtroom at once to call Manson. They decided Manson would go to the prison with a bunch of flowers, so that the minute Janise saw him, she would know they had won without enduring another second of anxiety.

VINDICATION

Only later did they get the reasons for judgment for study. The reasons for the majority were written by Justice Wilson. It is clear from her reasons that she was less than impressed with the procedural barrage thrown up by the three levels of the Crown (Alberta, Ontario, federal), and she had no hesitation in characterizing them as mistaken positions. In her review of the applicable law, she did not confine herself to the cases referred to by the appellant. There are many cases that were not cited on Janise's behalf, but one advantage that Supreme Court judges enjoy is that the court's own legal staff or the judges' clerks prepare what is referred to as a "bench memo." This canvasses all of the jurisprudence on the points raised by the appeal, which may include cases that counsel have not relied upon, which may well have been the situation in this appeal. It does seem clear, however, that most of the cases cited by the parties were referred to by the court.

Because of the many procedural issues thrown up by the various Crown attorneys, a considerable amount of legal detritus had to be dealt with before getting to the heart of the matter. Justice Wilson identified five issues for determination. The first was whether the application of the Charter in the circumstances of this case constituted its retrospective application to events prior to its proclamation. She first distinguished *Milne* on the basis that Janise was not seeking a review of her pre-Charter trial and sentence in the light of the new standards but rather seeking review and relief from the current operation of the parole ineligibility provision in her sentence; therefore, the appellant argued, the Charter was being applied prospectively. The Crown had insisted that the focus of the review should be on the soundness of the Alberta Court of Appeal's conclusion that, despite the fact that the appellant was tried and punished under the wrong law, section 27(2) of the transitional legislation prevented the remedy of a new trial under the old law.

The Crown had relied on *Milne* to show that a pre-Charter sentence could not be reviewed in light of new law. Justice Wilson rejected that argument, since that question specifically left open the issue of carrying out the sentence, as opposed to its pronouncement, as being retrospective. She then reviewed the authorities that considered the carrying out of the sentence, as opposed to its original pronouncement. For her the relevant act was not the conviction or sentencing, all of which had occurred prior to the Charter becoming operative. Instead it was the continuing execution of that part of the sentence that mandated a twenty-five-year period of parole ineligibility.[1]

The court, said Justice Wilson, should avoid an all-or-nothing approach that artificially divided the chronology of events into the mutually exclusive categories of pre- and post-Charter. Frequently, an alleged current violation would have to be placed in the context of its pre-Charter history in order to be fully appreciated. While Charter standards could not be applied to events occurring before its proclamation, it would be folly to exclude from the court's consideration any crucial pre-Charter history, which was often necessary when the court

---

[1] One of the interesting features of the case was that the majority of the court that determined that Janise should be declared eligible for parole had constituted the minority in *R. v. Stevens*, [1988] 1 S.C.R. 1153, where the test for determining whether a section 7 application was prospective or retrospective had been stated (by the minority) at page 1167 as: "Rather, the section seems to direct one to the point of time at which someone is about to be deprived of his or her life, liberty or security of the person. It is the projected deprivation which triggers the application of s. 7. We must ask therefore whether, at the time of the projected deprivation of the accused's right to liberty, that deprivation would be in accordance with the principles of fundamental justice or not."

exercised its broad discretion under s. 24(1) of the Charter, to formulate the remedy which was appropriate and just in the circumstances.

A constitutional remedy, to be fully appropriate and just, Wilson said, might have to take into account pre-Charter events. Another crucial consideration was the nature of the particular constitutional right alleged to be violated. Such an approach was consistent with the court's general purposive approach to the interpretation of constitutional rights. Different rights and freedoms, depending on their purpose and the interests they were meant to protect, would crystallize and protect the individual at different times. Some rights and freedoms in the Charter seemed to her to be particularly susceptible of current application, even though such application would of necessity take cognizance of pre-Charter events. Those Charter rights, the purpose of which was to prohibit certain conditions or states of affairs, would appear to fall into this category. Such rights were not designed to protect against discrete events, but rather to protect an ongoing condition of (sic) affairs.

Justice Wilson made it clear that Janise's Charter claim would fail were she to be invoking section 7 to reach back and reverse the liability that clearly existed on the basis of the facts and law in existence at the time the offences were committed. If the object was to overturn a pre-Charter conviction and sentence, it must necessarily fail, since she would then have been properly convicted and sentenced at a time before the Charter came into effect and she would be left to serve the sentence and pursue her appeal rights in the normal way. The difference with this appeal was that Janise was claiming a continuing current violation of her liberty interest, and it was the duty of the courts to consider her Charter claim and, in the context of that claim, to consider pre-Charter history to the extent that it explained or contributed to what was alleged to be a current Charter violation. This was especially true when the pre-Charter history was alleged to include unlawful conduct on the part of the Crown. Referring to the *Milne* case, where a pre-Charter conviction and sentence were not reviewed in light of subsequent changes in the law and the enactment of the Charter, it had been on the basis that Milne had been properly convicted and sentenced. In the case of Janise, the overwhelmingly significant fact was that she had not been properly convicted and sentenced because she was convicted and sentenced under the wrong law. In short, it was not a case in which an applicant was trying to avoid the law as it was at the time of the offence applied to her. It was instead that she had not had the proper law applied to her situation, nor could she have it now.

Justice Wilson then turned to the question of whether the Ontario Supreme Court had jurisdiction in this case, one of the central points of the resistance to the motion and the turning point in the courts below. She was unimpressed by the argument that the fact that Janise had been convicted and sentenced in Alberta deprived the Superior Court of Ontario of its traditional jurisdiction to issue a writ of *habeas corpus ad subjiciendum* to those in the province detaining a person in that province for the purpose of reviewing the legality of that detention or confinement. That, in addition, made good practical sense, since the writ would be served on those responsible for the confinement of the prisoner, in this case, the warden of the Prison for Women, so that the prisoner could be brought before the court. Superior courts would needlessly hinder the enforcement of rights if they refused to hear *habeas corpus* applications from prisoners within their jurisdictions. Relief in that form should not be withheld for reasons of mere convenience. There had been an argument by the federal government that perhaps the court to which application should be made was the federal court, but Justice Wilson said, "he (the Crown attorney) does no credit to that existing system by attempting to place procedural roadblocks in the way of someone like the appellant who is seeking to vindicate one of the citizens' most fundamental rights in the traditional and appropriate forum." She said the Ontario courts had the necessary jurisdiction to act in the matter.

The next question was whether the requested review of the period of parole eligibility could be undertaken on an application by way of *habeas corpus ad subjiciendum* with *certiorari* in aid under s. 24(1) of the Charter. Justice Wilson disposed of the arguments raised in opposition to such a procedure and said she was not persuaded by any of them in the context of the present case. They were all based on a misunderstanding of Janise's claim and a faulty characterization of what was sought. It was not a collateral attack on the sentence but on the continuation of the deprivation of liberty, which can be challenged by *habeas corpus*.

Irving and Manson, on Janise's behalf, had deliberately avoided framing her claim as an attempt to overturn her original conviction or sentence. This should not, however, be construed to her detriment, Justice Wilson said. Janise should be allowed, rather, to seek the relief she believed best suited to the vindication of her rights, and Justice Wilson could see no possible objection to a litigant's pressing her claim in its strongest possible light. Nor did she think that distinctions that had become uncertain, technical, artificial, and non-purposive should be maintained. There should certainly be no interest in protecting unlawful sentences, especially where they were apparent on their face, without the necessity of going behind the record. The quality of incarceration where a person may apply for parole is quite different from incarceration where this would not be possible for a further period of fifteen years. The fact that Janise's complete release could not be achieved through *habeas corpus* alone was not sufficient to deny its application in the circumstances, since the remedy should be flexible enough to continue to protect liberty interests now constitutionally protected under the Charter.

Next was whether Janise's rights under s.7 of the Charter were presently violated. It was fundamental to any legal system that recognizes the rule of law that an accused must be tried and punished under the law in force at the time the offence is committed. This had not happened in Janise's case. Under the new rules, the Crown enjoyed a lesser burden of proof than under those that applied when the crime was committed.

> Without embarking on the inevitably speculative exercise of considering what might have happened to the appellant had she been tried and punished under the properly applicable *Criminal Code* provisions, I am able to conclude from a comparison of the relevant legislation that the appellant *prima facie* was prejudiced by not being tried and punished under the proper law. I invoke in support of this conclusion the fact that it is due to the Crown's error that we cannot know for sure what would have happened to the appellant had she been tried under the proper law. She should accordingly be given the benefit of any doubt.

The final question was whether Janise was entitled to the relief requested and whether the courts in this matter could grant the remedy of a declaration that she was eligible for parole. Justice Wilson had little remaining sympathy for the Crown's position that, even if she had been tried under the proper law, she might have been condemned to death or ineligibility of parole for a period of ten to twenty years. Those were theoretical possibilities, but it was not for the court to speculate on an application such as this on what the verdict might have been. Given the submissions on the scope of the *habeas corpus* review, Justice Wilson noted that she found it ironic that the attorney general

for Canada and the attorney general for Alberta would invite the court
to do so. The final nail in the coffin was this statement:

> The real issue, it seems to me, is the one already mentioned,
> namely whether the Crown can take advantage of the uncertainty
> created by its own failure to give the appellant a fair trial in the
> first instance. I do not think it can. It is quite contrary to our
> legal traditions and to our obligations under the *Charter* to hold,
> as did the trial judge, that the appellant should only receive
> a remedy for the Crown's error if she proves that it was "in-
> eluctable" that she would only have received a sentence of life
> imprisonment with eligibility for parole after 10 years.

The court had the power to issue a declaration of parole eligibility.
Given the prejudice already suffered by the appellant, it seemed appropriate and just that she be declared eligible for parole forthwith. The
Parole Board, however, was the final arbiter of whether and when she
should be released on parole.

The dissenting judgment of the chief justice and Justice Beetz was
based almost entirely on the view that the effect of the application was
to engage in a retrospective application of the Charter. Chief Justice
Dickson, who wrote the reasons, having read the reasons of Justice
Wilson, concluded, "but, with considerable regret," that he could not
concur.

REACTIONS TO THE DECISION

The decision of the Supreme Court of Canada was not well received
in Calgary. Chief of Police Ernie Reimer, who was a close friend of the
murdered police officer, was quoted as saying, "My initial reaction is
one of disgust. I don't think there's any justice in this. I think it's very
unjust. She should be made to pay the full price and consequences."
Perhaps more understandably, Harrison's son, Kevin, reacted with a
statement that "capital punishment should never have been taken out."
"We were reasonably satisfied with 25 years. Now it turns out to be 13.
She got a cakewalk out of this." He might be forgiven his anger and
for not knowing that under the former law, since Janise had not, by her
own act, caused the death of his father, she would have been eligible

for parole much earlier. The Calgary Police Association president, Mike Dungey, said the decision added to the frustration of police, who sometimes feel unprotected under the law: "There are other crimes deemed less serious where people are serving more time. "I have a tremendous amount of difficulty and dismay with the system."

The Canadian Elizabeth Fry Society was happy with the decision. "Her case was one of the largest miscarriages of justice," said Bonnie Diamond, the society's executive director. "She killed nobody and she had the harshest sentence short of capital punishment." The society had supported Janise's position for years, and the Calgary office received several phone calls from angry opponents of that position. "The calls we received were from people who think we support cop killers. We don't," said Audrey Farrier of the Calgary Elizabeth Fry Society. "The laws need to be applied fairly and equitably. In her case, they weren't."

Jim Hogan, the Vancouver lawyer who carried in the methadone and helped negotiate the release of the hostages, said he was pleased by the Supreme Court decision because he believed Janise's role in the episode to be minimal. "I didn't see her as a main instigator. She was just involved with the wrong kind of people." One of the hostages, Diane Perry, however, said, "None of this was supposed to happen for 13 years. I can't believe the decision has been reversed. I can't believe it. I feel very strongly she was responsible for what went on."

Allan Manson said Janise was speechless after receiving the news. "She signed an application [for a parole hearing] this afternoon," he said. "It'll be day parole at first, but she's an easy parole case. I'm ecstatic. " Irving simply said, in response to reporters' questions, "I'm very relieved for her. She didn't kill the policeman or try to kill him. Her husband and another man her husband had met in prison had the shootout. She was over-punished for what she did."

A spokesman for the National Parole Board said that an application for parole had been received prior to Christmas, but that a hearing for Janise's release would not likely be held before five or six months. "We will be addressing risk as opposed to punishment," Simone Ferguson, regional director for the Ontario region of the National Parole Board, told the media. "The bottom line is we will be assessing what risk she presents to the community if any. There are no guarantees." Ferguson said it would probably be several months before a hearing would be set. The hearing would be conducted by four officials, who would receive material ranging from initial Calgary police reports from the case to the most recent psychiatric and psychological reports. They would also accept reports from other people – such as the victims – interested in the parole hearing.

Manson kept up his view that Janise would be most deserving of parole. "I've done parole cases for many years, and this is one of the easiest cases I've ever done. She never hurt anyone in her life. She is a bright, serious young woman." In the interim, now that there might be a more imminent future for Janise, announced Dennis Curtis, spokesman for Correctional Services Canada in Ontario, she, along with fifteen other female inmates, was put into a work program that took her out of the prison each morning Monday through Friday. The women were bussed about twenty kilometres to a minimum-security prison where they microfilmed documents for various government agencies.

IN RETROSPECT

In retrospect Irving was somewhat surprised that the decision was so close. Long after the case, he spoke with Jean Beetz and tried to find out whether Beetz would have signed the judgment he did if it would have ended up as being part the majority. Beetz gently dodged the question by saying that the court always had had difficulty with the retrospective application of the Charter, and there were many divisions of opinion. Beetz has since died. Chief Justice Dickson has also died, but the same question remains open for him, since he was always a great supporter of Charter rights. It is difficult to believe that he would have allowed the injustice to persist, had his view become the majority view of the court; it is more reasonable to speculate that he was content with the outcome, which still enabled him to hold his position that the Charter ought not to be applied retrospectively. Had he been part of a possible majority that might have kept Janise in prison for the full twenty-five years, it would have required very little for him to make his point of principle while distinguishing the facts of Janise's case as a current and ongoing injustice that warranted intervention. However, with the particular division that produced the "right" outcome, both he and Justice Beetz were able to have their cake and eat it.

Bertha Wilson, when approached, did not wish to comment and preferred to let her judgment speak for her. Her biographer states that she was delighted when Janise was released. Antonio Lamer, who later succeeded Dickson as chief justice of Canada, remembered the case well and said he thought the prosecution and sentencing under the old law were plainly wrong and that there must therefore be some remedy available to her in such circumstances.

In retrospect as well, the composition of the panel that heard the appeal was certainly the one most likely to produce the desired result. The three judges who made up the majority were the same three who had been the minority in the *Stevens Laviolette* appeal; this telegraphed what they might do if faced with a case like Janise's, namely to look at the situation at the time a Charter right might be affected, not necessarily at the time the sentence had been imposed. It is interesting to wonder whether the chief justice might deliberately have chosen the particular five-person bench to hear this case, knowing their predisposition to view matters from that perspective. He might well have been content with a majority decision to grant the relief sought, but with a small and divided bench, there would be a precedent that might not carry too much general weight in the future. When such a suggestion was made to Antonio Lamer, he said that he did not think it likely that Dickson had loaded the court with a view to getting the eventual result. There had been several illnesses on the court during that period and it was hard to get seven-judge benches, let alone full benches to sit, even on important cases. Still.

The case is not a landmark case, although it is often cited when there is a discussion of the retroactive application of the Charter. Its application has been whittled down by the courts, but it still remains an important case that calls for a liberal interpretation of the Charter, especially in matters of *habeas corpus*. It has certainly been blunted in immigration cases but remains particularly important when remedies are being sought that are outside the traditional (and especially common law) remedies, as a demonstration that the courts are entitled, and have a duty, to show more flexibility when constitutional issues are involved.

Irving received a number of congratulatory letters following the publication of the decision. One was from Peter Hogg, a law professor at the Osgoode Hall Law School at York University on 9 April 1989, who said he had finally read the decision of the Supreme Court of Canada.

I am astonished at the battery of technical arguments that the

Crown put up against you. In my naivete I would have expected
Gamble's eligibility for parole to be agreed to by the Crown, since
her conviction under the wrong law seems to overwhelm all other
considerations. If the Charter did not exist, I would expect the
Crown to be actively seeking the pardon or other discretionary
measure that would secure her release. Obviously, I do not live
in the real world!

As we discussed over the phone, the division of the court is a
puzzle. Dickson C.J. has been so solicitous of Charter rights in
other cases – in fact, I think he often exaggerates the civil libertar-
ian interest – that it is hard to see why he would walk away from
a rare real case of injustice.

A more personal response was the generous note from Allan Manson dated 3 January 1989.

In thinking back over the past few years, and in talking with
Janise about the future I am continually impressed with my gratitude to, and respect for, you.

You have been extraordinarily generous with your time and
expertise. For Janise, the benefit is obvious. None of this would
have happened without you. For me, it has been a pleasure and
a learning experience working with you. (I wasn't kidding when I
told a newspaper you are Canada's leading constitutional lawyer.)
When I re-think the various arguments we have had – s. 7, jurisdiction, remedy, retrospectivity – I appreciate the depth of the
intellectual dimension of Janise's case and the enormous value
of your participation.

My only regret is that co-operative undertakings are rare, rarely
enjoyable – and rarely successful. This one was terrific! And I
thank you.

But undoubtedly the one Irving most enjoyed was his Christmas
card from Janise, still in prison but now with hope, not endless despair,
ahead of her.

To you and all your family Colin
Veni, vidi, vici
That is certainly what you have done Colin and the words seem

so unnecessary as you have lived this hurricane with me. Therefore ... Thank you says it all.
The very merriest of Christmas' & the most joyful New Year ever!

Janise.

Nichols, ever the opportunist, filed his own application along the
lines taken on behalf of Janise by Irving and Manson. The only authority presented to the British Columbia Supreme Court was the decision in her case rendered by the Supreme Court of Canada. On 14
September 1989, following hearings on 5 and 6 September, the application was dismissed by Justice Raymond Paris. Whatever the circumstances that might have been particular to Janise, Nichols was unable
to take advantage of them, since he was the person who had killed
the police officer. If he had been tried under the law in force when the
offence was committed, he would necessarily have been convicted of
murder punishable by death. The effect of the new amendments would
have meant that, instead of being convicted of murder punishable by
death, he would have been sentenced to life imprisonment without eligibility for parole for twenty-five years. That was the sentence he got
and the sentence he was serving. There was no ongoing violation of
his Charter rights.

UNLUCKY TO THE END

With the judgment of the Supreme Court of Canada in hand, Janise had applied at once for parole. That it would be granted in the circumstances was all but a foregone conclusion. She clearly posed no ongoing threat to society. The major social problem was that she had by then been incarcerated for some fourteen years, most of the time in a maximum security institution where she had no freedom of action and no interaction with anyone other than fellow inmates and prison authorities. She had lost the ability to function normally in a free society, and it would have been as traumatic for her to simply walk away with no preparation for her re-entry into society as it had been to remove all her freedoms in the first place. She would have been completely unequipped.

By the middle of May 1989, she was granted day parole. The National Parole Board ruled that she would receive two temporary seventy-two-hour unescorted passes from prison and that, if she met all the requirements of those passes, she could then become eligible for up to six months of day parole in Ontario. The trips could be taken almost at once. One was to be to her mother's home in Peterborough and the other to a halfway house operated by Kingston's Elizabeth Fry Society.

The visits would be followed by a review and a possible extension of her parole.

Even with these gradual steps, it was hard for her to do some of the most simple things. Imagine having spent fourteen years never being able to open a door for yourself or to move from one place to another without the specific permission of someone in authority, usually someone who was armed. She was constantly terrified that she might do something that would lead to being put back in prison, perhaps for some reason she did not understand.

Harrison's family was still embittered by her eligibility for parole, and the day parole seemed to them to be a further aggravation. Kevin Harrison said, "She was given a life sentence. She should carry out a life sentence. The courts don't even think of the victim – only the one that caused the crime and their rights and freedoms. We don't have our father any more. We're without somebody we love very much. She can go on with her life. We can't. We're held back." He went on to say emotionally, "If capital punishment had been in, none of this would have happened because she'd have been hung a long time ago."

When news of the parole appeared in the media, victims groups, especially Victims of Violence in Calgary, put together a campaign of posters, one of which showing Janise and convicted cop-killer Real Chartrand. Chartrand's sentence had been reviewed after fifteen years, and he had been granted parole. "I feel a lot of criminals are not being punished enough for crimes," said *Maclean's* Richard Oakey. "Some Canadian laws are really a joke when it comes to murder and other violent crimes." He announced that he planned to mount the poster in his office. Another, Derek Bardell, voiced the feelings of many Calgarians, "This has really irritated me. I'm a firm believer that if you do the crime, you do the time." Mike Dungey, president of the Calgary Police Association, announced that he was disgusted by Janise's parole. "Because of a glitch in the judicial process she is now eligible for parole," he said angrily. "How long can Canadians stand for this type of system?" Calgary West MP Jim Hawkes felt that parliament should change the judicial process to take into account the Charter of Rights so that sentences for people like Gamble weren't changed later. He stopped short of being willing to quarrel with the Parole Board's decision, saying that he recognized the agony of Harrison's family but if criminals are rehabilitated and become productive people, it is to society's advantage not to pay to keep them locked up.

Manson stayed out of the discussion about the poster campaign, of which Janise was aware. She refused to comment on it and was unwilling to deal with the media at all. The Elizabeth Fry Society of Kingston, which had been dealing with her case, responded through Sally Wills, its executive director, who said that the hostility aimed at Janise was "most unfortunate," since she had served her debt to society. "She has been a victim of our society. She was sentenced incorrectly and has suffered for that. It's not going to help anybody reintegrate into society," Wills said.

By the end of June, Janise began day parole at the Kingston halfway house on the basis of a grant of a maximum of six months, having successfully completed the two seventy-two-hour unescorted passes. During the day she was free to go out, go to school, or do any number of things at her discretion. She was required to report nightly to the supervisor of the halfway house during the period of her day parole and, if she successfully completed the period, she would be considered for full parole. This further step continued to anger the Harrison family. Kevin Harrison said that all members of the family had sent victim impact statements to the National Parole Board in the hope that it would rescind the day parole decision. "This is sick. Our justice system is a farce," he said. "I wrote a letter to the parole board based on my feelings. I lost my father. It still hurts as much as when I was 16 years old."

FULL PAROLE

By early January 1990 Janise was close to completing her six months of day parole, and a hearing on whether to grant her full parole would probably be held very shortly. Jacques Belanger, manager of public affairs for the National Parole Board, speaking to the Calgary media who were paying close attention, confirmed the likelihood of the new hearing very early in the new year. "Normally if a person successfully passes day parole, the chances of full parole are better," he said, but it was up to the members of the Parole Board to reach a judgment as to how successful the day parole had been. When Dennis Curtis as Correctional Services spokesperson was asked if Janise had met all requirements of day parole, he simply said, "Yes, or she wouldn't still be out."

On 18 January 1990, a four-member panel of the National Parole Board granted Janise full parole, thirteen and a half months after the Supreme Court of Canada declared she was eligible. This decision came as no particular surprise to anyone, since it was obvious she represented no threat whatsoever to society and she would have to report to the police and to her parole officer for the rest of her life. But it continued to rankle the Calgary community and was especially bitter for the Harrison family. "She should've been given the death penalty," Harrison's widow, Pat, told the *Calgary Herald* the following day. "She should not be out there. Obviously they [Canadians] better start standing up and speaking to the government. The parole system is really out of whack." Michael Dungey branded the parole decision "abhorrent" and said, "My only comment to Ms. Gamble is that she better stay where she is because we don't want the likes of her, or people like her, anywhere near here."

Not all of the Calgary community was that harsh, and at least one person wrote a letter to the editor of the *Calgary Herald* about the angry tone of its reporting of the parole decision. On 22 February, Milda Rysan wrote:

> I read with dismay another angry report in the Herald on the parole of Janise Gamble ...
> While I sympathize with the family of the dead policeman, I abhor the hatred that they [seem to] have been cultivating over the 14 years. That is a long time to come to terms with the event and go on with living. Gamble did not kill the policeman ...
> My heart goes out to Gamble – I hope that she did not waste completely the time in the prison and that she will find enough help and support around her to help her to put the past behind her and do something useful with what is left of her life. I suggest the same to the family of the victim ...

UNLUCKY TO THE END

Janise moved into an apartment together with Fran Chiasson, a friend she had met in prison. They bought a dog they called Scoobie-Doo and were getting along as best they could. In her post-parole phase, Janise signed up for a course at a business college, but later called Manson, who got her out of a horrendously burdensome contract. By now she had no judgment about matters of that nature.

On the weekend of 29–30 September 1989, she and Fran were driving together on Highway 401, near Coburg, Ontario, about 120 kilometres

west of Kingston. Janise was at the wheel. They had thought the steering had been a bit loose the previous week. Janise, never a good driver,
lost control of the car and crossed the median. Their car was hit by an
oncoming vehicle. Janise was killed instantly; Fran was uninjured. Fran
had become a Buddhist in prison, and Janise had converted to that re-
ligion as well, but the funeral service, organized by her mother (who
has since died) was Christian. Irving and Manson attended, and Irving
recalls that Fran fled the funeral in a state of near hysteria.

On 13 November 1990, Irving wrote to *the fifth estate* about the se-
quel to their 7 December 1982 program entitled "Janise." He recount-
ed briefly the series of court decisions and advised that she had been
released on at least partial parole in May 1989. "She was, as your program made her appear, a lively and courageous person who had never
done anything to warrant spending thirteen years of her life in prison."
His concluding paragraph began with the words "Unlucky to the end."
It is an apt title for this account of her life.

Janise's death also seemed to bring some sense of closure to Calgary,
despite the depth of animosity it showed whenever her name came up.
"It's been an ongoing thing and this is the finality of it," said Mike
Dungey for the Calgary Police Association. Ernie Reimer, the former
Calgary police chief, who had publicly voiced his anger at the time of
the Supreme Court ruling, was subdued on learning of her death but
no less critical. "She was no innocent victim," he said from Regina,
where he was then chief of that city's police force. "She knew what was
going on, and was very much a part of things." He had been equally
unhappy with the parole decision and had little sympathy with Janise,
believing that she had been responsible for the death of his friend and
fellow police officer. He had helped train Harrison as a junior officer,
played football with him, and shared the occasional beer. "He had
both men out with their hands on the roof of the car," Reimer recalled.
"You can't relive it and determine just what happened, but there's good
reason to believe he [Harrison] had things under control." Then Janise
Gamble burst from the car with a gun, screaming. "She distracted
him," Reimer said.

The inmates and prison officials at Kingston were distraught at
Janise's sudden death. "I feel sorry for the people there [Calgary] who
didn't get to know the Janise we knew," said Kas Fehr, an inmate at the
Prison for Women who knew Gamble for six years and at times shared
a living unit with her. "She had gone through a lot of changes and a
did a lot of growing up here – and this is not the ideal place to grow

up. In here people were ecstatic for her when she got out. There's a lot of lifers in here who watched her fight the battle and she inspired them. " The prison's inmate committee sent flowers to Gamble's family in Peterborough and planned a memorial service for her. "It's really heartbreaking," said Fehr. "She was just beginning her life, just beginning to live and learn what life is all about."

Donna Morrin, deputy warden of Kingston's Prison for Women said, "When she first came here she was very young, very scared, very impressionable. She was terrified and it was a difficult adjustment for her. She had nothing going for her. She was doomed to spend the next 25 years of her life in jail." She grew to become a "very likable, bright" inmate, Morrin said. "Finally she gets a break for a normal life, and this car accident befalls her."

Allan Manson echoed that sentiment. "It's very, very sad that she won't have that opportunity. She was working very hard to be a serious and responsible person in our society."

CHAPTER 14

CONCLUSION

We may have to accept that we will never know for certain what knowledge Janise had of what was going on at the Inglewood Credit Union on 12 March 1976 and what she may have done at the scene of the shooting that followed. Gamble and Janise are both dead. Tracie Perry, huddled on the floor of the front seat of the car, saw nothing.

Nichols, himself now out on parole, declined to participate in the preparation of this book. I had hoped that he might be willing to shed some light on what really happened and perhaps confirm – or deny – that Janise had not been involved in the events of 12–14 March 1976, other than to have been the wrong person in the wrong place at the wrong time. Nichols was the first person in Alberta to get parole on the basis of section 745, the so-called "faint hope" provision, of the Criminal Code, which is designed to encourage better behaviour and rehabilitation among long-term prisoners. If such inmates know that no matter what they do and how they behave, it will make no difference to their sentences, there is a tendency not to improve and to move to the lowest common denominator, resulting in increased risk to corrections staff. Nichols was given day parole under this provision in 1993 and full parole on 13 March 1996.

All too predictably, this did not sit well with many in Calgary, although there was more objection voiced when Janise got her parole, perhaps because it was that much sooner. Harrison's widow issued a statement through a retired Calgary police superintendent, Ron Tarrant: "I'm very distressed at the decision and disappointed with the justice system. It seems to be very unfair." Tarrant himself, president of the Calgary Police Veterans' Association, said, "It's shameful … they replaced capital punishment with the promise of 25 years and then they caved in. What bothers me is if you replace capital punishment with 25 years without parole and then you start handing out parole, some people might suggest that's a signal to police officers not to be as thoughtful and considerate as Keith Harrison – but to fire first and ask questions afterwards. With the prevalence of handguns and weapons in the '90s, we may see people in uniform taking less risks."

Calgary Police Chief Gerry Borbridge, said, "I'm pleased they did not release him immediately. The death of Staff Sgt. Keith Harrison was cold blooded and we have to have penalties which are consistent with this type of crime."

RETROSPECTIVE POLICE INTERVIEW

Nichols did, however, give a videotaped interview after his conviction to police officer M. Miller, for purposes of a police training exercise. In the interview he makes it clear that neither of the women knew what was going on and that the gun beside the road was Gamble's.

> MILLER: You are about to see the convicted slayer of Detective Sergeant Keith Harrison. Bill Nichols will describe the events which took place on the 12th of March, 1976, as he and his partner held up the Inglewood Credit Union in Calgary, Alberta.
> We pick the story up at approximately 15:15 hours. John Gamble and Bill Nichols have just held up the Credit Union of approximately $1,600 and are running towards their getaway car parked at the rear of that same Credit Union.
> NICHOLS: As we were walking up to the car there was a car parked behind us just about half a car lengths behind the guy and the guy says out his window, "Hey, what are you doing?" Well, who's he? You know, some green Chevelle and a guy in a suit,

brown suit, who's he? We got in the car. The girls were sittin' in the back. Well, Janise was, Tracie was in the front passenger's. We come back and Janise had moved to the front so, it's not the time to argue about who's driving.

MILLER: Yeah.

NICHOLS: Well, let's go.

MILLER: Is this a four-door car? So Janise is sitting in the front?

NICHOLS: Right, in the driver's seat.

MILLER: Oh, she's in the driver's seat.

NICHOLS: Yeah.

MILLER: And you're in the –

NICHOLS: Now I get behind her.

MILLER: In the –

NICHOLS: Driver's side in the back.

MILLER: In the back. And John is sitting in the front?

NICHOLS: No, in the back on the passenger side.

MILLER: And the other, and the girl –

NICHOLS: Tracie, Tracie is in the front.

MILLER: Gotcha.

NICHOLS: So I said, "Let's go," so she just drove off.

MILLER: Yeah.

NICHOLS: I was directing – ah, first of all, before she drove away, like she is not in any hurry.

MILLER: No.

NICHOLS: She doesn't know, they don't know there's a bank been robbed.

MILLER: That's right. (*laughter*)

NICHOLS: So she's not in any hurry to get going and we're kind of settin', twiddling our thumbs as she's starting it up and getting it in gear and stuff, huh? And, ah, this guy who'd yelled at us, uh walked up beside the car, and sort of stood beside the car and looked at us.

MILLER: Yeah.

NICHOLS: Kinda strange. We looked up at him, he looked back and then he walked back and got in his car.

MILLER: Yeah.

NICHOLS: And we drove off. I directed Janise where to drive, and this guy started following us. So I looked back when he started following us and saw his licence plate and then I knew he was a cop.

MILLER: Oh, he was the car that come right beside you?

NICHOLS: Yeah. This was Harrison, Keith Harrison. I knew he was as soon as I checked his licence plate.

MILLER: How did you know from looking at his licence plate that it was a cop?

NICHOLS: Because you people, generally, [buy] all your licence plates at once.

MILLER: (*Laughter*)

NICHOLS: So, you know, your first two letters are always the same.

MILLER: Yeah.

NICHOLS: Whether a cruiser or a ...

MILLER: That's interesting.

NICHOLS: There're all close to the others to begin with.

MILLER: Yeah, that's right exactly, 'cause the guy goes out and buys them all at the same time.

NICHOLS: Yup.

MILLER: Yeah.

NICHOLS: So that's one sure way of keeping the identification.

MILLER: Yeah.

NICHOLS: So now I know we are in trouble. Now at this point, being as screwed up as I was both mentally and emotionally, I am into this head space where I'd made a deal with my partner that we go all the way. No one stops us.

MILLER: Yeah.

NICHOLS: So, I am actually a bomb being driven along in a car.

MILLER: Yeah.

NICHOLS: I'm just thinking, you know –

MILLER: Were you drugged up at the time?

NICHOLS: No. I don't have to be, I'm just crazy without it.

MILLER: Yeah. Oh yeah.

NICHOLS: At that point being to, my logic and my emotion being so out of kilter I'm –

MILLER: Yup.

NICHOLS: I'm sorta on a trip by itself.

MILLER: Yup.

NICHOLS: I'm not functioning as normal, eh? So I told Janise to make a left turn at this light.

MILLER: Yup.

NICHOLS: She did, she went through the light. She went

through it on an amber. She was going to stop … told her to go through.

MILLER: Yeah.

NICHOLS: And she went through.

MILLER: Yeah.

NICHOLS: And when she went through and made the left and when he came through on the red, then that confirmed that he was a police office, proof positive that this was a cop.

MILLER: Yup.

NICHOLS: So now I told Janise, well, pull over, let me drive. She still doesn't know what's happening.

MILLER: Yeah.

NICHOLS: This is cool. She pulls over to the side. I open the passenger door on the driver's side.

MILLER: Yeah.

NICHOLS: I steps out, and as I'm getting out, I say to Janise, I said, "Just jump over," like over the seat.

MILLER: Yeah.

NICHOLS: So I get out and I close the door. Now this, when I was gettin' out, I took the gun out.

MILLER: Yeah.

NICHOLS: And I don't know whether she seen it or not, but I think she did and she sort of went, "Wow, what's going on?" She had no idea what began …

MILLER: Yup.

NICHOLS: She figured we were going to Toronto. (*laughter*)

MILLER: (*laughter*) Yeah.

NICHOLS: I got out of the car. I closed the door and I got the gun in front of me and I opened the driver's door. Harrison at this time had gotten out of his car, drawn his gun and aimed it at me and yelled, "Drop your gun" and when I looked back at him, he's a car length, two car lengths, away

MILLER: Yeah.

NICHOLS: And he's, this is, really threw me off here. I wasn't sure he was a cop anymore because he's screaming.

MILLER: Well, very excited.

NICHOLS: Very excited, very agitated and he's screaming, "Get out of the fucking car, get out of the car, drop your guns, drop your guns!" He hasn't identified himself, he isn't in uniform, he is in some little junky Chevelle that you can't tell is a police car, the last thing you would expect the licence plates, now I'm starting to think twice, it doesn't matter to me anyways, really, when it come down to it, at that point, I'm going to figure a way out of this no matter ...

MILLER: Who you cornered.

NICHOLS: Yeah.

MILLER: Yup.

NICHOLS: I'm on a stuck trip anyway.

MILLER: Yeah.

NICHOLS: So he start yelling, "Get out of the car, drop your guns!" so I wasn't going to drop it on the ground. If I had of, chances are, he still would be alive today.

MILLER: Yeah.

NICHOLS: What I did was place it on the roof of the car.

MILLER: Yeah.

NICHOLS: I assumed the position with one hand on each side of the gun, so my hands are here ...

MILLER: Yeah.

NICHOLS: And the gun between.

MILLER: In the middle of them.

NICHOLS: Yeah. He switched his attention to Johnny getting out of the car.

MILLER: Johnny's on the passenger side, rear passenger.

NICHOLS: Now he took my other .38 and threw it into the snow.

MILLER: Who did? The fellow getting out of the car?

NICHOLS: Yep.

MILLER: Getting out of the side of the car.

NICHOLS: Yes.

MILLER: Threw it out.

NICHOLS: Yeah, he takes the .38 and he throws it in the snow.

MILLER: Yeah.

NICHOLS: There is this Luger in his belt.

MILLER: Right.

NICHOLS: Puts his hand on the trunk and he looked over at me and he said, "What now?" and Harrison starts yelling, "Get out of the car, get out of the fucking car!" Tracie opened the front door to get out, I put my head down and told her, "Get on the floor, don't get out of the car, get on the floor." Janise, meanwhile, was getting out the back door and she's ah, pretty rambunctious trying to get out of the car.

MILLER: Yeah.

NICHOLS: I guess she was pretty scared, as Tracie was, Tracie was crying.

MILLER: And excited, yeah.

NICHOLS: I hear some shots, I don't know to this day why. I don't know if Johnny had made a move or just the act of Janise scrambling out of the car like that or what it was when he took a shot. I was, because I am already looking for an opening, I grabbed the gun off the roof and turned and started exchanging shots with him. He couldn't shoot back at us very well. Johnny pulled his gun and started shooting because we sort of have him in the crossfire from the rear right trunk to the front driver's door.

MILLER: Right.

NICHOLS: At his car which he's behind the driver's door.

MILLER: He's still behind his own driver's door.

NICHOLS: Yeah.

MILLER: Did you both, were you shooting at, did you, did you consciously make a – do you remember where you were shooting?

NICHOLS: I was shooting to hit him.

MILLER: What part of the, for example?

NICHOLS: Chest area.

MILLER: Chest area, yeah.

NICHOLS: The biggest area to hit. Like the movies I see, guys shoot a gun ...

MILLER: Yeah.

NICHOLS: The guy falls down, well, I don't think that's all too accurate.

MILLER: Yeah.

NICHOLS: Unless you're Gene Kelly in a movie or something.

MILLER: Yeah.

NICHOLS: It's just, you shoot to get to the biggest area.

MILLER: Biggest area, so he must have been shooting through the window, eh, if he was standing behind the door?

NICHOLS: Well, he was behind the door, no, he was down below the door, he was crouched and he is shooting like this over the door.

MILLER: Yeah.

NICHOLS: Between the frame and the frame of the windshield.

MILLER: And standing on the ground.

NICHOLS: Yeah, so I guess firing – crossfire – sort of got him

nervous and he started to move back towards the rear of his vehicle.
MILLER: Yeah.
NICHOLS: When he did that, he left the protection of the front door and I could see him.
MILLER: Yeah.
NICHOLS: I shot him.
MILLER: Maybe, just before we end it, is there something that you, Bill Nichols, would like to leave with the audience, maybe just as something generally, like to leave …
NICHOLS: Just to always, always, be aware, totally aware, that you can't do things on your own.
MILLER: Yeah.
NICHOLS: In any situation, forcing something too soon will only cause chaos.

This is completely contrary to what Nichols had said to Detective Goetjen, which had been ruled as admissible evidence during the trial. In this version, Janise had no idea of the robbery and had no gun, but was responding to the directions of Harrison to get out of the car – probably, and with good reason, terrified. Her knowledge of and indeed participation in the robbery and the possession of a gun at the time of the shootout were essential links in the Crown's case against her for the murder of Harrison. Remove those two planks, and a conviction would have been far more difficult to achieve. Nichols's statement about recognizing the police licence plates is obviously complete nonsense; it is inconceivable that he would have been noting the licence plate numbers of Calgary police vehicles at the time.

On the other hand, Nichols, at the time leading up to the trial, would probably have said anything, whether true or not, that he thought might have helped his defence. He would hardly have been worried about perjury. What would they do – put him in prison for longer-than-life? The subsequent statement in the interview was made at a time when there were no competing interests and he had nothing to gain from lying as opposed to telling the truth. It does not, however, square fully with some of the evidence obtained from the wiretaps at the time (which, fortunately for Janise, had been ruled inadmissible at the trial) and with the evidence of Diane Perry, in which it seemed clear, to Perry at least, that Janise was looking for her own gun.

Her conduct may have been reconcilable with the suicide pact and the need to make it look like she had been involved, but that was a construction of events framed long after the fact. Still, it is difficult to imagine that someone in her position, from her background, with no evident knowledge of firearms, could have been transformed so thoroughly in the space of a few months – even living with a monster like Gamble – into someone who would come charging out of a car to confront an armed police officer. The particular gun, with the pearl handle, which had been found beside the road, was, according to Nichols, not even one of the guns that had been stolen in Vancouver in the break and enter before they had so precipitously left. It was one that Nichols had purchased in Coquitlam some time before. There are, nevertheless, some unanswered questions that remain troubling.

There was an eyewitness who identified Janise as someone outside the credit union and who picked her out of a lineup that included Tracie Perry, the person who was acknowledged to have left the car during the time of the holdup. Unreliable as such evidence may be, the witness was not shaken or moved from her identification of Janise. Regardless of who fired the first shot at the scene, it seemed indisputable that it was her exit from the car, with or without a gun, that was the immediate cause of the destabilization of the situation. It is true that no witness ever saw her with a gun and the one found by the roadside had not been fired, but it is not impossible to see what a jury might think. The fingerprint on the envelope could easily have been explained, especially in the circumstances of her jumping from the front seat to the crowded back seat where Gamble had the envelope from the credit union. It was probably more likely than not that she would have touched it at some point in the confusing circumstances, so a reasonable doubt could easily have been created as to the significance of the fingerprint.

Nichols certainly did not help, and even if his statement to the police was intended to be self-serving in the futile self-defence argument and was admissible only with respect to him, the jurors all heard it and would have had an impossible job to dismiss it from their minds when they came to consider Janise's portion of their verdict. He was more helpful when cross-examined by Macdonald, but by then it seems pretty clear that the jury would have had trouble believing him about even what day of the week he might have said it was.

It is not fair to second-guess trial counsel regarding decisions made under the pressure of that process, and there is no doubt that Macdonald and Pope did what they thought was in the best interests of their client at the time. At this stage, whether they were right or wrong is not important. They were dealing with a young woman who had been incarcerated for eight months, thousands of miles from her home, whose husband had killed himself in the course of the events for which she had been charged, who was twenty-two years old and completely over her head in the midst of a murder trial. It had been their plan, as part of her defence, to have her testify on her own behalf. The lawyers knew full well that, legal theory of the presumption of innocence notwithstanding, most juries want to hear from the accused and to form their own opinion of the person whose guilt they may have to determine. Of course, the accused is entitled to rely on the right to remain silent, but counsel know it is generally best to put their clients on the stand.

It is easy to imagine the dread with which Janise faced the trial. Throughout the entire time, she had been moderately to heavily sedated with 50 mg of Gravol, injected every morning at 8:30, and with Anafranil, 25 mg, as well as Dalmane, 30 mg, for seven days from 19 November. Whatever the case, on 1 December, the day she was supposed to testify, she was so distraught – shaking, her eyes rolling wildly in her head – that Macdonald determined she would be unable to be of any use to her own defence. He told her he was afraid she would break down. He may have been right. Another view was that she knew she would be cross-examined by Chrumka and that she had enough guilty knowledge that she was afraid to give evidence. The end of that road and, with it, the only opportunity for her to have told her story, came that afternoon, when Macdonald stood up to say, "My lord, Janise Gamble calls no evidence." He would have to deal with that decision when he addressed the jury.

In retrospect, there was some element of good fortune for Janise in the makeup of the particular panel of the Supreme Court of Canada that heard the final appeal. It was only five judges when it might have been seven or nine, and of the five judges, three – enough to compose a majority – were the dissenting members of the Court in the earlier appeal of *Stevens, Laviolette*, on the basis of which the chief justice had asked whether Irving and Manson still wanted to proceed with their application for leave, given the decision in that matter. Designation of the panels is the nominal responsibility of the chief justice. Depending on the level of mind game one might wish to play, it would have been easy to ensure that a majority of the panel had been part of the majority in

the *Stevens, Laviolette* appeal, or to designate a seven-judge panel, so
that the dissenters in that case could not have prevailed. We may never
know whether the choice of the panel, of which the chief justice was a
member, might have been deliberately designed to achieve the humanitarian outcome contended for in the special circumstances – with
strong dissents, so that the effects of the decision could be whittled
down in later cases. That outcome has in fact occurred, although the
case still stands for the principle of a liberal interpretation of the Charter where *habeas corpus* is involved.

Eventually the procedural barrage put in the way of examining the
real question – a tactical decision by the three levels of Crown attorneys – backfired. Had they focused on the meat of the issue, that no
matter how it was positioned by Irving and Manson, Janise's application to be declared eligible for parole prior to the expiration of twenty-
five years was in reality an indirect attack on the conviction, they
might have fared better. They could also have argued that the whole
matter of Janise's having been charged under the wrong provision had
already been dealt with by the Supreme Court of Canada when it had
denied leave to appeal back in 1978, even though the Charter of Rights
and Freedoms was not yet in force.

But the positioning Irving and Manson adopted on Janise's behalf
was particularly seductive. They took no issue with the conviction and
did not seek a new trial. They simply argued that the wrong section of
the Criminal Code had been used to charge her and that the current
effect of the sentence imposed was, in the circumstances, a cruel and
unusual punishment under the Charter. They did not seek to overturn
the conviction but simply to have her declared eligible for parole, following which her case could be considered by the National Parole
Board, using its standard criteria for the purpose. It was in the early
days of the Charter and the courts were working their way through its
ramifications. They knew that rights created under the Charter had to
be clothed with appropriate remedies, some of which might require
changes in the traditional approach to enforcement of rights.

Whether or not Janise played any part in the death of Keith Harrison on 12 March 1976, she paid a huge price. In any comparison with
Nichols and Gamble, she was at best an insignificant player and was in
all probability simply dragged along in the vortex they created. They
were hardened recidivists, both demonstrably capable of violent crimes,
including murder. She was in the thrall of a brutal sociopath, desper-

ately hoping that she could change his ways and provide an anchor that he seemed never to have known. That such an effort was doomed was apparent to almost everyone but her. Gamble's final demonstration of his so-called love for her was to push her out of the house on 13 March, knowing that she would be facing a murder charge that he and Nichols, the guilty parties, were intending to escape through suicide. Why would she even consider staying with someone like Gamble? The human condition is difficult, at best, to comprehend. A battered-wife syndrome is even more so:

> And I didn't get a chance. I didn't get a chance. Like there were so many questions in Calgary like that they asked me if she was so afraid of this man, why didn't she leave him? Why didn't they ask me what I'd been through for ten months with this man? If you had someone sitting there telling you that you were the only hope in the world that they had, and that without you they would just die and fade away to nothing, then could you walk away from someone like that? Especially someone you married, someone you in church married and said that I vow that I will help you whether it's good or it's bad? Could I walk out on him when the times got bad? Because the times were good. We used to go for snow walks in the middle of the night, make snowmen, you know. I made him decorate Christmas trees. He hadn't had Christmas since he was eleven. Could you leave someone like that when he really needed you? I couldn't. I couldn't. It wasn't a case of right or wrong then with me. I wasn't thinking that. All I was thinking was need and devotion. I loved him an awful lot for what he was inside, not the bad part I saw, because they were always over with. Like when they were through, they were through, and he was always the man I loved and the man I married, the man that wanted kids, the man that tried to make it but just never had any background to base it on. I love him still today for what he was.

She spent fourteen years behind bars, most of that time in the toughest women's prison in Canada, during which time there was, deliberately, nothing available to help prepare her for eventual return to society. She was obviously no danger to the community. Ironically, not long after the lengthy legal battle to get her declared eligible for parole,

she might have been able to avail herself of the same "faint hope" provision on which Nichols, by far the more guilty of the two, relied to
get out on parole.

Had this been the case, she would not have been at the wheel of her
car on that fall weekend in 1990.

Unlucky to the end.

INDEX

Note: In order to distinguish Janise from John Gamble, the latter is referred to as JFG in subheadings. Janise Gamble is referred to as Janise.

acquittals, 138, 141, 149
adopted admissions, 117, 121
aiding and abetting, 145–6, 164
Alberta: attorney general, 199, 203, 209–10; Court of Appeal, 160–9, 174, 182, 185, 192, 193, 194–5, 196, 200, 202; Crimes Compensation Board, 88; Janise's conviction and sentence in, 208
Alcan, 89
alcohol, 55
Alex Cristal Tool Town Ltd., 11
Anderson, Holly, 111
André, Harvie, 90
anti-social personality disorder, 6
appeals, 138, 139, 155–7, 164–5, 169, 172, 193–4, 195, 199, 213, 231, 232
Arbour, Louise, 176
Armstead, Joan, 32

bail: JFG and, 22, 23, 87, 89–90, 154; Nichols and, 22, 23, 61, 89–90, 154; reform, 90
Bardell, Derek, 217
Barnes, John, 39
Basford, Ron, 90
battered-wife syndrome, 233
Bechtold, Roger Allan, 113, 116–17
Beefers, Gerry, 39
Beetz, Jean, 202, 203, 205, 210, 212
Belanger, Jacques, 218
bench memos, 205
Black Friday, 37–8
Borbridge, Gerry, 223
Brinks robbery (proposed), 22–3, 26, 46, 61
British Columbia Supreme Court, 215
Browning, Ruth, 173–4
burden of proof, 140–1, 209
Bureyko, Michael, 16, 17
Burns Funds, 89
Butlin, James A., 94, 129
"by his own act," 181–2, 183n

Cairns, Richard A., 94, 132–3
Canada Evidence Act, 100–1
Canadian Charter of Rights and Freedoms, 186, 187, 232; cruel and unusual punishment under, 232; Dunbar and Logan killings and, 191; *habeas corpus* and, 213; retrospective applications of, 192, 200, 205–7, 210, 212, 213; section 7, 189, 207, 209; section 11(i), 200; section 24(1), 208
capital punishment, 70–1, 168–9, 209
Casey, Jeff, 202–3
Chartrand, Real, 217
Chekaluck, G.M., 94
Chiasson, Fran, 219–20
Chrumka, Paul: appeal by, 159–60; and ban on publicity, 101; and charges against Tracie Perry, 87; closing statement, 135–8; and compulsion defence, 151; and Galloway, 115, 116; and Homan's identification of Janise, 109–10; on Janise and guns, 121; and Janise as lookout, 98; and Janise's coat, 108; and Janise's not testifying, 231; opening statement, 102–3; and police lineup, 106; and severance application, 100–1; before Supreme Court of Canada, 169
cigarettes, 64, 65–6
civil trials, criminal trials vs., 104
Coates, Sid, 40–1, 42–3
Cole, David, 171
Cole, Janice, 184
collateral attacks on court decisions, 192, 200, 202
common intention, 101, 146, 158, 159, 164–5, 182
compulsion, defence of, 150–2. *See also* duress, defence of
Connelly, Al, 80
convictions, 139
Copeland, Paul, 171
Correctional Law Project, 171
Coté, Denis, 86
courts of appeal, 156. *See also names of courts*
Cox, John, 32, 178
credibility, 141–2

crimes compensation legislation, 89
Criminal Code: changes to bail, 90; "faint hope" provision, 222–3, 234; in judge's charge to jury, 143; section 17, 150, 151–2; section 18, 151; section 21, 148, 152; sections 25–27, 162; section 213 (d), 164; section 214, 166–7; section 218(1), 99; section 576.1, 101; section 617, 172, 177; section 669, 152–3; section 672, 183; section 745, 222–3, 234; wiretaps in, 163
Criminal Law Amendment Act No. 2, 166–7, 168, 174–5, 183, 194
criminal lawyers, 63, 70, 72, 93–4
Crosbie, John, 182–3, 186, 187, 188
Crossroads Motor Hotel, 89
cruel and unusual punishment, 189, 232
Curtis, Dennis, 212, 218

Dale, Holly, 184
Davidson, Boyd, 38
Davies, Jack, 39
death penalty. *See* capital punishment
defence counsel, 135, 139; objectives of, 103–4
DeLong, Manfred, 203
Demerol: D. Perry and, 96, 124; delivery of, 66–7, 68–9, 124; in exchange for hostage, 66, 124, 129; Hogan and, 79, 86; JFG and, 59, 77; Knowler's interview and delivery of, 63; Nichols's request for, 48, 53, 54, 62; quantity of, 65; as substitute for heroin, 55–6, 59
Denis' Trucking, 89
Diamond, Bonnie, 211
Dick, Tom, 37–8
Dickson, Brian, 202, 203, 205, 210, 212, 214
Dilaudid, 80
Dredge, Ann, 106, 111
drugs, 5–6, 47, 58, 62, 63, 64–5, 68, 72, 75–6, 81, 84–6
Dubienski (surgeon), 137–8
Dunbar and Logan, R. v., 191–2, 196
Dungey, Michael, 211, 217, 219, 220
duress, defence of, 173, 182. *See also* compulsion, defence of

Elizabeth Fry Society, 170, 205, 211,
216–17, 218
envelope, 113–17, 134, 136
Estey, Willard, 199, 201, 202
evidence, 139; admissibility of, 99, 100,
101, 121, 129; appeals and, 156; credibility
of, 141–2; in Crown opening statement,
102–3; direct vs. circumstantial, 142–3;
jury assessment of, 141–2; in murder trials, 103; prejudicial, 104; review of,
143–4; of witnesses, 103
eyewitness reports, 31–4, 95, 98, 103,
112–13

Fainstein, S. Ronald, 177–8, 182, 199,
200–1
Farran, Roy, 84–5, 90
Farrier, Audrey, 211
Federal Court of Appeal, 208
Fehr, Kas, 220–1
Ferguson, Simone, 211
fifth estate, 74, 172, 179, 181, 184–5, 220
fingerprints, 113, 114–17, 128, 133–4, 136,
147
flight, resisting arrest by, 162, 163–4, 182
Foster, Jim, 86–7
Fraser, Bruce, 196
Fritz, Lanny, 33–4

Gagnon, Philippe, 37–8
Gallagher, Pat, 4
Galloway, Robert John, 113–16
Gamble, Janise Marie: abuse by JFG, 9–10,
11–12, 12, 25, 112, 173, 178; admissibility
of evidence against, 100; and Alberta
Court of Appeal, 155, 157–8, 164–5;
amnesty for, 72–3, 75, 77, 78–9, 80, 81,
137, 180; appeals to Supreme Court of
Canada, 169, 172, 199; in Calgary, 25–40;
charges against, 82, 84, 98, 187; in closing statements, 133–8; coat, 106, 107,
108, 111, 118, 125, 137; compulsion defence and, 150–1; conviction of, 152–3,
174–5; Crown's case against, 105; and D.
Perry, 117, 122, 126, 136, 137, 181, 211;
death of, 219–21; depression, 204–5; as
driver of getaway car, 27, 28, 96–7, 98,

100, 104, 112, 128, 129, 134, 136; duress,
defence of, 173, 182; early life, 3–4; and
envelope, 113–14, 116, 136, 165, 178; family of, 93; fingerprints, 100, 113, 114,
115–16, 136, 147, 178, 230; and guns, 29,
34, 93, 98, 100, 112–13, 117, 118, 119–21,
124–7, 128, 130, 134, 137, 147–8, 178, 229;
and Hogan, 85; and hostage-takings, 35,
36, 42, 62, 100, 117, 123, 124, 148; identified by Homan, 107–10; imprisonment
of, 169, 175–7, 189, 203, 232, 233–4; indictment, 98–9; involvement of, 77, 78,
80–1, 104–5, 130–1, 143–4, 165, 173,
229–30; and JFG's fight with Molinaro,
17–18, 20; and JFG's suicide, 72, 74–5;
leads no evidence at trial, 130–1, 133,
134–5, 172–3, 175, 182, 231; leg run over,
29, 96, 124, 147; in lineup, 136, 178, 230;
as lookout, 27, 98, 147, 165; marriage,
6–7; and media, 218; miscarriage of justice for, 168, 172; and mother, 75, 180–1,
182; new trial for, 172; and Ontario
Court of Appeal, 193–5; parole for,
209–10, 211–12, 216–19; police lineup,
105–6, 110–11; preliminary hearing, 94–8,
108; purse, 118, 126, 137; relationship
with JFG, 4–5, 22, 74, 81, 134, 137, 181,
182, 232–3; and robbery of Inglewood
Credit Union, 26–7, 76, 98, 100, 104,
114, 129, 134, 144, 179, 222, 229; Royal
Prerogative of Mercy for, 172, 175–83;
sentencing of, 165–9, 175, 195, 196, 201,
206, 207, 208; in Shannon's charge to
jury, 143–4, 145–8; and shooting of Harrison, 34, 76, 104, 112, 128, 135–8, 143,
145–7, 148–9, 152, 158, 174, 179–80, 181,
222, 224–8, 230; and suicide, 72, 74–5,
82, 137, 180–1, 204; in Vancouver, 8–24;
in work program, 212
Gamble, John Frederick: abuse of Janise,
9–10, 12, 25, 112, 173, 178; and bail, 22,
23, 87, 89–90, 154; break-and-enter at
Alex Cristal Tool Town, 11; in Calgary,
25–40; childhood of, 8–9; and D. Perry,
36–7, 95, 122, 123–4, 126; drinking of, 8,
9–10, 11, 12, 13; and drugs, 5–6, 10, 59,
62, 77; exit strategy, 75–6; fight with

Molinaro, 16–20; fingerprints of, 116; and guns, 113, 119–21; history of imprisonment, 5; and Hogan, 76–7, 79–80, 181; hostage-takings, 35, 123–4; house robbery in Vancouver, 23; leaves Vancouver, 23–4; in Millbrook Reformatory, 4, 5; mother, 6, 8–9; negotiations with police, 39, 40–1, 46–7, 48–53, 58, 59–60, 180, 181; and Nichols, 21, 22, 54, 55, 71–2; in Ontario Institution for the Criminally Insane, 5; psychology of, 6; relationship with Janise, 4–5, 6–7, 22, 74, 81, 134, 137, 181; in Richmond General Hospital, 14–15; robbery of Inglewood Credit Union, 26–7; and shooting of Harrison, 28–30, 34, 227, 228; suicide of, 72, 74–5, 81, 82, 83–4, 128, 129, 180, 181, 233; surrender of, 77–8, 79–80, 83, 124, 128; temperament of, 134; and Tidsbury, 15–16, 17, 18–19; in Vancouver, 8–24

Gertler, Franklin, 202

getaway car, 27, 28, 30, 95–6, 98, 100, 104, 112, 128, 129, 134, 136, 137, 162

Goetjen, Leslie Herbert, 105–6, 110–11, 112, 127–8, 130, 133, 144–5, 157, 229

Gordon, Garde, 90

Gorman, John, 87–8

Goulard, Guy, 199, 200, 201

Graham, Nick, 38

Green, Doug, 58, 68–71, 179

Greene, James, 188

Greenwood, R.G.T., 33–4, 106, 179

Gregorish, Harvey, 38

guns: Harrison's, 95, 113; in hostage siege, 41–2, 56–7, 60–1, 77, 79; and Ingram house, 39; Janise and, 29, 34, 93, 98, 100, 112–13, 117, 118, 119–21, 124–7, 128, 130, 134, 137, 147–8, 178, 229, 230; JFG and, 77, 79, 113, 119–21; Nichols and, 41–2, 56–7, 60–1, 112, 113; ownership of, 121; in shootout with Harrison, 28–9, 112–13; Tracie Perry and, 125

habeas corpus, 187, 189, 192, 194, 197, 200, 201, 208, 209–10, 213, 232

Hanachuk, Marcia, 111

Hansen Interior Decorators, 89

Harrison, Allan Keith: in Chrumka's closing statement, 135; death of, 61, 62, 68, 180, 181; emergency surgery, 36–7, 45; funeral of, 90; guns, 113; killing of, 179–80; knowledge that he was a police officer, 158, 159, 161, 163, 164, 174; penalty for murder of, 71; Reimer on, 220; and robbery of credit union, 27–8, 61; shooting of, 31, 32, 33, 34, 93, 95, 112–13, 127–8, 159, 178–9, 223–9

Harrison, Kevin, 210–11, 217, 218

Harrison, Pat, 219, 223

Hartford, J.J., 130

Hautzinger, Joe, 41, 44–57, 58, 59–60, 61–3, 64, 65

Hawkes, Jim, 217

hearsay, 117

helicopter, 44–5, 47, 57, 61

heroin, 6, 55, 59, 77, 78, 79, 80, 85, 180

Hewko, Lawrence, 114, 115

Hogan, Jim, 76–82, 83–4, 85–6, 91, 130, 137, 179, 181, 211

Hogg, Peter, 213–14

Homan, Sharon Lea, 106–10, 111, 134, 136, 147, 178, 230

hostages and hostage-takings: admissions made to, 160; D. Perry taken, 35–6; Hogan and, 76; Janise and, 35, 36, 42, 62, 100, 117, 123, 124, 148; Jivrajs taken, 35; killing threats, 63, 64; media and, 91; numbers of, 64; police standoff and, 37, 38–9, 58–9, 69, 70; release of, 63, 64–5, 66, 67, 68, 72, 77, 79, 81, 82, 84, 85, 129; Tracie as, 64; tying-up of, 123

Houlden, Lloyd, 193–4

Hunter, John, 32, 178

Imperial Oil, 89

Inglewood Credit Union robbery, 26–7, 96, 100, 178; Galloway and, 113; Harrison and, 61, 162; Homan's evidence, 107, 108–10; Janise and, 26–7, 76, 98, 100, 104, 114, 129, 134, 144, 179, 222, 229; money from, 46; Tracie Perry's evidence, 112; women and, 72, 129, 222.

Ingram, David, 36, 88–9

Ingram, Elaine, 36, 89
investigative journalism, 184–5
Irving, Colin, 232: congratulatory letters to, 213–14; contacts Manson, 186–7; correspondence with Janise, 185–7, 188–9, 190–3, 195–6, 201–2, 204, 214–15; and *the fifth estate*, 185, 220; at Janise's funeral, 220; and judgment of Supreme Court, 204–5; and *Milne* decision, 199–200; and Ontario Court of Appeal, 193–4, 195; and Ontario Supreme Court, 190–1; seeks meeting with Crosbie, 188; on Supreme Court decision, 211, 212; visits to Janise, 188, 192, 204

Jivraj, Laila, 35, 36, 43, 64, 88, 97–8, 118, 123, 125, 148
Jivraj, Rahim Kassam, 35, 64, 66, 80, 97, 98, 123, 124, 148
judges, 138–9, 156
jury: charge to, 138–49, 156; closing addresses to, 132; discharge of member, 173–4; and facts, 140, 141, 164–5; judge's instructions to, 101–2, 160; media and, 154; secrecy of deliberations, 102; selection of, 99; sequestration of, 101; verdict(s), 149, 155, 164

Kain, Irene, 174
Keller, Doug, 81
Kerr, R.B., 90
Kingston Prison for Women, 3, 169, 176, 188, 203, 233
Kirby, Shaun, 111
Klein, Ralph, 37, 57
Knowler, Jim, 63–4, 70, 72, 145, 157, 163
Konechny, R. v., 200
Koster, John Frederick. *See* Gamble, John Frederick

Lamer, Antonio, 202, 203, 213
LeDain, Gerald, 199
L'Heureux-Dubé, Claire, 202
Lidster, Cathy, 11–12, 13, 16–17, 23–4
lineup, 105–7, 107–8, 110–11, 136, 178
Lozinsky, Walter, 14–15
Luffman, Ernest, 171

Lund (detective), 105–6, 111

Macdonald, Webster, Jr., 230–1: application for severance, 101; closing address, 133–5; cross-examination of D. Perry, 119–21, 126–7; cross-examination of Homan, 108–9; and D. Perry's evidence, 117; decision not to have Janise testify, 131, 231; and defence of compulsion, 151; and Galloway, 114–15; in hostage-taking, 81; Irving contacts, 185–6; Janise contacts, 93–4; and judge's charge to jury, 149–50; Manson and, 172; and police lineup, 106; in preliminary hearing, 94, 98; severance application by, 99–100; before Supreme Court of Canada, 169
Macdonald, Webster, Sr., 94
MacGuigan, Mark, 177
McKay, William John, 32
MacKenzie, Lloyd, 22
McMurtry, R. Roy, 171
McNeill, Don, 63
Manitoba Court of Appeal, 182, 183n
Manitoba Court of Queen's Bench, 182
Manson, Allan S.: and Irving, 186–7, 214; and Janise, 172–6, 186, 211, 219, 232; and Janise's death, 220, 221; and Ontario Court of Appeal, 193–4; and Ontario Supreme Court, 190–1; and parole for Janise, 212, 218; and prison law, 171–2; and Supreme Court of Canada, 202, 205, 211
Mathison, Jim, 18
Mayor, Dwight, 39
media: and admissibility of evidence, 101; and hostage-takings, 37, 42, 57, 63, 64, 65, 91; Janise and, 218; jury and, 154
memoranda, 139–40, 156
methadone, 82, 86, 130
Millbrook Reformatory, 4, 21
Miller, M., 223–9
Millhaven Institution, 171
Milne v. Her Majesty the Queen, 199–201, 206, 207
miscarriages of justice, 172
misdirection, by judge, 158, 161–2
Mitchell, 200–1

Molinaro, Dominic (Nick), 11–12, 13, 16–20, 18
monetary demands, 46–7, 58, 84, 86, 124
Monkman, Lorraine, 106, 111
Morrin, Donna, 221
Morrison, John ("O.J."), 10, 11, 22
Motyl, Ewa, 111

National Parole Board, 210, 211–12, 216, 218, 232
negotiations, 39, 40–1, 44–57, 81–2, 85, 86, 180, 181
Nelson, Barry, 72
Nichols, William John, 20–2: admissibility of evidence against, 100; appeal by, 155, 156–7; application to Supreme Court, 215; armed robbery plan, 22–3, 24, 26, 61; and bail, 22, 23, 61, 89–90, 154; bomb-making, 21; charges against, 93, 94, 98; in Chrumka's closing statement, 135; claims regarding guns, 41–2; closing address for, 132–3; conversation with Knowler, 72, 145, 157, 163; conviction of, 152–3; criminal record, 100; and D. Perry as hostage, 36–7; and death of Harrison, 129; defence of provocation, 157, 162; as driver of getaway car, 30, 137; early life, 20–1; exoneration of Janise and Tracie, 62, 77, 148; extortion by, 21; flight of, 163–4; on giving names to police, 118–19; guns, 112, 113; and handwriting on envelope, 116; hospital statement, 127–8; house robbery in Vancouver, 23; identities given to police, 125–6; on imprisonment, 71; indictment, 98–9; and Janise's involvement, 77, 78; on JFG's state of mind, 54, 55; knowledge that Harrison was police officer, 158, 159, 161, 163, 164, 174; leaves Vancouver, 23–4; meets JFG, 21, 22; Miller interview with, 223–9; negotiations with police, 39, 40, 41–3, 44–8, 53–7, 58, 59, 60–72, 123–4, 180, 181; parole, 222–3, 234; preliminary hearing, 94–8; robbery of Inglewood Credit Union, 26–7, 112; self-defence argument, 104, 129, 145, 156–7, 159, 160–2, 230; shootout with Harrison, 28, 29–30,

31, 34; statement to Goetjen, 112, 144–5, 157, 229; statements given to detectives, 159; statements to reporters, 179; and suicide, 70, 71–2, 75–6, 82, 83, 128, 129, 180, 181, 233; surrender of, 77–8, 79–80, 81, 83, 124, 128; taking of hostages from Thunderbird Restaurant, 35; taking of taxi, 35, 96; temperament of, 134; and Tracie, 22, 62, 64, 72

Oakey, Richard, 217
Ofirskey, Beryl, 3–4
Ogg, Don, 39
Okalla, 22, 41
Ontario Court of Appeal, 191, 192, 193–5, 196
Ontario Supreme Court, 188, 190–1, 208

parole, 216–19: eligibility for, 153, 168, 175, 189–90, 192, 194, 206, 209–10, 232; quality of incarceration and, 209
Penner, Alex, 66
Percival, Barry, 171
Perry, David, 42, 45, 123, 124
Perry, Diane: car taken, 35; and Coates, 42–3; evidence of, 95–6, 117–20, 121–7, 147–8, 179; fear of JFG, 126; in *the fifth estate*, 179; and Hautzinger, 53–4; as hostage, 35–6, 42–3, 45, 53–4, 57, 64, 67–8, 95–6, 97; and Janise, 117, 122, 126, 136, 137, 181, 211; Nichols's appeal to, 129; and Reimer, 67–8
Perry, Tracie, 122; amnesty for, 72–3, 75, 77, 78–9, 81, 82, 85, 86–8, 180; evidence at trial, 111–12, 113, 162; and guns, 125; and hostages, 35, 36, 42, 62, 64, 123, 124, 148; and identification of Janise, 136; and JFG's abuse of Janise, 11–12; and JFG's fight with Molinaro, 17, 18; in lineup, 105–6, 110, 111, 178, 230; lives with the Gambles, 11, 12; meets Nichols, 22; at preliminary hearing, 96–7; and robbery of Inglewood Credit Union, 26, 27, 129, 134, 147; and shootout with Harrison, 29, 34, 227–8; and trip to Toronto, 23
points of law, 99, 139
police: and 1974 shootout, 38–9; exposure

to risk, 30–1; and hostage-takings, 37, 39, 43, 44, 58–9, 84, 85, 86; killing of, 69, 71–2, 84; pursuits by, 36

Pope, Dale B., 94, 101, 149–50, 230–1

poster campaign, against parole, 217–18

preliminary hearings, 94, 108, 118, 119–21

presumption of innocence, 102, 104, 231

Price, Ron, 171

Priddle, Tom, 86

prison law, 170, 171, 197, 208

prosecuting counsel, 102–3, 104, 139

Queen's University Faculty of Law, 170–1

R. v. Dunbar and Logan, 191–2, 196

R. v. Konechny, 200

R. v. Prince, Hewitt and Craib, 182, 183n

R. v. Stevens, 206n

ransom. *See* monetary demands

reasonable doubt, 102, 103, 104, 135, 149, 155

Reed, Henrietta, 107

Reelie, Gary William, 13–14

Reimer, Ernie, 37, 43–4, 58, 63–8, 81, 85, 210, 220

robberies: of Brinks (proposed), 22–3, 26, 46, 61; home in Vancouver, 23; Inglewood Credit Union, 25–7

Royal Prerogative of Mercy, 172, 175–83, 187

Rusco Industries, 89

Russell, Daniel, 94

Ryan, H.R.S., 170

Rysan, Milda, 219

Sanderson, Kenneth, 3, 6–7

Sanderson, Mary. *See* Yerek, Mary

Sawyer, Brian, 38, 44, 85, 88, 90, 91

Schlossberg, Harvey, 44

Selfe, James, 22

sentencing, 165–9, 175, 187, 195, 196, 201, 206, 207, 208

Servicemaster, 88–9

severance of accused application, 99–101, 104

Shannon, M.E., 99, 101; charge to jury, 138–49

shootouts, 30–1, 112–13, 178–9

Short, John, 72, 179

Simpson, Bob, 86

Snaith (detective), 127, 128, 144, 145

standoffs, 37–9

Stevens, Laviolette appeal, 213, 231, 232

Stilwell, William, 94

Supreme Court of Canada, 169, 172, 175; 1978 appeal to, 202, 232; 1987/1988 appeal to, 199, 201–2, 202–3; appeal of Ontario Court of Appeal decision to, 196; designation of panels, 231–2; hearing of cases by, 198; judgment of December 1988, 204–5, 205–10; prisoners' cases and, 197; role of, 198–9

Sykes, Rod, 57, 84–6

Sylvestre, Kit, 38

TACT (Tactical Armed Combat Team), 39, 54, 56, 63

Tarrant, Ron, 223

Thunderbird Restaurant, 35, 97, 100, 148

Thurgood, Judge, 98

Tidalgo, Rutfy, and Estrella, 37

Tidsbury, Gary Thomas, 15–16, 17, 18–19

transportation, 47, 58

verdicts, 149, 155, 158, 164

Victims of Violence, 217

voir dire, 99, 117, 118, 122, 127–8

Watt, David, 190, 192, 193, 195

Western Aluminum Company, 89

Whitehall, Ivan, 190, 193–4, 202

Wills, Sally, 218

Wilson, Bertha, 199, 202, 205–10, 212–13

wiretaps, 43, 163, 229

witnesses in trials, 103, 114, 115. *See also* eyewitness reports

Wooliams, Eldon, 90

Yerek, Mary (later Sanderson), 3, 6–7, 12, 75, 180–1, 220

Yerek, Robert, 3

Zimmerman, Edward Murray, 32–3, 149, 178